MW01070625

Steven W. Mosher

THE DEVIL AND
COMMUNIST CHINA

THE DEVIL AND COMMUNIST CHINA

FROM MAO DOWN TO XI

STEVEN W. MOSHER

TAN BOOKS
GASTONIA, NORTH CAROLINA

Unless otherwise noted, Scripture quotations are from the Revised Standard Version of the Bible—Second Catholic Edition (Ignatius Edition), copyright © 2006 National Council of the Churches of Christ in the United States of America. Used by permission. All rights reserved.

Excerpts from the English translation of the *Catechism of the Catholic Church*, Second Edition, © 1994, 1997, 2000 by Libreria Editrice Vaticana—United States Catholic Conference, Washington, D.C. All rights reserved.

Cover design by Caroline Green

Cover image: Propaganda poster of Mao Tse-Tung, leader of the Chinese Communist Party. 1969. Color lithograph. © The Chambers Gallery, London / Bridgeman Images.

Library of Congress Control Number: 2023945281

ISBN: 978-1-5051-2650-1
Kindle ISBN: 978-1-5051-2651-8
ePUB ISBN: 978-1-5051-2652-5

Published in the United States by
TAN Books
PO Box 269
Gastonia, NC 28053
www.TANBooks.com

Printed in India

*I dedicate this book to my wife of nearly four decades,
Vera Lorraine Mosher.*

*When God decided that my soul was worth
saving, he brought Vera into my life.*

CONTENTS

"Morality begins at the point of a gun."

—Mao Zedong

"Both the theory and practice of Communism are completely inhuman."

—Aleksandre Solzhenitsyn

FOREWORD

As author of *The Devil and Karl Marx*, I regrettably know a few things about Communist China. Worst among them, here is a country that, according to the seminal 1999 Harvard University Press volume *The Black Book of Communism*, was responsible for the deaths of sixty-five million people under Communism in the twentieth century. Within the first two decades of Communist China's existence, primarily under Mao's Great Leap Forward (1957–60) and the Cultural Revolution (1966–69), tens of millions of innocent people perished. They died from purges, malnutrition, starvation, the collectivization of agriculture, and an overall wrenching transformation of society through militantly atheistic, totalitarian Communism.

The ghastly death estimate for China in *The Black Book*—which, according to the latest research on Mao's reign of terror, might actually be low—exceeds that of any country in history, including the Soviet Union, once rightly dubbed by President Ronald Reagan as an "evil empire." And when one adds in the horrific number of unborn babies snuffed out in the womb, especially via China's lethal one-child policy, the actual number of deaths under the nation's long march of Communism is unthinkably still larger. Add in the vast homicide against the unborn, and the killing field grows from tens of millions to hundreds of millions. Indeed, Steven Mosher estimates that 400 million human beings were killed off by the one-child policy.

Communist China has produced more deaths than any nation in the history of humanity. In the large sweep of history, that is no small accomplishment. It is downright diabolical.

I am prompted to quote Karl Marx here, specifically one of his chilling poems about the devil—namely, an 1841 work called "The Player."

There, the morbid Marx waxed perversely about a "blood-dark sword" that stabs "unerringly within thy soul. . . . The hellish vapors rise and fill the brain, till I go mad and my heart is utterly changed." "See the sword," declared Marx, "the Prince of Darkness sold it to me." Marx said of this dark prince, "For he beats the time and gives the signs. Ever more boldly I play the dance of death."

Marxism in China has been just that, a dance of death, one that could only please the Prince of Darkness.

There is no one who knows this better than Steven Mosher. Mosher, who began fighting Communism in China as a graduate student over forty years ago from inside the belly of the beast itself, calls this death apparatus the "Chinese Communist Killing Machine" and dubs Chairman Mao "the killingest man in history." Mosher notes of Mao that there are "lies, damned lies, and then Mao's lies." Like Lucifer, the Father of Lies, Mao Zedong (1893–1976) thrived on lying. The late Václav Havel once spoke of "the communist culture of the lie," but few Communists could live up to Mao's deceit. Like Lucifer, Mao built his kingdom on lies.

That, too, was no small accomplishment. It meant that billions suffered, and not just inside the walls of the Chinese Marxist empire.

From the Chinese Civil War in the late 1940s to the Korean War in the 1950s, the Vietnam War in the 1960s, Pol Pot's Cambodia in the 1970s, Tiananmen Square in 1989, and the one-child policy across multiple decades, Mao has bequeathed death, death, and more death. And he did not do so alone. There have been plenty of handmaidens. Various Communist successors have stepped in to take a turn cranking the wheels of the killing machine. Red China's blood-dark sword has laid out corpses not only among those who starved to death from collectivization policies, or among pro-democracy students gunned down or smashed by tanks in Beijing in June 1989, or among the expectant mothers forced round-the-clock into abortion factories, but also through the COVID-19 nightmare unleashed upon an entire unsuspecting world. China found a way to spread the plague of Communism to all countries, affecting all of our lives.

Well, Karl Marx did close the *Manifesto* by saying that Communists had a "world to win."

If only the Chinese Communist Killing Machine could have just stayed home. It was bad enough cranking along there. But like the devil unchained, Communism in China could not contain itself within the nation's geographical boundaries. Of course, such has been the ideology of Communism. The ideology has blown across borders. Like a phantom, it could not be contained.

"A specter is haunting Europe—the specter of Communism," wrote Karl Marx and Friedrich Engels in the opening lines of *The Communist Manifesto*. "All the powers of old Europe have entered into a holy alliance to exorcise this specter: Pope and Tsar, Metternich and Guizot, French Radicals and German police-spies."

It was fitting that Marx and Engels called their ideology a specter, one that needed to be exorcised. It was also fitting that they first listed the pope among those poised to confront the specter. The Catholic Church described Communism as a "satanic scourge," one that "conceals in itself a false messianic idea." Communism orchestrated a form of "class-warfare which causes rivers of blood to flow," a "savage barbarity." Marxists were "the powers of darkness." The Church declared: "The evil we must combat is at its origin primarily an evil of the spiritual order. From this polluted source the monstrous emanations of the communistic system flow with satanic logic."[1]

As Steven Mosher notes, Mao's enduring specter continues to haunt. Even as the one-child policy was finally changed, abortion became a way of life. Today, Chinese people are freer to have children than they were thirty years ago. But now, they are choosing not to. And still more unelected Communist leaders have taken the reins from Mao to repress the citizenry and harm lives.

Here again, the culprit is clear: this evil that we must combat is, at its origin, primarily an evil of the spiritual order. Steven Mosher is the rare international observer that understands that the force we face in

---

[1]   Pius XI, Encyclical *Divini Redemptoris* (March 19, 1937), nos. 20, 57, 77.

China is not just a political one, or even strictly an ideological one, but a spiritual one, a diabolical one.

Going back to the late 1970s, few have taken on that specter like Steven Mosher. Read this book and join him in that worthy battle.

—Paul Kengor, PhD
August 21, 2023, Feast of Saint Pius X

INTRODUCTION
THE CHINESE COMMUNIST KILLING MACHINE

"It is important to start with a presentation of the numbers. . . . Any ideology with a trail of rot like this is not of God but of the forces against God. It is not of God's creation but a fallen angel's anti-creation. It is not of the light but of the dark,"[1] wrote Paul Kengor in *The Devil and Karl Marx*. As Kengor suggests, no treatment of Communism should begin without mentioning its defining characteristic: mass murder.

Communism—the pernicious idea that man could create his own heaven on earth—is, quite simply, the most deadly idea ever conceived in the history of the world. It is no exaggeration to say that this misbegotten faith, once it came to power, has killed more people than any war, famine, or pestilence in human history.[2] Over the course of its bloody existence, Communist Parties have quite often been the chief cause of the wars, famines, and diseases that have racked other nations and, upon occasion, the world. The COVID-19 pandemic, caused by a virus that the Chinese Communist Party (CCP) deliberately spread around the world, is only the latest example of how the bloodbath that is Communism often spreads beyond its borders.

Nowhere has the death toll from this tyrannical system been higher than in China. This was not a necessary consequence of the country's

---

[1]   Kengor, *The Devil and Karl Marx*, xv.
[2]   See Mosher, *The Politically Incorrect Guide to Pandemics*.

large population. Rather, it followed directly from the proclivities of the evil genius who imposed Communism on the Chinese people. As we will see, Mao Zedong spent his nights thinking of new ways to terrorize the Chinese people to get them to obey the dictates of his adopted faith, ways that invariably involved the stigmatization, torture, and execution of millions of people. The Communist killing machine that he operated was more than capable of cutting a wide swath through the population.

One could fill a library with books about the manifold suffering and death caused by Communism's bloody century, and the section on the CCP depredations in China alone would require an entire wing.[3] Fortunately, we have *The Black Book of Communism*, which ably summarizes the carnage.[4] One of the authors, Stephane Courtois, writes, "Communist regimes turned mass crime into a full-blown system of government." And the result was murderous.

"Communist regimes did not just commit criminal acts," observes Professor Martin Malia of the University of California at Berkeley, "but they were criminal enterprises in their very essence: on principal, so to speak, they all ruled lawlessly, by violence, and without regard for human life."[5] And they were led by lawless, violent men—Lenin, Stalin, Pol Pot, and the North Korean Kim—who killed wantonly, violently, and with zero regard for human life. But none of these mass murderers, or even all of them put together, come close to matching the magnitude of Mao and the CCP's crimes against the Chinese people.

The Black Book of Communism estimated that the total death toll from twentieth-century Communism approached 100 million.[6] And China tops the list:

---

[3]   The Victims of Communism Foundation, based in Washington, DC, has made a good start at such a library. It is worth a visit if one is ever in our nation's capital.

[4]   Courtois, *The Black Book of Communism.*

[5]   Malia in Courtois, *The Black Book of Communism*, xvii–xviii.

[6]   Courtois, *The Black Book of Communism*, 4.

- China: 65 million deaths
- USSR: 20 million deaths
- North Korea: 2 million deaths
- Cambodia: 2 million deaths
- Vietnam: 1 million deaths
- Eastern Europe: 1 million deaths
- Africa: 1.7 million deaths
- Afghanistan: 1.5 million deaths
- Latin America: 150,000 deaths

The thought that two-thirds of the total victims of Communism died at the hands of the criminal enterprise known as the CCP is horrifying enough. But forty years of studying the People's Republic of China (PRC) has convinced me that sixty-five million casualties is a gross underestimate. Others agree. Jung Chang and Jon Halliday, in their brilliantly researched book *Mao: The Unknown Story*, give a figure of more than seventy million deaths attributable to Mao during his time in power.[7]

But I believe the figure is even higher, and not only because the killing has continued since Mao went to be with Marx in 1976. Two major campaigns, each producing millions of additional fatalities, must be added to the list. The first major addition to this figure is the correct number of Chinese who were starved to death by the communists from 1960 to 1962 in the worst famine in human history: up to 45 million (chapter 7).[8] The second and even greater addition to this number is the 400 million tiny victims, both born and unborn, of the CCP's long-running one-child policy, of which Mao was the godfather (chapter 13). Only God knows the exact number of those killed by Chinese Communism, but by my calculations, the number is close to 500 million, a truly insane level of butchery.

---

[7]   Chang, *Mao*.
[8]   The two best studies of the famine are Frank Dikötter's *Mao's Great Famine* and Jasper Becker's *Hungry Ghosts*.

The title of this book is *The Devil and Communist China*, but it could just as accurately be called *The Devil and Chairman Mao*. Mao Zedong looms too large in the history of the CCP not to have several chapters devoted to his crimes. If one adds together the years that Lenin (1917–1924) and Stalin (1924–1953) governed the Soviet Union, this still does not match the span of time, from 1935 to 1976, that Mao controlled the party.

As alluded to already, his forty-one-year reign was one long killing spree, with the vast number of deaths caused by his direct orders. He led some of the CCP's earliest terror campaigns, carried out in the "Red Base Areas" that he controlled in the 1930s, and was responsible for millions of civilian deaths during the Chinese Civil War in the years following. Moreover, in the fifties and sixties, after he had conquered all of China, he repeatedly executed bloody campaigns to target, isolate, and destroy different elements of Chinese society. He did this not just to eliminate potential opposition but, as he freely admitted, to terrorize the rest of the population into unquestioning obedience.

The use of terror as a tool for political control continues in China to the present day. Mao's ghost can be seen at work in the genocidal attacks on the Uyghurs, the persecution of the Falun Gong, and the insane COVID-19 lockdowns of entire provinces. The Communist system that Mao created in China—inspired by Marx, weaponized by Lenin, and exported to China by Stalin—continues to devour large numbers of victims to the present day. It is a criminal enterprise that, like its chief progenitor, kills willfully, violently, and with zero regard for human life. "How can you make a revolution without executions," Lenin decreed,[9] and people have been dying by the millions in China ever since.

As always, there will be those who attempt to exonerate Chinese Communism by blaming Mao alone for its excesses. But Mao the man is inseparable from the ideas and organization that empowered him. In

---

[9]   Fischer, *The Life of Lenin*, 435.

Marxism, Mao found the perfect ideology to justify his long-running reign of terror, while in Leninism, he discovered the blunt instrument that he would use to bludgeon the people into obedience. In Mao's hands, Communism became a weapon of mass destruction.

Yet while Mao and Communism were clearly a match made in hell, it is also true that the devil is a busy matchmaker. If Mao had not emerged victorious from the CCP's vicious intra-party struggles of the 1930s and '40s, some other lawless, narcissistic, power-hungry megalomaniac would have fought his way to the top. Marxism-Leninism breeds such creatures as surely as scum forms on the surface of a stagnant pond. Lenin's dictum—"Whatever furthers the revolution is ethical"—attracts cold, heartless psychopaths like honey attracts flies.

This is why China's current leader, Xi Jinping, takes Mao as his model in all things. It is why he and other top leaders continue to commit crimes against people and groups in China not all that dissimilar from his long-dead master. He, like Mao, believes that "morality begins at the point of a gun."[10]

Mao made no secret of his lawlessness when he was interviewed late in life by the American journalist Edgar Snow. In fact, he used a common Chinese expression—"I am a monk holding an umbrella; I have neither hair [law] or heaven"—that meant he rejected the laws of both man and God. Snow was either taken aback by this admission or failed to understand it at all. In any event, in his 1938 hagiography, *Red Star Over China*, he merely wrote that Mao lacked "religious feeling."[11] In fact, the lawless Mao was echoing the *non serviam* of the very first rebel, Satan himself. By saying he was lawless and godless, he was admitting that he served only himself.

To say that Mao was a sociopath or a psychopath does not capture the essence of the man. He certainly had elements of both in his personality.

[10] AZ Quotes, "Mao Zedong Quotes."
[11] Snow, *Red Star Over China,* 112. Although not a member of the Communist Party, in both the public press and in private letters, Snow distained capitalism and fervently argued for putting "the control of the means of production in the hands of the people." See Mosher, *Chinese Misperceived,* 57.

Like a classic sociopath, he had few friends and was antisocial in his attitudes and behavior. Like a classic psychopath, he was cold, heart-less, and even inhuman to others, including his own children. For Mao, nothing was sacred except his own being. Among the ancient Chinese philosophers, the only ones who rejected all authority—the laws of both man and God—were Lao Tzu and Chuang Tzu. Chuang Tzu, especially, is known for his bold declaration—almost a self-deification—that "I, heaven, and earth were born together, and I share the same body with the universe."[12] Chuang Tzu was, not surprisingly, one of Mao's favorite sages.

I am not going to argue that Chairman Mao or his chief followers were possessed by the devil, although, as Paul Kengor persuasively argues in *The Devil and Karl Marx*, some of Communism's past adher-ents certainly seemed to be. I have come across no evidence that Mao himself directly engaged in anything resembling a séance, a satanic ritual, or black magic. Still, as a child, he was once dedicated to a stone "god" of sorts that was thought to have protective powers.

When one puts the thoughts, acts, and words of the late Chairman Mao Zedong under a microscope, one sees a human being behaving at his absolute worst. Mao seems to have convinced himself that the universe and everything in it existed solely for his own satisfaction. And in this—his own private metaverse, as it were—good and evil did not exist. To call Mao's godlike conception of himself megalomania does not do it justice. Lucifer, the enemy of God and the author of evil, must have been proud of this aspiring antichrist and of the bloody path he carved through history.

The question that we must ask about such a dark soul is this: If Mao and his ilk *had* explicitly made a Faustian bargain with the devil, would they have said or done anything differently? Clearly, the answer is no.

When we examine the lives of Mao Zedong and his followers, we are not just looking at rapacious psychopathic monsters, we are look-ing at one of the human faces of Satan. And we must never do this unless we simultaneously look also into our own hearts.

---

[12] Chuang Tzu, "The Chuang Tzu."

There are lessons to be learned from studying the motives and actions of Mao and his successors, but only if we do not allow ourselves to be mesmerized by the horrors that we behold. This book is, above all, a cautionary tale about the evil that awaits us if we abandon God and embrace evil. We must not only recoil from Mao's embrace of Satanic thoughts and practices, which brought death to the Chinese people, but also deliberately move in the opposite direction, toward the life-giving truths of Jesus Christ, who is the Truth incarnate (see Jn 14:6).

Christ should be our exemplar in all things. Undaunted by the evil in the world, He lived to glorify His Father in heaven, was obedient to His earthly parents, embraced little children, kept Himself pure in every way, always told the truth, and in an act of breathtaking generosity, laid down His life for us so that we might have salvation.

Before we go explore the dark abyss of evil that Mao wrought in China and in his own life, let us resolve to enthrone Jesus in our hearts and live for Him on earth. Embrace that which is true, beautiful, and worthy of praise and live a life filled with love, compassion, and mercy.

Now, to Mao.

PART 1
THE ANCIENT DRAGON
ENTERS THE MODERN AGE

"Every society's judgments and conduct reflect a vision of man and his destiny. Without the light the Gospel sheds on God and man, societies easily become totalitarian."

—Catechism of the Catholic Church 2257

Thanks to Christianity, the totalitarian impulse had been banished from the West for nearly two thousand years and only began to creep back in with the radical secularism of the French philosophers and the revolution that followed. It had never really left China.

CHAPTER 1

"A Specter Is Haunting Europe," but It Never Really Left China

"We are indebted to Marx, Engels, Lenin and Stalin for giving us a weapon. The weapon is not a machine gun, but Marxism-Leninism."[1]

—Mao Zedong

The opening lines of *The Communist Manifesto* read like a declaration of spiritual warfare. "A specter is haunting Europe—the specter of communism," wrote Karl Marx and Friedrich Engels in 1848. In what can only be described as a sympathy ploy, they went on to claim that "all the powers of old Europe have entered into a holy alliance to exorcise this specter: Pope and Tsar, Metternich and Guizot, French Radicals and German police-spies."

The implication was that their new ideology was the innocent victim of a religious war. The truth is that Marx and Engels were inciting one, though they might play the victim. Militant atheists both, they were self-consciously setting out to destroy Christian civilization, a civilization that had lasted nearly two thousand years at that point. It should not surprise anyone that this, the opening declaration of a war that continues to the present day, turns the truth on its head. Bearing false witness, like mass murder, is one of Communism's chief characteristics.

---

[1] Mao Zedong, "On the People's Democratic Dictatorship," in *Selected Works of Mao Zedong,* vol. 4, 412.

There is no doubt that Marx and Engels intended to replace all existing religions with a secular one of their own. As Paul Kengor writes, the two even "viewed the initial draft of their manifesto as a revolutionary 'catechism' for an awaiting world. More than that, they saw it and referred to it, certainly in the initial draft stage, as a literal Communist Confession of Faith before later opting for the title that stuck. 'Think over the Confession of Faith a bit,' Engels wrote to Marx in November 1847. 'I believe that we had better drop the catechism form and call the thing: Communist Manifesto.'"[2]

The original title—a Communist Confession of Faith—would have been a more accurate reflection of what they were up to. It was a vision of man and his destiny that completely rejected the light of the Gospel. In its place, they created a false Gospel, one that promised to create heaven on earth for those who believed in them and followed their commandments. Marx even suggested that he and his movement would, as Kengor writes, "play the role of sacrificial savior on behalf of a new covenant for the new world." The current generation of Communists, wrote Marx, "resembles the Jews whom Moses led out of the wilderness. It must not only conquer a new world; it must also perish in order to make room for the people who are fit for a new world."[3] Of course, in "perishing" they would take a couple hundred million innocents with them.

In a strange resonance with the Ten Commandments delivered by God to Moses on Mount Sinai, the *Communist Manifesto* also listed exactly ten Communist commandments. Here they are in full:

1. The abolition of property in land and application of all rents of land to public purposes.
2. A heavy progressive or graduated income tax.
3. Abolition of all right of inheritance.
4. Confiscation of all property of emigrants and rebels.
5. Centralization of credit in the hands of the state, by means of

---

[2]   Kengor, *The Devil and Karl Marx,* 4.
[3]   Quotes from Kengor, *The Devil and Karl Marx,* 28.

a national bank with state capital and an exclusive monopoly.

6. Centralization of the means of communication and transport in the hands of the state.

7. Extension of factories and instruments of production owned by the state; the bringing into cultivation of waste land, and the improvement of the soil generally in accordance with a common plan.

8. Equal obligation of all to work. Establishment of industrial armies, especially for agriculture.

9. . . . gradual abolition of all the distinction between town and country by a more equitable distribution of the population over the country.

10. Free education for all children in public schools.[4]

Note that while each and every one of the original Ten Commandments dealt with matters of personal morality, not a single one of the manifesto's ten Communist commandments did. There is not a "thou shalt" or a "thou shalt not" in sight. The individual had no importance in his own right. There were only two options: be subsumed into the masses or be killed.

Marx and Engels were drawing up a grand blueprint for the complete reordering of society. And the role of the masses in their factory plan for the human race was to serve as interchangeable cogs in a giant machine. The public had no choice in the matter because, according to the diabolical duo, they were "obligated" to serve wherever the state required them to. Their individual views were unimportant unless they tried to flee or rebel. At that point, they would have to be eliminated and replaced on the societal assembly line by those who had been properly indoctrinated in the "free public schools."

Not only wealth but the population itself would be redistributed in accordance with the needs of the state. According to the blueprint laid out by Marx, the state would create "industrial armies" for agriculture.

---

4   Marx, *Manifesto of the Communist Party.*

Mao Zedong attempted to operationalize this idea in his "people's communes," which failed so spectacularly that forty-five million or more Chinese died along with them from 1960 to 1962.

Vladimir Lenin and his Bolsheviks, and, later, Mao and his Chinese Communist Party (CCP), would follow the manifesto in broad outline, especially in their militant atheism, abolition of private property, antagonism toward the family, and treatment of "the masses" as a disposable commodity.

Godless to the Core

Perhaps the single most salient ideological feature of Communism is its utter hatred of God. The one truth that Marxist believers despised more than the existence of heaven, a true utopia infinitely superior to their earthly one, was the idea of a being superior to themselves. Marx and Engels were not merely atheists who denied the existence of God. Rather, like their direct ideological descendants, as progressives of the present age, they believed that religion was nothing more than an artifice of mankind. To them, it was the cause of most, if not all, of man's ills.

The "social justice" Christians who, even today, still believe that it is possible to reconcile Communism and Christianity would not have received a warm welcome from Karl Marx himself. In Marx's opinion, "the social principles of Christianity preach cowardice, self-contempt, abasement, submission, humility. . . . So much for the social principles of Christianity."[5] Christians "abased" themselves by submitting to what Marx considered to be a false God. He considered them to be "cowards" because they refused to face life without the crutch of religion.

Marx's most famous quote concerning faith was that "religion is the opium of the people." Mao shared this view. He once told the Dalai Lama, the leader of Tibetan Buddhism, that religion is "poison." On another occasion, he compared Christian missionaries in China to the Nazis in Europe.

---

[5]   Quoted in Kengor, *The Devil and Karl Marx*, 29.

Marx's attitude toward religion was even harsher than his "opiate of the people" remark would suggest. He was fully on board with the sentiments of his sometime friend, the anarchist Mikhail Bakunin, who wrote, "If God really existed, it would be necessary to abolish him." In the words of Paul Kengor, Marx was onboard with Bakunin's "nasty, angry, cynical view of God and religion, [with Bakunin] stating that religion enslaves, debases, and corrupts, and that 'all religions are cruel, all founded on blood.'"[6]

If that is the standard we must use, then Communism has turned out to be the cruelest religion. It was founded on more blood than would have been shed in ten thousand Spanish Inquisitions. The total number of people sacrificed to pagan gods from the beginning of time—from the ancient Canaanites who burned infants alive in Baal's ovens to the bloody sacrifices offered up to the Aztec temple gods—is only a fraction of those murdered by the Communist killing machine in the last century.

The wages of not just ignoring but viciously trampling upon the first three commandments, which outline the love, respect, and time owed to God, have resulted in countless deaths, including spiritual ones.

Abolition of Private Property

Second only to their hatred of God was the determination of the founding fathers of Communism to ban the holding of property. Marx was unequivocal on this point: "The theory of the Communists may be summed up in the single sentence: Abolition of private property."[7] In the *Communist Manifesto* itself, he and his partner in crime insisted on this point. They argued to doubters that it was wholly justified, saying, "In one word, you reproach us with intending to do away with your private property. Precisely so; that is just what we intend. . . . You are horrified at our intending to do away with private property. But in your existing society, private property is already done away with for nine-tenths of the population."[8]

---

6   Kengor, 18–19.
7   Kengor, 8.
8   Kengor, 8–9.

Those who believed, like Marx, that all property was theft[9] were prepared to right this imagined injustice by committing a real one: they would use the power of the state to steal the people's property from them, forever. The confiscation of property by Communist states represents a radical break not just with Judeo-Christian tradition but also with the cultural practices of every human society that has ever existed on the planet. The hunter has a natural right to his kill, just as the farmer has a natural right to his crop. To be sure, the exactions by the ruling authorities grew progressively more severe as societies grew more complex. The leader of the clan demanded less from his clansmen than the tribal chief did from his tribe, whose levies were in turn dwarfed by the taxes that the local prince imposed on his people. But no society's rulers had ever sought to reduce every single inhabitant to a propertyless slave of the state. Until the advent of Communism, that is.

The Communists' problem is that people instinctively understand that private property is a natural right. In the Judeo-Christian tradition, it is enshrined in the seventh commandment, "Thou shalt not steal."[10] As the *Catechism of the Catholic Church* explains, "The seventh commandment forbids unjustly taking or keeping the goods of one's neighbor and wronging him in any way with respect to his goods. It commands justice and charity in the care of earthly goods and the fruits of men's labor. For the sake of the common good, it requires respect for the universal destination of goods and *respect for the right to private property*."[11]

And again: "A system that 'subordinates the basic rights of individuals and of group to the collective organization of production [i.e., Communism] is contrary to human dignity.'"[12] One of the corollaries that follows naturally from this commandment is the prohibition of slavery: "The moral law forbids acts which, for commercial or

---

9 The phrase is Proudhon's, a socialist who later turned against Marx for the latter's radical views. See Kengor, 10.
10 See Ex 20:15; Dt 5:19.
11 *CCC* 2401 (italics added).
12 *CCC* 2423.

totalitarian purposes, lead to the enslavement of human beings, or to their being bought, sold or exchange like merchandise."[13]

There is no doubt that Marx the totalitarian intended to virtually enslave the population. Immediately after declaring that everyone would be deprived of their property, Marx and Engels dictated that people would be "obliged" (read: forced) to labor and that the labor would be performed whatever and wherever the state assigned them. The people's labor, no less than its property, was to be stolen from it by the Communist state and redistributed for its own purposes.

Saint Paul, in his First Letter to the Corinthians, calls out such people: "thieves, nor the greedy, . . . nor robbers will inherit the kingdom of God" (6:10). Communists, who worship the material world, are quite prepared to rob everyone of their property and freedom in order to build an illusory kingdom of man. Together, they constitute the largest criminal conspiracy, comprised of the greediest class of people, that has ever existed.

Those who would unjustly rob us of both our property and our freedom still prowl the world. Repackaging themselves as progressives, these modern-day Communists may have abandoned traditional Marxist terminology, but their underlying goal remains the same. "You will own nothing and be happy" is nothing more than a clever restatement of the two-century-long Communist delusion of totalitarian societal perfection.

Abolition of the Family

The first and most fundamental unit of social organization is the natural family, consisting of a father, a mother, and their natural or adopted children. The success of the family throughout history is due to the complementarity of the sexes, as well as the love and mutual respect that unites parents and children. Aside from those who have voluntarily adopted a monastic existence, the family is the only truly "communist" society, one in which everyone ideally works for the common good.

---

[13] *CCC* 2455.

It is no surprise that all Communists, starting with Marx and Engels themselves, see the family as an obstacle to their own plans to reorganize society. When in power, they invariably set out to weaken, if not entirely destroy, this God-given and highly fruitful social organization to make way for their own restructuring of society into a giant collective.

In the *Communist Manifesto*, Marx and Engels were not at all circumspect about their plans for the family. They wanted to abolish it completely. They anticipated that the reaction of their followers to this proposal would be shock and disbelief, noting, "Even the most radical flare up at this infamous proposal of the Communists [to abolish the family]."[14] But they do not relent.

Instead, they justify their attack on the natural family by claiming that the family is not a natural social unit at all. According to Marx and Engels, it is simply an artifact of "capital" and "private gain," and that it "exists only among the bourgeoisie." Once you expropriate everyone's property, they suggest, it will simply disappear: "The bourgeois family will vanish as a matter of course . . . with the vanishing of capital."

Abolishing the family among the proletariat will be even easier, the two conspirators contended, because it really didn't exist in the first place. That's right. Marx and Engels, in pursuit of their illusory utopia, dismiss the lived experience of tens of billions of men and women down through history who have joined together to create happy, fulfilling lives together for themselves and their children despite only having the bare necessities of life. Instead, they grasp at social pathologies like public prostitution, child labor, and family breakdown among the lower classes in mid-nineteenth-century England and claim that there is a "practical absence of the family" among the poor.[15]

The ready dismissal of the family by Marx and Engels—and, as we will see, by Mao—is surely a reflection of their own rejection of the bonds of marriage, family, and children. Marx sponged off his parents his entire life, and his failure to provide for his family left his wife and

---

[14]   Marx, *Manifesto of the Communist Party.*
[15]   Marx, *Manifesto of the Communist Party.*

children destitute. Engels, too, relied on his family for "capital" and for decades refused to marry at all. Mao had four wives, countless concubines, and a number of children, none of whom he was very attached to. Each of these Communist revolutionaries who wanted to abolish the family had already "abolished" their own.

Several of their Communist ten commandments were intended to weaken the family. To strip families of their wealth, private enterprises, including family-owned businesses, were to be obliterated. All right of inheritance was to be abolished. To raise loyal minions of the state, all children were to be educated in public schools. The ultimate goal was to remove children from their parents shortly after birth, raising them in state-run crèches, completely destroying the natural affection that binds children to parents.[16]

Abolition of National Identity

Not only the family but nations would fall before the leveling scythe of Communism. Marx and Engels make it clear that both "countries and nationality" are to be abolished on the grounds that "the working men have no country." They admit, however, that, as a practical matter, the proletariat would first have to seize control of the nations in which they reside. After that initial success, they must turn their attention to the entire world. The first nations captured would be used as launching pads for revolutions in neighboring countries, with the goal being to bring all nations under the banner of the hammer and sickle.

"United action," they insisted, would enable Communism to sweep across the planet. It would obliterate national boundaries and national identities in the process and create a global utopia. This grandiose plan was the fever dream not only of Marx and Engels, or Lenin and Stalin, but also many of those who followed them, including Mao Zedong. It is not generally known that Mao, in 1958, set up what was called an "Earth Control Committee" for the day when the whole world would be

---

[16] As we will see, Mao attempted this during the Great Leap Forward (1958–60), with predictably disastrous results.

red. Someone, after all, had to be in charge, and the ambitious chairman could think of no better candidate than himself and the CCP that he led.

The Devaluation of Life

Marx claimed that under Communism, all men would become renaissance men. Writing in his *German Ideology* (1845), he promised, "In Communist society, where nobody has one exclusive sphere of activity but each can become accomplished in any branch he wishes, society regulates the general production and thus makes it possible for me to be one thing today and another tomorrow, to hunt in the morning, fish in the afternoon, rear cattle in the evening, criticize after dinner, just as I have a mind, without ever becoming a hunter, fisherman, herdsman, or critic."[17]

To a worker laboring twelve hours a day in a noisy, smoke-filled factory, that would sound like paradise. But I suspect that Marx was here writing about himself, given that he spent his days doing exactly as he pleased, sometimes scribbling away in the British library, other times taking long walks.

In reality, Marx had little empathy for ordinary working men, with whom he almost never rubbed shoulders. To him and his ideological descendants, men like Mao Zedong, they were "the proletariat" or "the masses": a faceless mass of "units" of production whose individual members possessed little dignity or worth.

The "bourgeoisie" and "capitalists" had it even worse in the Communists' view, for they had forfeited their right to life itself by their exploitation of the masses. The "five bad classes," as Mao later called them, were to be terrorized into submission, if not destroyed entirely.

This subsuming of the individual to intellectual constructs like "the masses" and "class" goes a long way toward explaining why mass murder is one of the chief characteristics of Communism wherever it is found. Though it is mightily aided by the psychopathic, tyrannical character of its leaders.

---

17   Kengor, *The Devil and Karl Marx*, 7.

Communism Comes to Europe and China

These Communist proposals to destroy God, family, country, and life itself were rightly shocking to the Christian sensibilities of Europe as they existed in 1848. It was no wonder that in addition to "Pope and Tsar, Metternich and Guizot, French Radicals and German police-spies," the vast majority of society aligned against the Communists. A specter may have been haunting Europe in 1848, but it took the better part of a century for that specter to become powerful enough to take control of Russia and begin its reign of evil.

Marx had originally proposed that Communism required such a radical rupture in human relations, and such a deliberate destruction of the existing social order, that it could only be accomplished through a reign of terror. In reality, it took something far worse than that: a world war. It was World War I and the starvation, privation, and sheer terror that accompanied that conflict that brought Lenin's Bolsheviks into power in Russia.

It took a second world war to spread Communism to Eastern Europe and, eventually, to China. Were it not for the Japanese invasion of China and the chaos that followed, the Communists would never have succeeded in conquering China. The Red Army's ascension to power was further smoothed by an ancient Chinese totalitarian philosophy called legalism, which predisposed the people to accept the dominant role of the state.

In the West, the deification of Roman rulers and the glorification of the state had gradually given way to the teachings of Christ, who had revealed His authentic kingship over all humanity. The temptation of the ancient serpent—"You will be like God" (Gn 3:5)—was suppressed for a time among Western kings and princes by a broad popular understanding of man's subordinate place in the universe *and* his eternal destiny. After all, if everyone from peasant to king were mere creatures, answerable to a higher being, that put to rest the illusions of even the most megalomaniac of rulers.

Satan's whispers to Christian kings thus largely fell on deaf ears. Though when they didn't—when the king fell prey to the blandishments of his courtiers and began to imagine that he was something more than mortal—there were always those in the population at large to mock his pretensions. *The Emperor's New Clothes* is not merely a fairy tale but a popular metaphor for the fate of a man suffering from such hubris.

The satanic delusion of Communism arrived in the West in the nineteenth century after having taken, thanks to Christianity, a nearly two-thousand-year detour. But the East had remained ever in thrall to the ancient totalitarian dragon's practices. China had never been Christianized. The dragon had never been exorcised from China. On the contrary, he became the country's national symbol.

If the imposition of Communism in the West was a break with Christian civilization, in China one could almost say that it represented a continuity. The governing philosophy throughout dynastic times owed a lot to the ancient Chinese school of political theory called legalism. Developed during the period in Chinese history known as the Warring States, legalism was a kind of proto-totalitarianism that had long legitimized the encroachments of the state into the private lives of its citizens. Because of this confluence, the resistance to Communist ideas among both the intelligentsia and the population at large was much weaker than it otherwise might have been. The Communists in China found themselves on much friendlier ground than they had in Europe.

Not everyone saw the parallels between Imperial China's police state practices and modern-day Marxist-Leninism. But one young Communist did, and he wasted no time in taking advantage of it. Cloaking his imperial ambitions in Communist drivel about democracy, equality, and the withering away of the state, Mao Zedong mobilized the power of the state in his quest to become China's first Red Emperor. And against all odds, this man who took his lawlessness and godlessness as a point of pride succeeded.

CHAPTER 2
THE RISE OF REVOLUTION: A BRIEF HISTORY OF MODERN CHINA

Empires Fall, Empires Rise

The nineteenth century saw China's last dynasty, the Qing, in terminal decline. The corruption of the imperial court and the ineptitude of its officials had led to widespread poverty and runaway inflation. Rebellions broke out in different parts of the Qing Empire; chief among these was the Taiping Rebellion, which engulfed the country from 1850 to 1864. Russia, Germany, Great Britain, and other imperial powers all took advantage of the growing weakness of the Qing. They forced the emperor to sign "unequal treaties," ceding trade, territory, and legal rights to them.[1] Rapidly modernizing Japan was particularly aggressive, seizing Taiwan and a Qing tributary state, Korea, in 1895, and wresting Manchuria away from Russia a decade later. The tottering remains of the Qing finally fell to the republican revolution of 1911–12, and six-year-old Emperor Puyi was forced to abdicate.

Following the collapse of the Qing, most provinces in China were ruled by local warlords. The southern province of Guangdong—the most Westernized of China's provinces—was the sole exception. It was under the control of the Nationalist Party of China, also called the Kuomintang, or KMT, which was headed by a charismatic leader by the name of Dr. Sun Yat-sen. Almost alone among his contemporaries, Dr. Sun had studied in

---

[1] Schoppa, "From Empire to People's Republic," 47–50.

America and developed a clear understanding of our country's republican form of government. This understanding was immeasurably aided by his conversion to Christianity while he was there.[2] Dr. Sun was instrumental in establishing the Republic of China—he modeled its constitution on the US Constitution—and was elected its first president.[3] Dr. Sun had thought deeply about how to reunite and restore China to its proper place among nations, and he devised a program called the Three Principles of the People to accomplish this end.[4] The three principles in question were democracy, nationalism, and the people's welfare, or well-being.

To help China catch up to the modern world, many young Chinese joined Dr. Sun in seeking to bring Western democratic ideals into their country. This effort at renewal became known as the New Culture Movement. China also aided the Western democracies in a practical way during the First World War by sending over 100,000 workers to support the British and French armies as they were engaging in grueling trench warfare on the Western Front.[5] This only added to the outrage felt by the Chinese people when, at the end of the war, the German concession in the Chinese province of Shantung was not given back to China, as the Western allies had promised. Instead, it was handed over to Imperial Japan.[6]

Massive student protests against this betrayal broke out across the country. Key figures of this patriotic awakening, which came to be known as the May Fourth Movement, later emerged as important political leaders in the Nationalist government. Others, however, angrily rejected American-style democracy, blaming progressive President Woodrow Wilson for the loss of Shantung. Many of these individuals became Marxists, convinced that the Bolshevik Revolution in Russia offered a better model for freeing China from both imperialism *and* poverty than the West.[7]

2   Holcomb, *A History of East Asia*, 263.
3   Bergere, *Sun Yat-sen*, 17.
4   Bergere, 352.
5   Mosher, *The Politically Incorrect Guide to Pandemics*.
6   Wood, *Betrayed Ally*.
7   Schoppa, "From Empire to People's Republic," 59–60.

Marxism-Leninism also freed them from the moral restraints demanded by a republican system of government, including respect for the fundamental dignity and inalienable rights of the human person.

Lenin wasted little time in taking advantage of the opportunity to sow revolution in the world's most populous country. Following the establishment of the Communist International (Comintern) in 1919, Bolshevik agents were soon on their way to China. In July 1921, they convened a meeting of leading Chinese Marxists in Shanghai, where they established the Chinese Communist Party (CCP). The newly formed party followed Leninist lines, with power heavily concentrated in the hands of a few. Mao, who had only become a Marxist the year before, played a minor role in the meeting. But from his base in Hunan province, he immediately began plotting how to climb the power pyramid.

While financially supporting the CCP, Moscow also approached Dr. Sun, offering to help him build an army to unify China, but only on the condition that he would allow the Communists to join the effort. He agreed, and the first United Front was formed in 1924.[8] But before the Nationalist army was ready to march, Dr. Sun died. The KMT's senior military commander, General Chiang Kai-shek, was elected as his successor, and the following year, what would become known as the Northern Expedition got under way. Chiang's forces defeated one warlord after another as they made their way up the Chinese coast, successfully capturing Shanghai in early 1927.

Shanghai was the center of CCP influence and activity in China, and its agents began to secretly infiltrate Nationalist ranks, corrupting it from within. Chiang, who would soon become, like Dr. Sun himself, a committed Christian, decided that the time had come to break with the Communists. In April 1927, he struck. By the time the smoke cleared, the Communist Party had been virtually wiped out in its one-time stronghold. The Chinese Civil War, which was to last for more than two decades, had begun.[9]

---

[8]   Schoppa, 61.

[9]   Schoppa, 62–63.

Political Power Grows Out of the Barrel of a Gun

Up to this point, Mao had merely been a bit player in Hunan province, with no military forces under his command. But already Mao had learned, as he told one of Stalin's agents in late 1927, that "political power grows out of the barrel of a gun." And so he set out to get his hands on some. On the pretext of launching an uprising in the city of Changsha, he convinced Party Central to give him operational control of the CCP's only military force. As soon as he took command, he ordered them not to advance but instead to retreat into the hills. He led them deep into the rugged Jinggang Mountains and set up a Communist base area, with himself in charge, of course.[10]

It was the first time, but certainly not the last time, that Mao would deceive and betray not just the party leadership but even those he called comrades in order to advance his career. Over the course of the forced march to Jinggangshan, for example, many of his soldiers died of dysentery and disease, and large numbers deserted. But none of that gave Mao pause. He had gotten what he wanted, and that was the only thing that mattered.

The fortunes of the Red Base Areas in South China rose and fell in the years that followed, as did Mao's own. Wearied of his scheming, double-dealing, and blackmailing, other Communist leaders repeatedly tried to oust Mao from his position in the leadership, if not from the party itself. They failed, primarily because Moscow—which in those days meant Soviet dictator Joseph Stalin—was impressed by Mao's utter ruthlessness and correctly saw in him a proper son of Marx and Lenin, a kindred evil spirit. But the other leaders did manage to sideline Mao for a time by giving him the largely ceremonial post of head of state.

Chiang Kai-shek, determined to excise the cancer of Communism from China once and for all, launched an encirclement campaign against the largest Red base in 1933. As the noose gradually tightened

---

[10]   See Chang, *Mao,* esp. chapter 5, "Hijacking a Red Force and Taking Over Bandit Land."

around the Communist "capital" of Ruijin, the party leadership, facing annihilation, decided to make a run for it the following year. They hoped to make their way close enough to the border of the Soviet Union so their "Soviet Older Brothers" could resupply them with weapons and ammunition.

Constantly harried by Nationalist forces, it took the Red Army over a year to reach the northern city of Yan'an.[11] Only a few thousand troops survived the six-thousand-mile journey, but in the course of it, Mao's fortunes dramatically improved. For it was during this "Long March," as it was later romanticized in Communist propaganda, that Mao Zedong finally seized control of the CCP.[12] Only his death forty-two years later would finally end the tyrannical reign of the first Red Emperor.

The CCP was further saved from defeat by Imperial Japan, which sent its forces into China in 1938. While Chiang's Nationalist army heroically fought against the invaders for the next seven years, Mao refused to let his forces engage. Instead, working behind Chiang's back and behind the Japanese lines, he relentlessly fortified his forces and expanded the Red Base Areas under his control.

Following Japan's defeat in the Second World War by the United States, and using arms and equipment supplied by the Soviet Union, the chairman finally sent his long-husbanded armies on the march. Paying no attention to the mounting death tolls, Chairman Mao ordered city after city blockaded and their populations starved into submission. It was a campaign of unmatched brutality. After the Manchurian city of Changchun was encircled, for example, one of Mao's leading military commanders, Lin Biao, ordered his forces to turn

---

[11] Chang and Halliday argue in *Mao: The Unknown Story* that Chiang Kai-shek's forces were merely herding the rapidly diminishing ranks of the Red Army along rather than attempting to annihilate it. The most likely reason for Chiang's restraint, they explain, was that Stalin was holding the Generalisimo's son hostage in Russia and that Chiang was in effort proposing a kind of prisoner exchange. Give me back my son, he told Stalin, and I will let your miserable little guerilla force live. See chapter 12, "Chiang Lets the Reds Go."

[12] Chang, *Mao*, 65–66.

the capital into a "city of death."[13] During the siege that followed, an estimated 160,000 people died. General Lin's men then easily captured the city, declaring victory on October 20, 1948.[14]

Purge after Bloody Purge

On October 1, 1949, Mao stood on top of the Gate of Heavenly Peace overlooking Tiananmen Square and proclaimed the establishment of the People's Republic of China.[15]

The chairman of the CCP had posed as a simple "land reformer," even a believer in democracy, during the civil war.[16] Now he showed his true face, embarking on a brutal campaign to impose his vision of Communism on China. One group after another was targeted in nationwide campaigns of terror called "purges." In the cities, this meant targeting officials of the former government and successful businessmen ("capitalists"). While in the countryside, it meant anyone who owned more land than they could farm themselves ("landlords"). Those who were targeted lost their businesses, their farms, and often their lives as well.[17]

Farmland was redistributed equally to all, but the party soon took it away again. They forced the farmers into larger and larger collectives, where they were ordered to farm the land in common. But the purpose of the purges was not just the redistribution of wealth or land. Mao promoted the purges as official state policy to eliminate opposition to the CCP. According to Frank Dikötter, "Mao emphasized that terror should be 'stable,' 'precise,' and 'ruthless': the campaign should [therefore] be carried out with surgical precision, without any slippage into random slaughter, which would undermine the standing of the party."[18] At the same time, Mao cautioned against killing too few, saying,

---

[13] Dikötter, *The Tragedy of Liberation*, xi.
[14] Dikötter, xi.
[15] Cheek, *Mao Zedong and China's Revolutions*, 125.
[16] Mosher, *Chinese Misperceived*.
[17] Mosher, *Broken Earth*.
[18] Dikötter, *The Tragedy of Liberation*, 88.

"In provinces where few have been killed a large batch should be killed; the killings can absolutely not be allowed to stop too early."[19]

The Communist Party admits that two to three million people lost their lives to such purges in the first three years of the People's Republic.[20] Based on my own research in rural China in 1979–80, however, I believe the actual number is much, much higher, and others agree.[21] The official statistics released by Communist officials in China are constructed for political advantage and often bear little resemblance to the actual reality.

Political campaigns resulting in purges have remained a feature of life in the People's Republic of China down to the present day.

The Great Leap Forward

The end of the civil war and the strong work ethic of the Chinese people set the stage for rapid economic growth in the 1950s. Borrowing the Soviet economic model in the hope of quickly industrializing, the CCP introduced its First Five-Year Plan in 1953.[22] But even as China's economy grew, the party bureaucracy grew even faster, and Mao grew impatient with the pace of change.[23] He decided that both food and factory production could be greatly increased if China's peasants were forced into huge collective farms called "people's communes." This was the *Communist Manifesto*'s "industrial armies [for] agriculture" come to life.

Mao laid out his plans in the Second Five-Year Plan, which called for "launching the country into a race to catch up with more developed countries through breakneck industrialization and collectivization of the countryside."[24] Mao, who couldn't read a balance sheet but excelled at crafting clever slogans, announced that it was time for China to take a "Great Leap Forward." He declared that China must catch up to

---

[19] Dikötter, 88.
[20] Courtois, *The Black Book of Communism,* 481.
[21] Short, *Mao,* 436.
[22] Worden, *China,* 215.
[23] Worden, 215.
[24] Worden, 84.

industrialized nations like Great Britain in steel production within three years.

Mao's fantasy of overnight industrialization did not speed up China's economic development. Instead, it resulted in a cascading series of disasters. Many villagers were unhappy about being drafted into "industrial armies" and were tortured, or even beaten to death, for refusing to join the new "people's communes." More than 2.5 million people perished in this way as the communes were organized and the Great Leap Forward began.[25]

The quotas handed to commune officials for the production of iron— "to catch up to Great Britain in steel production"—set in motion another disaster. Since the vast majority of China's eighty thousand communes had no access to iron ore, or the coal they would need to refine it, this was the equivalent of being told to weave straw into gold. Fearful of failing to meet their quotas, commune officials ordered villagers to stop tending their crops and instead build crude "backyard furnaces."[26] To make up for the lack of iron ore, they were then told to throw everything made of iron they could find, including their own cooking pots and water buckets, into the furnaces. Finally, to make up for the lack of coal, they were told to fire the furnaces by stripping the surrounding countryside bare of trees and their own homes of furniture. In all, perhaps 10 percent of China's forests were cut down to use as fuel.[27]

But the real tragedy was just beginning. In their haste to produce "steel"—most of which had to be later re-smelted if it could be used at all—the cadres in charge of the communes had neglected their primary duty: to allow the villagers to produce enough food to feed China's massive population. By late 1959, the country was in the grip of the worst famine in all human history. During the following three years, forty-five million or more people starved to death.[28]

---

[25]   Dikötter, *Mao's Great Famine*, 298.
[26]   Brown, "China's Great Leap Forward," 31.
[27]   Brown, 31.
[28]   Courtois, *The Black Book of Communism*, 464.

The Cultural Revolution

The chaos, death, and destruction caused by the Great Leap Forward generated enormous resentment and anger toward the CCP and the leader who had ordered it. Hundreds of thousands of citizens wrote letters complaining about the lack of food, excessive working hours, poor housing, and more.[29] Even within the party, Mao faced a barrage of criticism.

Stung by this criticism, Mao was forced to retreat. The backyard furnaces were torn down, and peasants were allotted small plots of land on which to grow vegetables. Control over food production was shifted from the giant "people's communes" down to smaller, village-sized collectives called "production brigades" and "production teams." One thing didn't change, however. Communist cadres would continue to control most of the land, and wield all the power, in the countryside.[30]

The seething chairman, who would never admit that his critics were justified, plotted revenge for this loss of face. He had two aims. The first was to resolidify his grip on power by purging his enemies within the party. The second was to systemically destroy all traces of China's traditional culture and beliefs in order to replace it with a new Communist society according to his own vision. The Great Sloganeer—as he might be called—announced that China was in need of a Great Proletarian Cultural Revolution. For his shock troops—his brownshirts, as it were—he would use China's millions of young, impressionable students. He even coined a term for them. They were to be called Chairman Mao's Red Guards.

The Cultural Revolution began on May 16, 1966, when the *People's Daily* newspaper published an article claiming that "counterrevolutionary revisionists" had "sneaked into the Party, the government, the army, and various cultural circles."[31] Students across China were forced to study the "thought of Chairman Mao" because it was their

---

[29]   Courtois, 221.
[30]   Mosher, *Broken Earth.*
[31]   Chinese Communist Party, "The CCP's May 16th Circular (1966)."

duty to "make China Maoist from inside out . . . help the working people of other countries make the world red . . . and then the whole universe."[32] The youth were whipped into a frenzy by such propaganda and, organized into Red Guard units, began attacking anyone they suspected of being disloyal to Chairman Mao.

Mao himself encouraged the students to pursue violent revolution and forbade the police and the military from acting against them. Not surprisingly, Mao's enemies in the party and government were the first to come under attack by Red Guard units secretly under his direction. But the students soon turned on their teachers, their parents, and even on other Red Guard groups as well. This unrestrained violence led to mass killings across the country and, in some areas, something close to civil war.

By 1968, Mao's enemies within the party had been killed or imprisoned, and he decided to end the chaos. The army was brought in to disarm and disband the Red Guard units and restore order. "Revolutionary party committees" led by army officers were placed in charge of the government.[33]

To ensure that the millions of Red Guards he had trained and unleashed on his enemies would cause no further trouble, Mao eventually banished his young zealots to the countryside. They were told that they were being sent down to the countryside to "learn from the peasants," who would warmly welcome them as fellow revolutionaries.[34] In fact, the peasants saw these city youth, who were unused to working in the fields, as just more mouths to feed. It didn't take long for these "sent-down youth," as they were called, to realize that they had been betrayed by the leader they had formerly idolized. Instead of returning to their schools to finish their education, they found themselves condemned to a life of hard labor in a barren countryside that had been devastated by the Great Leap Forward.[35]

---

[32]   Chong, *China's Great Proletarian Cultural Revolution*, 105.
[33]   Dikotter, *The Cultural Revolution*, xvi.
[34]   Dikotter, 192–95.
[35]   Dikotter, 192–95.

The Cultural Revolution only came to an end with Mao's death in 1976. Over the course of this ten-year-long political campaign, according to the CCP's own numbers, "20 million people died [and] 100 million people were persecuted."[36]

Mao's passing, however, did not end the cycle of political campaigns and purges. From forced abortions in the one-child policy[37] to the persecution of Christians and Falun Gong Buddhists, from the crushing of the Tibetan independence movement to the genocide of the Uyghurs in China's far west, China remains today a totalitarian, one-party Communist state with one of the worst human rights records in the world.[38]

How did the Communists manage to seize power in China and, despite repeated disasters that caused tens of millions of lives, stay in power? And why does China, more than three decades after the collapse of Communism in Eastern Europe and the Soviet Union, still remain in thrall to this deadly ideology?

The answer lies in an ancient totalitarian political system called legalism, a modern abomination called Marxist-Leninism, and the bastard child that Mao spawned by crossbreeding the two.

---

[36] Ma Licheng, *Confrontation,* 261.
[37] Mosher, *A Mother's Ordeal.*
[38] Amnesty International, "China 2020."

CHAPTER 3

LEGALISM AND COMMUNISM: A MARRIAGE MADE IN HELL

"The working class, the laboring people, and the Communist Party . . . [are] working hard to create the conditions in which classes, state power and political parties will die out very naturally and mankind will enter the realm of Great Harmony."

—Mao Zedong[1]

"All men under the sun work with one heart. Morals have been standardized. Neighbors keep watch on one another, relatives inform on relatives, and thieves lie low!"

—An Inscription Lauding Qin Shi Huang,
First Emperor of the Qin Dynasty

Totalitarian from the Beginning

A Chinese emperor—the Eastern despot par excellence—wielded far more power than any Western monarch, however absolute. There is nothing resembling a *Magna Carta* to be found anywhere in the long stretch of Chinese history, much less the equivalent of an Athenian Assembly or a Roman Forum. Neither was there a religious authority comparable to the ancient Jewish prophets or the later Roman Catholic pontiffs who could impose moral sanctions on wayward kings and emperors. In China, political authority moved unchecked in the opposite direction, as the early despotism of the Shang and Zhou kings

---

[1] Mao Zedong, "On People's Democratic Dictatorship," in *Selected Works of Mao Zedong*, vol. 4, 412.

was perfected several hundred years before the birth of Christ, into the totalitarianism of the Qin, Han, and later dynasties.[2]

Confucius said, "Just as there are not two suns in the sky, so there cannot be two emperors on earth."[3] But what happened in ancient China went far beyond merely concentrating power in the hands of the sovereign. Rather, anticipating the Marxist-Leninism of our own day by roughly two thousand years, it involved the creation of an entire system of government to grind the population into utter submission. The ancient dragon, the enemy of human freedom, carried the day.

China's early rulers were guided in their quest for power by a school of Chinese Machiavellis collectively called Legalists. The leading Legalists reflected deeply on the nature of power and its employment. But as a class, the Legalists more closely resembled the *consiglieri* of Mafia chieftains, each plotting and conniving to advance the power of his local prince, duke, or baron against other local rulers. During the Warring States period of Chinese history—which was just as brutal as it sounds—the greatest Legalist of all, Han Fei, warned, "Today the competition depends on having the greatest power. He who has great power will be paid tribute by others, he who has less power will pay tribute to others; therefore the wise ruler cultivates power."[4]

---

[2]   Parts of the following chapter are adapted from my *Bully of Asia: Why China's Dream is a Threat to the World Order.*

[3]   One of Confucius's oft-quoted sayings, this appears twice in *Li ji (Book of Rites)*, in chapters 7 and 30, and once in Mencius, *Mengzi (Book of Mencius)*, in chapter 5a.4. Easily accessible online versions of these Chinese classics include Confucius, *The Book of Rites,* translated by James Legge, 249, 320, and *Mencius,* translated by James Legge, 80. In *Mencius,* the version is slightly altered to "Confucius said: 'Just as there are not two suns in the sky, so there cannot be two emperors on earth.'"

[4]   Han Fei Zi, chapters 47, 49, 50 in Fu, *Autocratic Tradition and Chinese Politics,* 20. What Professor Fu translates as "force," I translate as "power," which more accurately aligns with modern-day English usage. Among the forerunners of Legalism was a branch of Daoism called the Huang-Lao school (after the legendary Yellow Emperor Huang-di and Daoist philosopher Lao Zi), through which many Daoist prescriptions became Legalist statecraft. This connection came to light with the discovery of the *Huangdi sijing* ("Four Canons of the Yellow Emperor") during a 1973 excavation of a Han dynasty tomb in Hunan province. The views expressed in this ancient document accord with those of the Legalists; for example: "Possessing a

In pursuit of power, the Legalists designed and implemented a series of political "reforms" to strengthen the hand of the local monarch. Build and maintain strong armies, they advised, and organize the peasants to increase agricultural production. Replace the unreliable aristocracy with an appointed bureaucracy, increase taxes, and regulate commerce, they further suggested. Above all, they warned, the people must be intimidated into subjection. Any and all dissent must be crushed without hesitation. The "totalitarian regulation of society in the service of the state" is how Sinologist Charles Hucker has described this Legalist program.[5]

To strengthen the ruler's hand over the people, the Legalists recommended such policies as:

- Accumulation of people as an indispensable component of power: "Therefore the ruler of men desires to have more people for his own use. . . . The ruler loves the people because they are useful."[6]
- Suppression of all voluntary associations: "The early kings always made certain that the interests of their subjects diverged. Thus under perfect governance, spouses and friends, however close to one another, can neither refuse to report another's crimes, nor cover up for them."[7]
- Establishment of informer networks: "The wise ruler forces the whole world to hear and to watch for him. . . . No one in the world can hide from him or scheme against him."[8]
- Use of punishment instead of reward: "A well-governed state . . . employs nine punishments to one reward; whereas a weak state employs nine rewards to one punishment."[9]

---

large territory, a teeming population, and a strong army, the ruler is matchless in the world." See Fu, *Autocratic Tradition and Chinese Politics,* 37.

[5]　Hucker, *China's Imperial Past,* 92.

[6]　*Guan Zi,* chapter 16.

[7]　*Shangjun shu,* chapter 24; *Han Fei Zi,* ch. 45.

[8]　*Han Fei Zi,* chapter 14.

[9]　*Shangjun shu,* chapter 7.

- Harsh punishment for violations according to set laws: "If crimes are punished by execution, then the law wins over the people and the army is strong."[10]
- Mutual surveillance and collective punishment: "The people were commanded to be organized into groups of fives and tens. They must be under mutual surveillance and punished for crimes committed by other members of their group. Those who failed to inform against a crime were to be cut in half at the waist."[11]

The cynical, immoral advice of these Chinese Machiavellis grates on Western ears, but it found a willing admirer in Mao Zedong. Mao especially admired—and wanted to emulate—their most accomplished follower, the man who founded the Qin dynasty in 220 BC. The first emperor of the Qin Dynasty, Qin Shi Huang in Chinese, was one of the most ruthless rulers in human history.[12] Mao, of course, turned out to be a fitting acolyte.

The Qin Dynasty Model

During an age when the reach of even the most ambitious rulers almost always exceeded their grasp, the first emperor of the Qin Dynasty sought to make the entire population of China, at the time some forty million people, directly accountable to him. Acting through an enormous cadre of bureaucrats, a complex network of laws, and a highly elaborated ideology, he very largely succeeded. In so doing, the Qin emperor became the archetype of a political monster that has become all too common in our modern age. More than two millennia before George Orwell coined the term, ancient China endured the world's first Big Brother.

---

[10] *Shangjun shu,* chapter 5.

[11] *Shi ji,* chapter 68.

[12] In the following sections, I draw heavily upon the seminal work of Professor Zhengyuan Fu, especially his *Autocratic Tradition and Chinese Politics and China's Legalists.* Professor Fu was well-acquainted with not only China's totalitarian past but also its totalitarian present, since he spent the years from 1957 to 1979 incarcerated in Beijing Prison Number 1 for speaking out during the Hundred Flowers Campaign.

Qin Shi Huang is a household name throughout the Orient, yet few in the West, outside of a handful of Asian experts, have heard of this despotic son of the dragon. But his policies, crafted in conjunction with his Legalist advisers, stunningly anticipated those of Vladimir Lenin, who created the Soviet bureaucratic totalitarian empire more than two thousand years later, and those of Mao Zedong.

To begin with, a special cadre of commissars was established to keep watch over officialdom. At the provincial level, for example, there was a civil governor, a military commander, and a political commissar. The duties of the commissar—precisely like those of their latter-day counterparts in the People's Republic of China today—were to spy on the governor and military commander and ensure that they did not deviate from the official line or criticize government policy. All civil and military officials were centrally appointed and salaried, and they served at the pleasure of the emperor.

The emperor's Legalist credo was that "a wise prince doesn't ask his subjects to behave well—he uses methods that prevent them from behaving badly." Every area of life was regulated. The people were not permitted to bear arms, and all weapons were confiscated and sent to the capital. Trade, regarded as "parasitical activity," was made illegal. Wandering minstrels were banned and replaced by state-sanctioned troupes of singers and musicians whose very repertoires had to be approved by the Ministry of the Interior.

As laws proliferated, the bureaucracies charged with enforcing them fattened. Fierce punishments, calculated to squelch any murmur of resistance, were meted out to violators. For major capital crimes, both the offender and his entire family were annihilated. Those convicted of lesser crimes were sent by the millions to labor on government projects in a forerunner of the Soviet Union's Gulag or Communist China's Laogai camps.

For the construction of Emperor Qin Shi Huang's palace, for example, more than seven hundred thousand laborers were conscripted; a similar number were drafted for the construction of his tomb.[13] Hundreds of thousands more labored to build some four thousand miles of imperial highways, as many as were built by the Roman Empire. Countless others dug canals and widened waterways to allow water transport for the twelve hundred miles from the Yangtze to Guangzhou. Others were sent north to strengthen the walls that earlier Chinese states had built.[14] The state treated ordinary people as disposable resources.[15]

At the same time, anticipating later Communist leaders, the world's first cult of personality was invented. Clever ministers attributed godlike powers to the Qin emperor, and official bards spread stories of his fabulous accomplishments throughout the length and breadth of the empire. One minister had giant footprints four feet long and two feet wide carved in the rock of a sacred mountain and let it be known that these had been made by the august emperor's shoes. At the summit of another sacred mountain, another minister placed a set of chess pieces as tall as a man. The emperor, he avowed, had ascended the mountain and played chess with the gods. Everywhere, steles were raised with deeply carved inscriptions lauding the emperor and the accomplishments of his rule: "All men under the sun work with one heart. Morals have been standardized. Neighbors keep watch on one

---

[13] *Shi ji*, chapter 6.

[14] The Great Wall of China as we know it today was built by the Ming dynasty in the sixteenth century, as Arthur Waldron has conclusively shown in *The Great Wall of China*. Earlier walls were built by Qin, other Warring States, and later dynasties.

[15] There are those who would argue, even in the face of all this evidence, that the Qin state was not truly totalitarian since it was not able to achieve total control over the entire range of human thought and action. But this is like saying that the United States is not truly democratic because not everyone votes in elections. Totalitarianism, like democracy, is an ideal type, the real-world iteration of which can scarcely be without deficiencies. Intentions must be weighed alongside results. And the intent of the first emperor of the Qin dynasty, few would dispute, was to dominate his subjects totally. The Legalist system of government that he employed for that purpose came as close to achieving total control over the population as the relatively primitive means of communication and transportation then allowed; it can properly be judged totalitarian.

another, relatives inform on relatives, and thieves lie low!" Few among his fearful subjects dared disobey the Qin emperor's edicts.

Still, despite the harshness of his laws and the strength of his personality cult, occasional acts of sedition did occur. The only way to achieve perfect control over his subjects, Legalist Li Si informed the emperor, was to eradicate thought itself:

> Your Majesty . . . has firmly established for yourself a position of sole supremacy. . . . And yet these independent schools [Confucianists and others], joining with each other, criticize the codes of laws and instructions. Hearing of the promulgation of a decree, they criticize it, each from the standpoint of his own school. At home they disapprove of it in their hearts; going out they criticize it in the thoroughfare. They seek a reputation by discrediting their sovereign; they appear superior by expressing contrary views, and they lead the lowly multitude in the spreading of slander. If such license is not prohibited, the sovereign power will decline above and partisan factions will form below. It would be well to prohibit this. Your servant suggests that all books in the imperial archives, save the memoirs of the Qin Dynasty, be burned.[16]

Emperor Qin Shi Huang agreed, and he issued an imperial edict:

- Anyone owning classical books or treatises on philosophy must hand them in within thirty days. After thirty days, anyone found in possession of such writings will be branded on the cheek and sent to work as a laborer on the northern wall or some other government project. The only exceptions are books on medicine, drugs, astrology, and agronomy.
- Private schools will be forbidden. Those who wish to study law will do so under government officials.
- Anyone indulging in political or philosophical discussion will be put to death, and his body exposed in public.

---

[16] Li Si, "Memorial on the Burning of Books," in de Bary, *Sources of Chinese Tradition,* 154–55.

- Scholars who use examples from antiquity to criticize the present, or who praise early dynasties in order to throw doubt on the policies of our own, most enlightened sovereign, will be executed, they and their families!
- Government officials who turn a blind eye to the above-mentioned crimes will be deemed guilty by virtue of the principle of collective responsibility, and will incur the same punishment as that inflicted for the offense itself.[17]

The consequences of the edict were swift and devastating. Pyres of burning books lit up the cities and towns as China's ancient literature was reduced to ashes. For possessing forbidden texts, three million men had their faces branded with the stamp of infamy and were deported to the Great Wall. Numerous scholars committed suicide in protest, while others hanged or drowned themselves out of fear.

It is for his punishment of 463 famous Confucian scholars that the Qin emperor is most notorious. These were individuals that the emperor personally tried and found guilty of conspiracy, sabotage, and lèse majesté. In the supreme atrocity of a long record of brutality, he sentenced them to five tortures: beating, amputation of the nose, branding of the cheek, amputation of the feet, and castration. Only after being tortured and unmanned were they then buried up to their necks in the earth and their heads crushed by chariot wheels.[18]

Although the Qin dynasty did not survive the death of its founder, Legalism transformed China forever. Local kingdoms had been welded together into an empire. The aristocracy had been replaced by a bureaucracy. Power had been centralized into the hands of a "son of heaven." The autocratic political system that the Qin emperor and his Legalist adviser had designed—with its absolute monarch, centralized bureaucracy, state domination over society, the law as a penal tool

---

[17] Li Si, "Memorial on the Burning of Books," in de Bary, *Sources of Chinese Tradition,* 154–55.

[18] Derk Bodde, in *Cambridge History of China,* suggests that the 460 (not 463) scholars were not actually buried alive, only murdered, but this is a minority view.

of the ruler, mutual surveillance and informer network, persecution of dissidents, and political practices of coercion and intimidation—entered China's cultural DNA and continued to replicate itself down through the centuries and the dynasties.

Acting on the Legalists' frank, brutal, and cynical advice, China's first emperor had created the world's first totalitarian state. As the centuries unfolded, it continued to prove admirably suited to the ambitions of ruthless Chinese rulers. A young Communist by the name of Mao Zedong, who was well-read in the Chinese classics, took notice.

Mao also noticed that later dynasties balanced Legalist intimidation with Confucian indoctrination. Had not Confucius taught that one of a ruler's most important responsibilities was to educate his subjects in virtue through exhortation, persuasion, and, above all, moral example? "If a ruler himself is upright, all will go well without command. If the ruler himself is not upright, even when he gives commands, he will not be obeyed."[19] The emperors who followed Qin Shi Huang had made a great show of celebrating Confucianism and its rites in public, but they were "Confucianist on the outside, Legalist on the inside" (*wairu neifa*), just as Mao would be "Communist on the outside, Legalist on the inside." Mao sought to use Communism in the same way that previous emperors had: as a kind of secret force to police the mind far more thoroughly than cadres of informers ever could.

The official ideology of Imperial China was not "Confucian" as so often claimed, but rather a clever amalgam of Legalist principles and Confucian rhetoric. Similarly, the official ideology of Communist China is a melding of Marxist-Leninism and Legalist practices. As the emperors made a show of following the benevolent Way preached by Confucius, Chairman Mao and his successors justified their policies as being "for the good of the people." They made a great show of ruling with paternal solicitousness. But they kept the sword close at hand and were quick to use it on their enemies.

---

[19]   Confucius, *Lun yu,* chapter 13.6.

Some would compare China's Legalist traditions, still alive in present-day China, to Machiavelli's *The Prince*. The "end-justifies-the-means" views that Machiavelli espoused in *The Prince*, however, were never able to dominate Western statecraft to the same extent that the Legalists, ancient and modern, have dominated China. And *The Prince* was only published in 1513, nearly two thousand years after the Legalists came to dominate statecraft in China. Why the delay? The bulwark of Catholicism stood in the way.

Nothing like the Humiliation of Canossa—when the Holy Roman Emperor Henry IV walked on foot across the Alps to Canossa Castle in Tuscany, Italy, in January 1077 to beg Pope Gregory VII to lift his excommunication—ever happened in Chinese history. Nor could it have. It is difficult to imagine any Chinese emperor, at any point in Chinese history, publicly asking forgiveness from any religious figure, be he Taoist, Buddhist, or Confucian.

It is even more impossible to imagine that any occupant of the Dragon Throne would ever, like Henry IV, further humiliate himself by kneeling in the midst of a raging blizzard for three days and three nights before a castle begging an audience with that religious authority. The emperor, as the divine "Son of Heaven" and the highest religious authority in the land, would have had to kowtow to himself. And any religious figure who suggested otherwise would probably have had no head left to kowtow with.

First Emperor of the Red Dynasty

Growing up at the turn of the twentieth century, Mao had steeped himself in Chinese historical classics, absorbing the frank and brutal Legalist advice they offered to would-be hegemons.[20] "Know the future in the mirror of the past," as the Chinese say (*Jian wang zhi lai*).

---

[20] During the Cultural Revolution, PLA Marshal Peng Dehuai told the Red Guards who were persecuting him that "Comrade Mao Zedong is more familiar with Chinese history than anyone else in the Party. The first emperor of a dynastic era was always very wise, and very ferocious." Li Yizhe "On Socialist Democracy,"

Mao cast his eye over China's long history and decided that it was the brutal Emperor Qin Shi Huang that he would seek to emulate and the totalitarian "Qin order" that he would seek to recreate. Never mind that more than twenty-two centuries had passed since his "ancestral dragon" had walked the earth. Mao, too, would forge a new dynasty by naked force. He, too, would rule China with an iron fist, resurrecting and modernizing the totalitarian institutions earlier employed by his merciless hero.

To successfully establish the "Qin order" in the modern age, however, Mao needed two things: He needed to reconfigure Legalism for modern times, and he needed a replacement for Confucianism, a new overarching ideology that would soften the harshness of his governance in the eyes of the people. Communism fit the bill.

With the victory of the Communist revolution in Russia, Mao and the rest of China's revolutionaries found the perfect vehicle for their totalitarian ambitions. The imported Marxism-Leninism was every bit as statist as traditional Chinese political culture, while at the same time claiming to be even more "modern" and "progressive" than its chief ideological opponent: liberal democracy.

True democracy, after all, is the opposite of totalitarianism. It disperses power among elected representatives instead of concentrating it in the hands of the ruler. It weakens the state instead of strengthening it. And, worst of all for would-be dictators, it empowers the people instead of subjugating them.

Marxism-Leninism, on the other hand, while formally acknowledging civil rights and the equality of man, was an enabler for totalitarianism. It defended the monopoly of power by a tiny elite and defined a relationship between the state and society that was very much in keeping with China's autocratic tradition. It was a much more effective tool of indoctrination than Confucianism, and its pseudoscientific terminology provided a stronger defense for totalitarian rule. As a bonus, it

---

in *On Socialist Democracy and the Chinese Legal System.* Marshall Peng was certainly correct about the ferocious part.

even commanded a respectful audience in the very heart of Western civilization.

Even as Mao was importing Marxism-Leninism from the West, he was adapting it to China's unique totalitarian heritage. This wasn't as difficult as it might seem. The Leninist party structure was a natural fit with preexisting Chinese imperial practices at both the ideological and the organizational levels. Transitioning from the absolute authority of the emperor to the absolute authority of the Chinese Communist Party (CCP) and its leaders required only a minor mental adjustment. Mao would wield his power in a way very similar to the Chinese emperors of the past.[21]

As far as the highly bureaucratized nature of party rule is concerned, this was not all that different from the complex set of imperial offices that, under the control of the nine-tiered mandarinate, had been in existence in China for centuries. From an organizational point of view, all the Leninist party system did was enable the imperium to be concentrated even more effectively in the hands of the politburo than the traditional structures previously relied upon by the emperors. The new power structures were instantly recognizable, and largely acceptable, to many patriotic intellectuals eager to see China recover its lost glory.

For the illiterate or semiliterate villagers who became the foot soldiers of Mao's armies, the principles of liberal democracy were unknown and the abstractions of Marxist-Leninist ideology forever a mystery. But resonance with dynastic China's Confucian beliefs and imperial traditions helped to make Communism and its leader acceptable. Marxist dialectics militated for change, just as did the yin-yang theory and the *I Ching* (Book of Change). The state remained the grand provider on whom all ultimately relied for their survival. The paternalistic party, as the vanguard of the proletariat, was understood as a stand-in for the "father-mother officialdom" of imperial times. Its "chairman" was the omnipotent savior—the Red Emperor—upon whose benevolent rule all of his subjects depended.

---

[21] Zheng Yongnian, *The Chinese Communist Party as Organizational Emperor,* 16, 22.

Mao's "personality cult" was already flourishing by April 1945, when the new party constitution declared the "thought of Mao Zedong" essential to "guide the entire work" of the party. The chairman was praised as "not only the greatest revolutionary and statesman in Chinese history but also the greatest theoretician and scientist." Much of this fulsome praise came from Mao's own hand.[22]

Mao Zedong was better versed in Chinese history than in Marxist dialectics; he saw himself more as the founding emperor of a new dynasty than the ruler of a Communist state. His most famous poem "White Snow" reveals not only his imperial ambitions but also his boundless narcissism. Mao begins by exalting the beauty and majesty of the north China landscape in winter and ends by exalting himself—and denigrating the founding emperors of previous Chinese dynasties. Written at a time when the Long March had reduced the chairman's ragtag Red Army to fewer than eight thousand men (but not published until many years later), the poem stands as an extraordinary exercise in egotism and self-aggrandizement:

> How beautiful these mountains and rivers,
> enticing countless heroes to war and strife.
> Too bad that Emperors Qin Shi Huang and Han Wudi
>   lacked culture
> and that Emperors Tang Taizong and Song Taizu lacked romance.
> Genghis Khan was the pride of his time,
> though he was only good at shooting eagles with his bow.
> They all belong to a time gone by,
> Only today is a True Hero present.[23]

The "True Hero" was proposing himself, more or less accurately as it worked out, as the superior in both ability and ruthlessness to

---

[22] Schram, *Chairman Mao Talks to the People.*
[23] Mao Zedong, *Mao Zhuxi shici sanshiqi shi.* Translation by the author. "True hero" is a phrase taken from the famous Chinese novel *Romance of the Three Kingdoms,* in which Liu Bei says to Cao Cao that "the only true heroes in the world are you and I."

other dynastic founders. If Mao was offended by comparisons that many made between himself and Emperor Qin Shi Huang, arguably the most hated figure in Chinese history, it was only because he saw himself as Emperor Qin's superior in cunning and cruelty.

By the Second Plenum of the Eighth Party Congress in May 1958—after twenty years of persecuting and purging his enemies inside and outside of the party—Mao was bragging about this success. "Emperor Qin Shi Huang was not that outstanding," he scoffed. "He only buried alive 460 Confucian scholars. We buried 460 *thousand* Confucian scholars. [Some] have accused us of being Emperor Qin Shi Huang. This is not true. We are a hundred times worse than Emperor Qin. To the charge of being like Emperor Qin, of being a dictator, we plead guilty. But you have not said nearly enough, for often we have to go further."[24]

In another of his poems, Mao contrasted his admiration for Emperor Qin Shi Huang and the Legalist order to his utter disdain for Confucius:

> Please don't slander Emperor Qin Shi Huang, Sir
> For the burning of the books should be thought through again.
> Our ancestral dragon, though dead, lives on in spirit,
> While Confucius, though renowned, was really rubbish.
> *The Qin order has survived from age to age.* (Emphasis added.)

Mao's disdain for Confucianism was rooted less in his Marxism-Leninism than in his Legalism. Mao despised the old Confucian orthodoxy for its impracticalities, for its moral niceties, and for its preachiness about virtue and benevolence. Even more, he despised it because its tottering remains stood in the way of building a strong state that would dominate not just the Chinese people but neighboring peoples as well. Mao's respect and admiration were reserved for the

---

[24]   Mao Zedong, *Selected Works,* vol. 4, 195; cited in Fu, *Autocratic Tradition and Chinese Politics,* 188. Some sources have 46,000 instead of 460,000.

"ancestral dragon," the Emperor Qin Shi Huang of the Qin Dynasty, who just happened to be one of the greatest tyrants in human history.

And Mao clearly continued the emperor's cult. The party went to extraordinary lengths to prey upon the superstitions of the people in this way. Mao was endlessly exalted as a larger-than-life figure, a kind of living god who would rescue the people from all manner of suffering and oppression. As soon as the Communists captured a village in the civil war, its buildings would blossom with slogans such as "Mao Zedong is the great savior of the Chinese people." "Chairman" (*zhuxi*) became a modern-day synonym for emperor (*huangdi*).

Mao may have paid lip service to Communism, but he only did so because it served his own purposes so well. As cynical and sophisticated as the most ruthless Legalist rulers, he took full advantage of China's millennia-long totalitarian tradition to consolidate his rule. Mao Zedong had become what he had long admired: the founder of a new dynasty, an emperor of the Legalist school.[25]

As the chairman of the CCP, Mao controlled an organization that even Qin Shi Huang would have admired for its rigid discipline, its highly elaborated organizational structure, and its designs on the total control of society. A Communist party, Mao instinctively understood from the beginning, is a "war party."[26] War is its element, protracted conflict its means, and the seizure of power its ultimate end. It is so admirably suited to these martial purposes that it is, in effect, a force multiplier. By organizing his initially tiny base areas—first in Jinggangshan and later in Yan'an—along military lines, Mao was able to

---

[25] Mao Zedong and the Chinese Communist Party had adopted a pose as "agrarian reformers" during the last decade of the Chinese civil war, advocating a "New Democracy" in local governance and promising to rule "democratically" when they came to power. But as Nationalist resistance collapsed in early 1949 and a Chinese Communist Party victory appeared certain, Mao decided the time had come to abandon this pretense. The new national government would not be a democracy after all, he declared on 1 July 1949, but a "people's democratic dictatorship."

[26] Selznick, *The Organizational Weapon,* especially chapter 1, "The Combat Party," 17–73.

punch well above his weight, vanquish his intra-party enemies, and eventually conquer the entire country.

The Legalist Restoration

Mao may not have been the first to realize the parallels between China's ancient Legalism and modern Marxist-Leninism, but he was the first to put it fully into practice. Mao's evil genius was to amalgamate the two in a new and deadly way.

With the establishment of the People's Republic of China on October 1, 1949, both the Chinese people and the world were told that the future had come to China. Viewed from a long-term historical perspective, however, it looked suspiciously like a case of *Back to the Future*.[27]

The ideological justifications used to legitimate Communist rule differed in many particulars, to be sure, from those of its Confucian predecessors. The central political myth of imperial China was that the emperor held his place by divine sanction and led by moral example, and that as long as he maintained Confucian standards of public virtue, he would continue to enjoy this "Mandate of Heaven."

The central myth of the People's Republic of China, at least for decades after its founding, was identical to that of other Communist states—namely, that the CCP ("the Vanguard of the Proletariat") and its leaders were temporarily exercising dictatorial power on behalf of the "masses" for their own good and in anticipation of the eventual "withering away" of the state. Or as Mao put it, the CCP was "working hard to create the conditions in which classes, state power and political parties will die out very naturally and mankind will enter the realm

---

[27] The Chinese Communist Party led "a counterrevolution against the first Chinese republican revolution of 1911," argues Professor Zhengyuan Fu, and following its victory, it restored a revitalized traditional autocracy. Fu, *Autocratic Tradition and Chinese Politics*, 2. Former President Lee Teng-Hui of Taiwan holds a similar view: "What did the Communist revolution accomplish? It did not bring the continent out of stagnation or free the people of stifling, oppressive tradition; what it did do was resurrect 'hegemony' and imperialism." Teng-hui, *The Road to Democracy*, 53.

of Great Harmony."[28] In fact, the reality underlying this Communist fable was a Marxist-Leninist totalitarian state that was not all that different from China's Legalist past.

The Communist revolution in China restored the traditional Chinese pattern of state-society relations in which society is almost totally subservient to the state. Legalism was reborn in China, although it was veiled in Communist terminology and gave formal deference to a theory of civil rights that the emperors would have scorned. Communist to all outward appearances, the new Chinese state was Legalist in essence, continuing the autocratic tradition of the imperial Chinese state by:

- imposing an official ideology (Marxism-Leninism-Maoism) with interesting functional parallels to Chinese imperial orthodoxy (Legalism-Confucianism);
- concentrating political power in the hands of a tiny minority, often of one, with power deriving ultimately from control of the military and wielded without appreciable institutional constraints;
- treating the penal code and the legal system as tools of governance wielded by the ruler, who acts above legal constraints;
- dominating most, and at times all, aspects of domestic commercial and economic life;
- controlling all forms of social organization outside the nuclear family, which itself is severely restricted;
- engaging in political practices familiar from dynastic times, such as censorship, large-scale persecutions, purges of the bureaucracy, court intrigues, and elite factional conflicts; and
- regarding the people as its property, as subjects rather than citizens.

---

[28] The world of Great Harmony is a utopian vision of a world in which everyone and everything is at peace. The Chinese Communists cynically identified their own ideology with this Confucian ideal in order to win popular support.

The nascent civil society that had grown up during the republican era (roughly 1910 to 1949) was eradicated. Those formerly in leadership positions were "re-educated" or simply executed. The organizations they had formerly headed were either co-opted or destroyed. Newspapers and magazines were brought under state control or closed down entirely. Private and Christian schools were taken over by the state. Voluntary associations were disbanded or merged into party-led front groups.

By the end of the five-year period following 1949, few vestiges of Nationalist China's once-flourishing civil society still survived. Chinese society had come to resemble that of an archetypal Communist state—or equally, that of a Chinese imperial dynasty. Still, the terror campaigns continued.

Mao was characteristically blunt about his aims. Under the guidance of the CCP, the masses would exercise a "democratic dictatorship," whose first and most important task would be to liquidate bad or "antagonistic" classes, defined as "the running dogs of imperialism—the landlord class [and] the bureaucrat-bourgeoisie, as well as the representatives of those classes, the Kuomintang reactionaries and their accomplices." Eventually, all class distinctions would cease to exist, Mao promised, but before that could happen these two "antagonistic" classes had to be "eliminated." Nor was Mao coy about how this class war was to be prosecuted. "Our present task is to strengthen the people's state apparatus," he wrote. "The state apparatus, including the army, the police and the courts, is the instrument by which one class oppresses another. It is an instrument for the oppression of antagonistic classes." Interestingly, Mao still felt obliged to pay lip service to democracy. "The people" would "enjoy freedoms of speech, assembly, association," and would have the right to vote and "elect their own government." But only on one condition: none of this was to interfere with the primary task of the new government, which was to exercise a dictatorship over the enemies of the people. It did not take a political philosopher to see that, even if the rights enumerated by Mao were inalienable, the right to membership in "the people" was not. Those who vigorously exercised their freedom of speech (or assembly, or association), or took seriously their right to "elect their own government," would run the risk of being declared "enemies of the people" by the state apparatus, which would then punish, imprison, or execute them with impunity.[29]

As an emperor of the Legalist school, Mao believed that the Mandate of Heaven gave him license to dominate, well, *everything*. First, there was the matter of firmly subjugating the Chinese people. The incessant political campaigns of the People's Republic of China's early years came about because of Mao's determination to emulate China's "ancestral dragon" and eliminate, utterly and without mercy, all possible opposition to his absolute rule within China.

This ten-year campaign of revolutionary terror was a prototypically Communist thing to do. For had not Marx himself written, in the close of the *Communist Manifesto*, that "the Communists . . . openly declare that their ends can be attained only by the *forcible overthrow* of all existing social conditions"? And, again, "There is only one way in which the murderous death agonies of the old society and the bloody birth throes of the new society can be shortened, simplified and concentrated, and that way is revolutionary terror."[30]

At the same time, however, this ongoing terror campaign is exactly what China's ancient Legalists would have advised Mao to do. Legalism, down to the fall of the Qing Empire, had been the ruling philosophy of China. And now, after a short hiatus, China's ancient dragon had been reborn, like a phoenix from the ashes. His plumage was now red, but aside from the rhetoric, he really hadn't changed all that much. He was still hungry for power and thirsty for blood.

Mao's Evil Genius

Mao Zedong was one of the most evil men who ever lived. Mao and his minions wove a path of destruction through modern China that

---

[29] Mao Zedong, "On the People's Democratic Dictatorship," in *Selected Works*, vol. 4, 417–18.
[30] Kengor, *The Devil and Karl Marx*, 10

was unprecedented in its sheer destructiveness. His efforts to remake China's political economy, obliterate China's history, and even reinvent human nature led to disaster upon disaster. The totalitarian regime that he created continues to pay its dues to the devil on a regular basis, dealing out death to unborn babies, persecution to Christians, and genocide to restless minorities.

Evil is an unpleasant reality, but Christians can grow in virtue by confronting it. Indeed, we are called in Scripture to do exactly this: "Do not be overcome by evil, but overcome evil with good" (Rom 12:21). One way to ensure that we are opposed to Satan and his demons is to understand and expose the sins of an evil genius like Mao, and then ask God to empower us to do the opposite.

With that in mind, let us examine what we know about this man who conquered China, killed tens of millions, and set in motion a perpetual killing machine called the CCP. Where did Mao come from, what did he believe, and was he, consciously or unconsciously, in service to Satan?

PART 2
MAO ZEDONG:
MONSTER AND DEMON[1]

"And one of them, a lawyer, asked him a question, to test him. 'Teacher, which is the great commandment in the law?' And he said to him, 'You shall love the Lord your God with all your heart, and with all your soul, and with all your mind. This is the great and first commandment. And a second is like it, You shall love your neighbor as yourself. On these two commandments depend all the law and the prophets.'"

—Matthew 22:35–40

"I do not agree with the view that to be moral, the motive of one's action has to be benefiting others. Morality does not have to be defined in relation to others. . . . People like me want to . . . satisfy our hearts to the full, and in doing so we automatically have the most valuable moral codes. Of course there are people and objects in the world, but they are all there only for me."

—Mao Zedong[2]

---

[1]   What follows is not a biography but a review of some of Mao's actions that shine a light on his personal morality or, in this case, his lack of it. Nearly all of these incidents I recount occurred early in his political career and on his direct orders. The Communist Party invariably blames the brutality of its leaders on "the excesses of lower level officials," but no such defense can be mounted here: these sins against God and man were clearly committed by Mao himself. And, as we will see, his successors are cut from the same cloth.

[2]   Chang, *Mao,* 13.

CHAPTER 4

THIRD SON OF THE MONOLITH

"And what rough beast, its hour come round at last,
Slouches towards Bethlehem to be born?"

—W. B. Yeats, "The Second Coming"

Chairman Mao and His Inner Demons

The religion of China was a potpourri of primitive animism, folk practices known as Taoism, with an overlay of Buddhism. Animism is the belief that features of nature—rock formations, giant trees, mountains, or seas—are inhabited by powerful spirits. The ancients would call them demigods. Christians would call them demons.

The pagan Germans annually sacrificed a small child to "Thunder Oak," a sacred oak dedicated to mighty Thor, a practice that only ended in the eighth century when Saint Boniface cut it down in a demonstration of the power of the Christian God.[1] Pacific Islanders cast young maidens into the volcanoes that formed their islands in order to propitiate and pacify the angry god they believed periodically tried to kill them with eruptions of ash and lava. Mao Zedong's mother was to take her infant son to a haunted rock formation—a monolith—near her village to beg for the protection of the spirit, or demon, who lived there.

Mao was born into a peasant family in the Hunanese village of Shaoshan on December 26, 1893. It was the day after Christmas, not

---

[1] Laux, *Church History,* 221. Tree worship is also found in China. There was, for example, a sacred banyan tree, complete with a good-sized cement altar with an incense burner, and bearing the inscription "Old Banyan Tree," in 1950s Hong Kong. See Burkhardt, *Chinese Creeds and Customs,* 119.

that anyone took notice since Christianity had not reached the remote part of the province where Shaoshan was located. There, people still followed the old lunar calendar. By its calculations, a boy was born into the Mao family on the nineteenth day of this eleventh month of the Year of the Snake.

The snake is one of a dozen common animals that appear in the Chinese zodiac. These are, in order of appearance, the rat, ox, tiger, rabbit, dragon, snake, horse, goat, monkey, rooster, dog, and pig. Starting with the rat and ending with the pig, each of the twelve dominates the year that is named after it.

This may seem like merely a simple way to keep track of the cycle of years, but to the Chinese, it is freighted with astrological meaning. The Chinese term for the zodiac is *Shengxiao*—the two characters of which literally mean "born resembling"—and the Chinese of the time firmly believed that a person's character and personality were determined by the animal presiding over his birth year. A child born in the Year of the Rat, for example, is expected to be clever, energetic, and quick to take advantage of new circumstances, much like the rodent itself. At the same time, they are thought to lack courage and to be ill-suited for leadership positions, just as a rat tends to scurry away from danger.

In other words, the Chinese zodiac served as a kind of parenting guide in traditional times because it often determined how Chinese parents would approach a particular child born under a particular sign. It is easy to see how such would become a kind of self-fulfilling prophecy, if you will, as the child "born resembling a rat" conforms to the expectations of those around him and indeed becomes more "rat-like" over time.

But as mentioned above, Mao Zedong was born in the Year of the Snake. In the West, snakes are held to be the primordial symbol of evil. In China, on the other hand, people think of snakes as "small dragons." But that doesn't mean they are generally well-regarded. Their character is ambiguous, mysterious, and seductive; they are often used as symbols of witchcraft.

As for those born during the snake's reign, they are held to be intelligent and wise, but at the same time calculating and inscrutable, keeping to themselves and hiding their designs from others. They may appear to be slow and serene, but they are actually alert and observant as they chart their own course in life. They especially thrive in chaos, holding their ground and calmly thinking through solutions. If they are the eye of the storm, it may be because they themselves unleashed it.

These are the traits that Mao's relatives would have expected him to display as he was growing up. It is curious, to say the least, how many of these same traits are manifested by Mao the man. The American Communist Agnes Smedley, who met with him shortly after he seized control of the Chinese Communist Party (CCP) in late 1934, found him an unreadable and forbidding figure. "His dark, inscrutable face was long, the forehead broad and high, the mouth feminine," she wrote. "I had the impression that he would wait and watch for years, but eventually have his way. . . . His humor was often sardonic and grim, as though it sprang from deep caverns of spiritual seclusion. I had the impression that there was a door to his being that had never been opened to anyone."[2]

Some may scoff at the thought that a mere sign of the Chinese zodiac could play such a formative role in shaping Mao's serpent-like personality. How could anyone take a mere horoscope that seriously? They fail to understand that for thousands of years, up to the last days of the Qing Empire, the Lunar Calendar governed life in rural China. The calendar supposedly dates back to 2254 BC, when Emperor Yao ordered his astrologers to fix the seasons so that farmers might know when to plant their crops. But it had grown over the ages into a sixty-page farmer's almanac that dictated precisely how everyone was to live

---

[2]   Smedley, *The Battle Hymn of China,* 121–23.

their lives according to their sign. The 1954 Chinese Lunar Calendar, for instance, states that:

- Lucky days for traveling on the First Moon . . . are the 3rd, 5th, 6th and 10th for all but those born under the sign of the Pig, Rat, Ox and Snake.
- For good fortune and wealth the 5th, 8th, 15th and 17th are lucky except for Rabbit, Dog and Rat folk. If not born under the sign of Rat, Rabbit, Dragon or Cock a profitable business can be opened on the 5th, 8th, 9th or 14th of the month.
- Asking gods for blessings can best be accomplished, with a good hope of success, on the 3rd, 8th and 15th, but this does not apply to Dog, Rat or Rabbit people.[3]

In other words, Mao's snake-like character would have been reaffirmed continually by the expectations of those around him. And to some extent, he became how he was beheld. By the time he reached adulthood, he had become inscrutable to friends and enemies alike. He had mastered the art of lying in wait, biding his time until his enemy revealed his hand and it was time to strike. He called this "luring the snakes out of their holes and then chopping their heads off." He steeped himself in the countless stories of deception and betrayal that populate Chinese history, and he brought them back to life in his own time.

As an infant, Mao was given an unusually propitious name consisting of two characters: Ze, which means "to shine on" or "to anoint," and Dong, which means "the East." So his full given name meant, rather grandiosely, "the Mao who shines on the East" or "the Mao who anoints the East." Mao's hagiographers—atheistic Communists for the most part—have made much of this grand name, seeing it as prophetic of his future political career as the ruler of all of China. Of course, Mao did not go on so much to "anoint" the East as to defecate on and despoil it, at least that part of it that he controlled.

---

[3]   Burkhardt, *Chinese Creeds and Customs,* 3.

Now it was not unusual for a boy child to be given, in addition to his formal name, a humbler handle so that the gods would not, in their jealously and wrath, destroy him. Because her first two sons had died in infancy, Mao's mother was particularly eager to protect her third born from their baleful eyes.

Mao's mother was not content, however, just to give Mao a nickname. She also took her young son on a kind of religious pilgrimage. There was a monolith about eight feet high some distance from the village that, both because of its prominence and the spring that issued from its base, was thought to be inhabited by a spirit. There, before the spirit of the monolith, she made her toddler kowtow and perform obeisance, as one would bow and scrape in front of a statue of Buddha or before the tablets of one's own ancestors. She rechristened him *Shi san ya-zi,* which means "The Third Son of the Monolith." After this ceremony, Mao was considered to have been adopted by the spirit of the monolith.

Most of those who have written about this episode—and there aren't that many—have translated *Shi san ya-zi* as "The Boy of Stone." However, this is misleading.[4] The "stone" in question is not the toddler Mao, as much as his admirers would like to claim that tough, resolute-sounding nickname for him. Rather, "stone" is a reference to the monolith—actually to the spirit of the monolith—to whom he had been dedicated, and by whom he was now thought to have a spiritual connection.

Few on either side of the Pacific attribute any real significance to this "second baptism," as Jung Chang and Jon Halliday aptly referred to it in their biography of Mao. But a kind of baptismal rite it was, although one with a very different meaning than its Christian counterpart. A Christian baptism is conferred "in the name of the Father and of the Son and of the Holy Spirit," at which time the baptized receives his name in the Church, usually the name of a saint. This patron saint

---

[4]   See, for example, Chang, *Mao,* 5. *Shi san ya-zi* could also be translated "The Number Three Boy of the Monolith."

not only provides a model of charity but intercedes for us in heaven.[5] Little Mao also received a name in the course of this pagan ritual, but it was a name totally foreign to Christian sentiment. "Third Son of the Monolith" has echoes of the demonic.

Communist Chinese historians have generally sought to airbrush this second baptism out of history as an embarrassing feudalistic hold-over. Secular Western historians, on the other hand, have viewed this act as just another quaint custom of Chinese folk religion, like setting off firecrackers to ward off evil spirits or burning paper money by the gravesides of deceased ancestors so that they might have spending money in the spirit world. There is even a children's book on the shelves of some American school libraries called *The Boy of Stone*, which is such a cutesy portrayal of the young Mao that it would make a Communist propagandist blush.

But the animistic views of Mao's mother cannot be so easily disdained and dismissed. The belief that natural phenomena, such as trees and rocks, have resident spirits has been shared by billions of human beings from the beginning of time, including hundreds of millions of rural Chinese. Rock formations have been at the heart of pagan ceremonies throughout history, from giant Uluru in Australia to the Standing Stones of Scotland.

Mao's mother was clearly seeking supernatural protection for her young son. But establishing a relationship with a non-corporeal spirit entity can be, shall we say, problematic. Catholics are cautioned against such practices for good reason. The *Catechism of the Catholic Church* warns against "all practices of *magic* or *sorcery*, by which one attempts to tame occult powers, so as to place them at one's service and have a supernatural power over others—even if this were for the purpose of restoring their health—are gravely contrary to the virtue of religion."[6]

---

[5]   *CCC* 2156.
[6]   *CCC* 2117.

Mao's mother, invincibly ignorant of such things as she was, was only trying to protect her little son's health by her "second baptism" of Mao as *Shi san ya-zi*. But a Christian must view such an act differently. Placing young Mao under the monolith's protection may have opened him to demonic influence at an early age.

Calling it a "second baptism" may not be all that far from the mark. In contrast with a Christian baptism, in which a child is named and offered to the Triune God, it was a kind of anti-baptism in which the infant Mao was given a false name and offered to a false god.

As we will see, the Third Son of the Monolith certainly behaved as though he was at least "infested" with an unholy spirit that was constantly goading him to evil, for at every turn, he invariably took the darkest path. One can almost hear Satan screeching that "Mao Zedong is 'stone,' and upon this 'stone' I will build a demonic temple of horrors."

As for Mao, he remained oddly fond of the name given to him at his second baptism at the Monolith, so much so that he continued to use it throughout his life. Chang and Halliday report that in 1959, when Mao returned to his home village of Shaoshan for the first and only time as CCP chairman, he held up the banquet thrown in his honor until his mother arrived. "So everyone is here except the mother of the 'Third Son of the Monolith,'" said Mao. "Shall we wait for her?" Coming from the ruler of all of China, it was not really a question.[7]

Calling this strange episode a satanic baptism would be going too far, but it certainly was a curious beginning to a life that, over the course of decades, repeatedly plumbed the depths of evil. The Third Son of the Monolith was to grow up into one of the most ruthless, pitiless individuals who ever lived. He was totally without compassion for other human beings.

You might say he had a heart of stone.

---

[7] Chang, *Mao,* 5.

The Man of Stone

The only person that Mao ever loved was his mother because she catered to his every whim. Chinese mothers in traditional times were wont to spoil their sons since having a son was the only way to gain status in the extremely patriarchal society of the time. Wives who did not, or could not, bear sons were often, after a time, replaced by concubines who could.

Even by the standards of the time, however, Mao's mother was especially loving and tolerant—so much so that Mao could not recall that she ever once raised her voice with him. Even as Mao grew older, he clung to her apron strings. He once recalled, "I worshipped my mother. . . . Wherever my mother went, I would follow. . . . Going to temple fairs, burning incense and paper money, doing obeisance to Buddha. . . . Because my mother believed in Buddha, so did I."

Young Mao was thus exposed to Buddhist teachings from his mother and from the monks at a nearby temple that they regularly visited.[8] This would have included very specific admonitions against killing, stealing, sexual contact, lying, deception, and pride, all elaborations of the more general moral guidance known as the Three Pure Precepts: "Avoid all evil, cultivate goodness, and act for the good of others."

None of Buddhism's teachings, which include a profound respect for all life, seem to have made any lasting impression on him. Mao recalls abandoning any belief in Buddhism as he entered his teens.

Nor did the works of the ancient Confucian philosophers, which also to a degree foreshadow Christian moral teaching, make any lasting impression on him. Indeed, many of the Ten Commandments find almost exact parallels in the Confucian tradition. Mao would have been familiar with these from his years of studying classical Confucian texts, such as the requirement to honor one's parents. China's ancient sage even laid down what is called the Silver Rule (to distinguish it

---

[8]   Chinese Buddhism was an amalgamation of Mahayana Buddhism and Taoist practices.

from the West's Golden rule): "Do not do unto others what you would not have them do until you."

All this means that one cannot defend Mao's actions by arguing that he was invincibly ignorant, or that he was merely "a product of his own time." It was of his own free will that he chose to reject everything good in the Confucian and Buddhist traditions, as well as the still, small voice in his own heart. It was by conscious choice that he immersed himself in Chinese history, familiarizing himself with the brutal Legalist practices of every evil emperor down through Chinese history. It was by deliberate intention that, throughout his long life, he emulated their evil at every turn—and counted himself clever for doing so.

Mao exempted himself from existing moral codes on his natural superiority, writing that he did "not agree with the view that to be moral, the motive of one's action has to be benefiting others. Morality does not have to be defined in relation to others. . . . People like me want to . . . satisfy our hearts to the full, and in doing so we automatically have the most valuable moral codes."[9] And then, as if he were a Greek god descended from Mount Olympus to toy with humanity, he added offhandedly, "Of course there are people and objects in the world, but they are all there only for me." Given what we know of Mao's penchant for mass murder, this may be one of the most chilling sentences ever written by a human hand. Tens of millions of people went to their graves because of Mao's unbounded pride and his presumption that their existence was meaningless.

Mao was steeped in the Chinese classics, but he rejected their counsel of Confucian moderation in toto. He was drawn instead to the classic stories of deceit, treason, and betrayal compiled in histories such as the *Comprehensive Mirror in Aid of Governance* published in AD 1084,[10] and in novels such as *The Romance of the Three Kingdoms.*

---

[9]   Chang, *Mao,* 13.

[10] The "Comprehensive Mirror in Aid of Governance" (*Zizhi Tongjian*) is a three-million-character chronicle of Chinese history from 403 BC to AD 959 covering sixteen dynasties.

The editor of the *Comprehensive Mirror*, Sima Guang, wrote it as an instructional guide to rulers, saying that he included "matters . . . related to the rise and fall of dynasties and connected with the joys and sorrows of the people, and of which the good can become a model and the evil a warning." Mao, who devoured its three million characters in search of ways to found his own dynasty, took the acts of evil rulers not as a warning but as a guide.

Mao may have loved his mother, but for the rest of the Chinese people, their joys and sorrows, the Man of Stone seems to have felt nothing. Other people were simply pieces to be moved around on his private chessboard in order to advance his own career. After arriving in Yan'an at the end of the Long March, he assassinated one rival, Liu Chih-tan,[11] poisoned another, Wang Ming,[12] and deliberately sent the forces of a third, Chang Kuo-tao, to be entrapped and annihilated by the Nationalist forces.[13] He butchered their followers by the hundreds and thousands. His rise to the top of the CCP owed a lot to his callous disregard for human life.

Mao had little interest in the well-being of the people under his control. Even though he himself came from peasant stock, he had no real compassion for China's vast peasantry. His writings may express concern for the "masses," or for "workers and peasants," but these were mere abstractions. The "workers" existed only as a class to be manipulated and mobilized against "capitalists" and other classes. The "peasants" existed only as a class to subdivide into rich and poor and set against each other. All of this was done for the Marxist purpose of abolishing private ownership of property and destroying the existing social order—a precursor to ushering in totalitarian rule by the Communist Party. The "masses" existed only to serve the interests of the state, which is to say Mao's interests.

---

[11]   Chang, *Mao,* 173.

[12]   Peter Vladimirov, one of Stalin's agents in Yan'an, believes that Mao ordered, and his secret police chief Kang Sheng orchestrated, the attempt to murder Wang Ming by means of mercury poisoning. Byron, *The Claws of the Dragon,* 174–76.

[13]   See chapter 7.

Human beings were nothing more than faceless objects to Mao. For example, in the mid-fifties, attempting to realize the *Communist Manifesto*'s call for "agricultural armies," he embarked upon a grand scheme to collectivize agriculture. Hundreds of millions of Chinese peasants were forced into huge people's communes. The peasants were understandably unhappy when the CCP took away their land, but Mao was not yet content: he wanted to dehumanize them further. The chairman seriously entertained the idea of simply assigning everyone a number, as they do in prisons, and thus doing away with names altogether. In *Les Misérables*, Inspector Javert released prisoner 24601 on parole; China's masses, like so many Jean Valjeans, came close to losing their identities altogether in the giant prison camp that Mao was constructing.

Mao's total lack of compassion for other people manifested itself in other ways as well. When the people's communes failed and famine struck the land in the early sixties, Mao was unmoved. The people could live on "tree bark and grass," he quipped. Later, when tens of millions of people began to die of starvation, he did not utter a word of sympathy. Instead, he dismissed their plight by matter-of-factly observing, "When there is not enough to eat, people starve to death. It is better to let half of the people die so that the other half can eat their fill."[14]

But it is Mao's heartless remark about human fertilizer that stands out in my mind. "Deaths have benefits," he observed. "They fertilize the ground."[15]

Given the trail of death and destruction that Mao wrought over the course of his long life, the spirit to whom his mother entrusted him must have been malevolent indeed. Mao launched the brutal Cultural Revolution by demanding that his Red Guards "Sweep Away all Monsters and Demons,"[16] ignoring the fact that he himself was the biggest "monster and demon" of them all.

---

[14] AZ Quotes. "Mao Zedong Quotes."

[15] AZ Quotes. "Mao Zedong Quotes."

[16] Literally "Sweep Away All Cow Monsters and Snake Demons." The editorial appeared in the *People's Daily* on 1 June 1966.

We will find out just how malevolent the Third Son of the Monolith himself was in the succeeding chapters as we follow him through the commandments. To paraphrase Yeats, here is the rough beast in the flesh—devoid of empathy, reveling in corruption, feeding on human suffering—slouching toward Beijing to be born.[17]

---

[17]   In the next chapters, we examine Mao Zedong in the light of this twofold yet single commandment of love as we go through the Ten Commandments of the Decalogue. To those who say it is unfair to judge Mao against commandments that he was never formally taught, I quote the *Catechism of the Catholic Church:* "Since they express man's fundamental duties towards God and towards his neighbor, the Ten Commandments . . . are fundamentally immutable, and they oblige always and everywhere. No one can dispense from them. The Ten Commandments are engraved by God in the human heart" (*CCC* 2072).

CHAPTER 5

MAO: LAWLESS AND GODLESS BY HIS OWN ADMISSION

*"You shall love the Lord your god with all your heart,
and with all your soul, and with all your mind."*

—Matthew 22:37

"I am only a lone monk walking the world with a leaky umbrella."

—Mao Zedong[1]

*"There seemed to be nothing in him that might be called religious feeling;
his judgments were reached, I believe, on the basis of reason and necessity."*

—Edgar Snow, *Red Star Over China*

In allowing Edgar Snow to become the first Western correspondent to visit the new Communist base area in 1936, Mao Zedong made an excellent choice. Like many Western intellectuals in the 1930s, Snow fervently believed that only socialism could produce and sustain democracy. He advocated putting "the control of the means of production in the hands of the people," and he was disdainful of capitalism, which he saw as leading inevitably to fascism. Arriving in Yan'an, he was convinced that he had "found [in Yan'an] a political movement that . . . harnessed people's energies for the common good."[2]

The reality was that the people of Yan'an had been enslaved by Mao and his Red Army for his own good, not for theirs, and anyone who

---

1   Snow, "A Conversation with Mao Tse-Tung."
2   Mosher, *China Misperceived*, 57.

questioned their rule was imprisoned and often executed. But Snow wasn't interested in discovering the truth about this Communist revolutionary. Instead, Snow copied down every word Mao spoke, and then even allowed Mao to edit it. Snow was totally captivated by the guerrilla leader.

Still, in his book *Red Star Over China*, and in later interviews, the real Mao occasionally came through.

On one occasion, in a rare burst of candor, Mao tried to tell Snow that he respected neither the laws of God nor the laws of man. The message was lost on Snow, however, because Mao had used a Chinese idiom—*Wu Fa, Wu Tian*—that his American scribe took literally.

"I am a monk holding an umbrella," Snow thought Mao was saying. "I have neither hair nor heaven." The saying was not meant to be taken literally, but Snow, who was as innocent as his name suggests, did exactly that. He wrote that the Communist leader was suggesting that he was leading a spartan, even monastic existence, had few possessions, and didn't care about his looks, like a shaven-headed monk with a leaky umbrella, see.

Chinese idioms are often difficult for Westerners to unpack. Like onions, they often contain layers of hidden meaning. It turns out that there is a word that in Chinese sounds exactly like "hair," tone and all. That word is "law." Any native speaker of Chinese would have instantly grasped that what Mao actually meant by saying *Wu Fa, Wu Tian* was this: "I respect the laws of neither man nor God."

Communist sympathizer Snow, like many who would follow him, was eager to put Mao in the best light for his Western audience. So, either out of ignorance or cunning, he covered up the Communist leader's damning admission about the lawlessness and godlessness that would characterize both his political and his personal life.

To be sure, Confucius never said anything resembling the first commandment, "Thou shalt love the Lord thy God with all thy heart and with all thy mind." Nor did he suggest, following the second: that one should not take God's name in vain. After all, he did not know

God. But he did say, when asked by his followers about beings of the spirit, that "he respected them but kept his distance." It is good advice to respect God and the angels while keeping one's distance from evil spirits. But it seems that Mao did neither.

First Commandment: "You Shall Have No Other Gods before Me"

"I am the LORD your God, who brought you out of the land of Egypt, out of the house of bondage. You shall have no other gods before me. You shall not make for yourself a graven image, or any likeness of anything that is in heaven above, or that is in the earth beneath, of that is in the water under the earth; you shall not bow down to them or serve them."

—Exodus 20:2–5

"People like me only have a duty to ourselves; we have no duty to other people. . . . I am responsible only for the reality that I know, and absolutely not responsible for anything else. I don't know about the past. I don't know about the future. They have nothing to do with the reality of my own self."

—Mao Zedong[3]

Edgar Snow's romantic account of Mao the revolutionary is mostly fictional. But the irreligious Snow was right when he wrote of Mao: "There seemed to be nothing in him that might be called religious feeling; his judgments were reached, I believe, on the basis of reason and necessity."[4]

Saint Paul, writing to the Romans, explains that such a refusal to "acknowledge God" is the source and explanation of all "unacceptable thoughts and indecent behavior" (Rom 1:18–32).[5] Mao not only rejected God but also seemingly believed that there was no creature in heaven or on earth who was higher, more exalted, more intelligent, or more worthy than he.

---

3   Chang, *Mao*, 13.
4   Snow, *Red Star Over China*, 112.
5   See also *CCC* 2087.

Mao was an atheistic humanist, and as such, as Snow noted, he was completely devoid of religious sentiments. He considered himself to be "an end to himself, and the sole maker, with supreme control, of his own history."[6] But he certainly didn't want his followers to be irreligious, at least where he himself was concerned. Emulating Chinese emperors down through history, he sought to be revered as a deity by the illiterate soldiers who comprised the bulk of his army. He wanted the village masses to acknowledge his authority, have faith in him, and obey his every utterance. He wanted to be regarded as the all-powerful, all-merciful, and all-good savior of China, concerned only about, as he wrote, "serving the people." He wanted, in short, to fill the God-shaped hole in the hearts of the Chinese people, even if he had to destroy them to do it.

As for Mao himself, he may have served Communism, but only because it served his own purposes so well. If the emperors had been Confucianist on the outside, Legalist on the inside, then Mao was effectively Communist on the outside, Legalist on the inside. As cynical and sophisticated as the most ruthless Legalist rulers, he took full advantage of China's millennia-long totalitarian tradition to consolidate his rule. A study of references and quotations in Mao's *Selected Works* is revealing in this regard. Some 24 percent come from Stalin, the most ruthless Soviet leader. But almost as many—22 percent—come from traditional Chinese sources. In his later speeches, references to traditional sources become even more common, while Stalin and his sayings disappeared down the memory hole. Mao Zedong had become what he had long admired: the founder of a new dynasty, an emperor of the Legalist school, regarded by the ignorant as something more than a mere mortal.

As the chairman of the Chinese Communist Party (CCP), Mao controlled an organization that even Qin Shi Huang would have admired for its rigid discipline, its highly elaborated organizational structure, and its designs on the total control of society. A Communist

---

[6]   Second Vatican Council, *Gaudium et Spes* (December 7, 1965), no. 20.

party, Mao instinctively understood from the beginning, is a "war party."[7] War is its element, protracted conflict its means, and the seizure of power its ultimate end. It is so admirably suited to these martial purposes that it is, in effect, a force multiplier. By organizing his initially tiny base areas—first in Jinggangshan and later in Yan'an—along military lines and claiming divine status, Mao was able to punch well above his weight, vanquish his intra-party enemies, and eventually conquer the entire country.

During the Cultural Revolution, his cult of personality reached its peak with over six billion of his pictures littering the landscape (ten for every person in China). When I first arrived in China in the late seventies, Mao's image was in every house, in every factory, and in every commune office. In the homes of villagers, to make the late chairman's exalted status clear at a glance, a poster of his face was placed above the altar on which the family's ancestral tablets rested. These bore the names of family members who had gone before, often going back several generations. But before people bowed down before their deceased grandparents and burned incense in their honor, the party demanded that they honor and make obeisance to Chairman Mao first.

This veneration of one of the greatest villains in history, encouraged by the Communist Party, continues in China today. Mao's mausoleum in Tiananmen Square in Beijing always has a line of people waiting to get in, and the numbers increase around the date of his birth, December 26. Some people have a small statue of Mao set up on their family altar as if he is a god or an ancestral spirit. Hundreds of thousands of visitors come to his place of birth in Shaoshan each year and take part in vigils remembering the late leader.[8]

Perhaps most surprising, given Mao's vicious and unrelenting attacks on religion during his lifetime, statues of Mao can even be found inside Buddhist and Taoist temples, especially in his home

[7]   Snow, *Random Notes on Red China (1936-46)*, 83.
[8]   "Mao Zedong, a persecutor of religions, is now worshipped like a god."

province of Hunan. There, the Great Helmsman, dressed in imperial yellow, smiles benignly down on supplicants offering incense, fruit, and spirit money in return for his supposed favor. Even in death, Mao continues to violate God's first commandment to the ancient Israelites, commanding from the grave that the Chinese people make graven images of him and that they bow down to him and serve him.

But Mao was not just an atheistic megalomaniac—although he certainly was that—he committed an even graver violation of the first commandment, one that was almost Luciferian in its implications. In his hunger to become the Prince of this World, or at least the Prince of China, he sought to convince his mostly illiterate followers that he was more than a man. It is bad enough to attempt to depose God by insisting that a rock, or an idol, is divine. But to attempt to supplant God by sowing the seeds of one's own deification is an act worthy of Satan.

Second Commandment: You Shall Not Take the Name of the Lord Your God in Vain.[9]

"You have heard that it was said to the men of old, 'You shall not swear falsely. . . . But I say to you, Do not swear at all.'"

—Matthew 5:33–34

Mao Zedong's language is often characterized by his Western admirers—and, yes, he does have some among the ideological and the innocent—as a product of his peasant background. They explain that Mao was simply being earthy, plain-spoken, and unpretentious. But having lived among Chinese country folk and spoken their language, I can tell you that his constant vulgarity was not normal. Ordinary village men do not constantly talk about their bodily functions or curse other people's mothers the way that Mao did.

Mao the Snake never did anything spontaneously. He carefully calculated the effect of his every word and act on others. His adoption of a peasant persona was obviously a conscious choice intended to suggest

---

[9]   Exodus 20:7.

solidarity with the peasants, upon whose loyalty his power rested but for whom he himself felt nothing. He could just as easily have adopted the accents of a Confucian scholar. He was well-read in the Confucian classics and Chinese history, and his poems are filled with classical allusions.

It's also clear that Mao's constant cursing also gave him a rhetorical advantage over his more refined political adversaries. Mao succeeded in wresting the leadership of the CCP away from the urbane Zhou Enlai in the 1930s because the man who later became his number two found it impossible to respond in kind.

Most of the other Communist leaders were, like Zhou, educated men who were originally drawn to Communism by its ideals. Mao saw Communism chiefly as a vehicle to seize power, and his lust for power found expression in his language. As Mao himself noted, "Communism is not love. Communism is a hammer which we use to crush the enemy."[10]

It is that same lust for power that led to his personality cult, and from there to his attempt to deify himself in the eyes of ordinary peasants and workers. Mao's pretensions to divinity constitute the clearest violations of the second commandment. Is it possible to more vainly abuse God's name than to misappropriate it for one's own use? I don't think so.

By 1943, this process of secular deification was well underway. The chairman's utterances began being referred to as "Mao Zedong Thought" (*Mao Zedong Sixiang*), while his speeches were compiled into the first volumes of the "Selected Works," which were to become the CCP's version of sacred scripture. This was the same year that the blasphemous hymn to Mao, "The East is Red," was composed:

> The East is Red, the sun rises.
> In China a Mao Zedong is born.
> He seeks the people's happiness
> He is the people's Great Savior.

To show that he enjoyed the mandate of heaven—that is, that he and his nascent dynasty had a divine right to rule—Mao even began

---

[10] AZ Quotes, "Mao Zedong Quotes."

mimicking some of the elaborate rituals earlier practiced by the emperors. In 1944, for example, he made a great ceremony of planting the first few seeds of millet, just as the emperors of the past had plowed the first spring furrow, and for the same reason: to use his heavenly connections to ensure the success of the year's crops.

Third Commandment: Remember the Sabbath and Keep It Holy

"Remember the sabbath day, to keep it holy. Six days you shall labor, and do all your work; but the seventh day is a sabbath to the LORD your god; in it you shall not do any work."

—Exodus 20:8–10

"The average person has the equivalent of five whole days of [political] meetings per month, and these are very good rest time for them."

—Mao Zedong[11]

Children in Chinese villages were expected to do chores from a young age, but Mao was ever averse to doing physical labor. Growing up, he got in frequent rows with his father over his unwillingness to do farmwork.

Mao the indolent boy grew up into Mao the indolent man. During his brief stint as a soldier in 1911 at the age of eighteen, he refused to perform the menial chores that he and the other soldiers were assigned, thinking them to be beneath his station in life. As he explained, "Being a student [that is, a man of letters, I] could not condescend to carrying [water or anything else]." Instead, he paid porters to carry items for him.[12]

Later, during the Long March, Mao refused to walk. Instead, with an eye to his own creature comfort, he bragged to others, "'Look, we have designed our litters . . . we will be carried.' . . . [The] litter had very long bamboo poles so it would be easier and lighter to carry while climbing over mountains. It had a tarpaulin awning . . . so [Mao]

---

[11]   Schram, *Mao's Road to Power*, 603.
[12]   Snow, *Red Star Over China*, 166.

would be shielded from the sun and the rain."[13] Needless to say, the poor bearers were not protected from either while they bore the reclining Communist Party leader over terrain so rugged they sometimes had to climb on their knees.

What did Mao do while he was borne across the landscape like an oriental potentate? The same sort of things he spent his entire life doing. He whiled away the hours reading Chinese history and historical novels, dreaming of founding a dynasty and plotting a coup against the party leadership, who, for good reason, had learned to distrust him. As always, he was more than willing to let others do the heavy lifting.

The Yan'an Way: Work until You Drop

While Mao, like Mandarins of old, shunned physical labor as beneath his station, he did not hesitate to squeeze every bit of food and labor out of those he controlled. Like Communists everywhere, he regarded his subjects as a disposable resource—an industrial army, as Marx put it—to be deployed with military discipline and precision to advance his cause. In his own mind, as one of Chinese history's self-described "Great Heroes," he had never been one of them.

The areas that the CCP controlled, like Yan'an, quickly came to resemble giant "reeducation through labor" camps. After seizing control of a territory, the Red Army set up a perimeter to control entry and egress. But while the sentries at the guard posts allowed people to enter more or less freely, no one was allowed to leave.

The Yan'an base area, on Mao's orders, was completely cut off from the outside world. Even the surviving Long Marchers, whose loyalty should have been beyond question, were never given leave to visit their families, even though years had passed since they had seen their wives and children. When two of them continued to insist, they were told they were "crazy" and sent to the hospital under armed escort for treatment. Seeing their Long March veteran's medals, one Communist

---

[13] Liu Ying, *Zai lishi de jiliu zhong* [In the Tidal Waves of History], 56. Cited in Chang, *Mao,* 139.

official warned them, "Remember your glorious revolutionary history." Glorious history or no, had they tried to escape, they would have been executed. Still, desertions from the front lines threatened to cripple the Red Army. One brigade in 1943 set a target of catching one thousand deserters—from its own ranks![14]

The people living throughout the Yan'an region had, before the arrival of the Red Army, largely managed their own affairs. "The mountains are high and the emperor is far away," goes the Chinese saying. There was a local warlord, of course, but his writ did not extend far beyond the walls of the city he controlled. Nine-tenths of the population lived in villages, and these, as they had from time immemorial, governed themselves. They had their own village head, usually the leader of the dominant clan, and their own local militia to defend the village against bandits and mete out justice to local ruffians. And, of course, they were free to plant and harvest their crops, celebrate their festivals and feasts, and generally come and go as they pleased.

All that changed in October 1935 when detachments of men with guns, wearing ragged uniforms and speaking an incomprehensible southern dialect, started showing up in their villages. "You are all now citizens of a revolutionary base area," a Communist official would announce to the surprised villagers, "and we will be in charge from now on." All local militias were then disbanded and disarmed, and all guns and other weapons were confiscated. Anyone who resisted was shot. Household registrations were created for each family in the village, and class status was assigned. Those owning more land than they could farm themselves were viciously attacked as "landlords," beaten, tortured, and killed.

Land was also parceled out to the landless, but it came with strings attached. Peasants were told not only what to plant but how much they would be expected to turn over to the government in taxes, exactions that were much higher than they had been used to paying to local landlords or warlords. To make matters worse, men of military

---

[14] Cited in Chang, *Mao*, 241.

age soon found themselves conscripted into the Red Army—it was not possible to refuse—while the women who were left behind were told it was their patriotic duty to take their place in the fields. Festivals were suppressed as feudal holdovers or wartime extravagances, as endless labor became the order of the day. Since life had become an endless grind of physical labor on short rations, there was little left to celebrate—or to celebrate with—in any case. Mao dismissed the peasants' complaints by claiming, "The average person has the equivalent of five whole days of [political] meetings per month, and these are very good rest time for them."[15] What he didn't say was that the meetings were held in the evenings, after a full day's work.

The evenings were now devoted to propaganda lectures rather than spending time with one's friends and family. And these lectures centered around criticizing the old ways while touting the many "improvements" that Communism had brought to the villages. This was a farcical claim but one that few villagers dared to question at the time. In fact, they had woken up one day to find themselves incarcerated in the functional equivalent of a "reeducation through labor" camp. It was a life sentence with no hope of parole. The only way out was by natural death or, if you tried to flee, execution.

Over the years, I have interviewed many Chinese on what the coming of Communism meant to them and their families. One elderly villager I spoke to in 1979 put it this way: "[Before the Red Army came,] times were good. People had money. You could buy anything. Goods have never been abundant since then. There are always shortages. Before, if you had money you could buy anything. Now a lot of things go through the back door, and only those with foreign currency [from remittances from relatives overseas] or officials can afford it. The people in power now have many more special privileges than before the liberation. They can purchase fish or high-quality rice that the masses can't now even if they have the money."[16]

---

15 Schram, *Mao's Road to Power,* 603.
16 Mosher, *Broken Earth,* 308.

"Another thing that they say about the old times is how the villager heads oppressed the masses," he continued. "You know, our village leaders then, the village gentry, were not bad men." He used the traditional term of respect for gentry, *shenshi*, rather than the word *dizhu*, or landlord, a term the CCP uses to smear landowners. "Even if one or two were bad men, they had little power. The brigade cadres now have much more power to control people than the old village leaders. Now they can fine you, or struggle you, or assign you to a difficult task. Now you even have to have their permission on a travel permit to leave the county or spend the night outside the brigade. They decide everything for their own benefit, even though they say it is for the people."[17]

But they were very much in evidence in Yan'an and the other Communist base areas before the revolution, and throughout all of China for decades following. Christians are enjoined to let others, especially the poor, enjoy a respite from work.[18] Mao, who pretended to embrace a Communist ideology that favored the poor, inflicted his people with a "reeducation through labor" existence that was not all that far removed from serfdom, or slavery. It was a life so devoid of ordinary pleasures that, risking death, they fled whenever they could.

Scripture instructs us: "The sabbath was made for man, not man for the sabbath; so the Son of man is lord even of the sabbath" (Mk 2:27–28). Chairman Mao, on the other hand, made himself a kind of "lord of the sabbath," and of every other day in the life of the masses he controlled, in some cases literally working them to death.

Clearly, Mao and his followers exemplify the evil opposite of how we are commanded to behave.

At the same time, Mao led a life of indolence. While others labored and bled, fought and died for his ignoble cause, the "True Hero"—as he styled himself in his poetry—enjoyed the best of what the enslaved population of the base area was able to produce.

---

[17]   Mosher, 308.
[18]   See *CCC* 2172.

CHAPTER 6

UNFILIAL SON, FAITHLESS HUSBAND, ABSENTEE FATHER

*"Either man governs his passions and finds peace, or he lets himself
be dominated by [his passions] and becomes unhappy."*

—*Catechism of the Catholic Church* 2339

*"When Great Heroes [like me] give full play to their impulses, they
are magnificently powerful, stormy and invincible. Their power is
like a hurricane arising from a deep gorge, and like a sex maniac on
heat and prowling for a lover . . . there is no way to stop them."*

—Mao Zedong[1]

Both Christianity and Confucianism emphasize the fundamental human relationships that are the building blocks of families, communities, and society as a whole. Christianity, of course, provides the fullest and most positive understanding of the mutual obligations of family members. It begins with the fourth commandment's universal obligation of children to parents, which includes respect for members of the extended family, elders and ancestors, and all those who exercise authority over others.[2] It continues on through the sixth and ninth commandments, which insist upon the loving, faithful, and exclusive communion between a husband and a wife that is to characterize marriage.

---

[1]   Quoted in Chang, *Mao*, 14.
[2]   See *CCC* 2199.

81

Confucianism, for its part, identified five key relationships, with the first four being strictly hierarchical: Fathers were above sons, husbands above wives, older brothers above younger brothers, and rulers above their subjects. The fifth relationship—between friends—was the only one where the two sides were equal. In all the others, power was wielded by the superior—morally, Confucius insisted—while the inferior was duty bound to obey.

Of all the relationships, that between father and son was the most important. The extended Chinese family was a kind of local government, and its successful function depended on the young obeying their elders. Filial piety was drummed into small boys in countless ways—by teaching them past stories of heroic filial virtue, by insisting that they always respect and honor elderly family members, by having them frequently venerate the family's ancestors before the family altar, and by the annual rites at the ancestral tombs on the day of the spring "Grave Sweeping Festival."

Mao Zedong, like tens of millions of other boys his age, would have done each of these innumerable times. He would also have memorized passages from the Chinese classics, such as this one from *The Analects of Confucius*: "The Master said, 'A youth, when at home, should be filial, and, abroad, respectful to his elders. He should be earnest and truthful. He should overflow in love to all, and cultivate the friendship of the good. When he has time and opportunity, after the performance of these things, he should employ them in polite studies.'"[3]

Mao rejected it all. He even publicly denounced China's ancient sage, with typical vitriol, in one of his poems: "Confucius, though renowned, was really rubbish." Over the course of his long life, he betrayed not only his father, his multiple wives, and his children, but all the families of China. All the while, he engaged in an endless circus of carnality with ever younger women.

---

[3] *Analects of Confucius* (*Lun Yu* in Chinese) is a collection of the sayings and ideas of Confucius (551–479 BC) that, following his death, were compiled by his followers into book form.

Fourth Commandment: Honor Your Father and Your Mother

*"Honor your father and your mother, that your days may be
long in the land which the Lord you God gives you."*

—Exodus 20:12

*"Children, obey your parents in the Lord, for this is right. 'Honor your
father and mother' (this is the first commandment with a promise), 'that
it may be well with you and that you may live long on the earth.'"*

—Ephesians 6:1–3

Of all the Confucian precepts, the obedience that sons owed their fathers was the most deeply rooted in Chinese culture. Every Chinese boy knew the stories of "The Twenty-Four Paragons of Filial Piety." This classic text was even reprinted in the Chinese Almanac every year and was, much like Grimm's Fairy Tales in the West, read over and over again to small children. Dating from ancient times, this was composed of stories of sons who engaged in heroic acts and exemplary deeds to show their fidelity and devotion to their parents.

Some of the stories are uplifting, such as the Emperor Wen of the Han dynasty who was so attentive to his mother, the empress dowager, that he personally cared for her when she fell ill and tasted all her medicines first to make sure they were safe to consume. Dong Yang of the Han dynasty had no money to give his father a proper burial, so he sold himself into slavery to raise the burial costs.

Other stories are the stuff of nightmares. If you thought that the wicked witch trying to put Hansel and Gretel in the oven might give children bad dreams, consider the story of Guo Ju of the Eastern Han dynasty, who decided to bury his son alive so that he would have enough food to feed his mother. Or consider the filial piety of Wu Meng of the Jin dynasty, who used to sit naked near his parents' bed at night so the mosquitos would suck his blood and not that of his parents.

Most sons and daughters conformed to the expectations that were drummed into them in this way. They understood that they were, if necessary, to literally sacrifice their own lives to save their parents' lives.

But in Mao the Snake's case, the lessons didn't take.

Mao Cursed His Father

"O son, help your father in his old age, and do not grieve him as long as he lives; even if he is lacking in understanding. . . . Whoever forsakes his father is like a blasphemer."

—Sirach 3:12–13, 16

"My father was bad. If he were alive today, he should be 'jet-planed.'"

—Mao Zedong, 1968, fantasizing about torturing his late father[4]

Mao was an unruly child who quickly made a name for himself in Shaoshan for being disrespectful to his elders. He began to study the Confucian classics at the age of eight, but he never remained with any one tutor for very long. By age ten, he had developed the bad habit of talking back, which was unheard of in those days, when teachers commanded great respect.

Mao was equally disrespectful to his father, Li-chang. Li-chang had quite reasonably expected his oldest son to succeed him in running the family farm. But Mao proved to be both arrogant and lazy. For Mao's thrifty, hardworking peasant father, who spent most of his waking hours working, this was intolerable. When he found him shirking, Li-chang would cuff his son.

Mao grew up hating his father, and by his early teens, he was fighting back with fist and tongue, scandalizing the entire village. He later recalled, with apparent pride, one such occasion:

---

[4]   During the Cultural Revolution, Mao encouraged the Red Guards to arrest and publicly denounce his political foes in "struggle sessions." While being "struggled," the victims were "jet-planed"—that is, their arms were wrenched behind their backs and their heads were forced down so that their backs were parallel to the ground. This was an agonizing position to be forced to assume, especially given that the struggle session often lasted several hours.

My father invited many guests to his home, and while they were present a dispute arose between the two of us. My father denounced me before the group, calling me lazy and useless. This infuriated me. I cursed him and left the house. . . . My father pursued me, cursing at the same time that he commanded me to come back. I reached the edge of a pond and threatened to jump in if he came any nearer. . . . My father backed down. My father insisted that I apologize and kowtow as a sign of submission. I agreed to give a one-knee kowtow if he would promise not to beat me.[5]

For a village boy of thirteen, this was a scandalous performance, especially as it took place in front of a house full of guests. The Mao family would have lost considerable face as a result of Mao's public defiance of his father. Mao, on the other hand, exulted in his rejection of paternal authority: "I learned that when I defended my rights by open rebellion my father relented, but when I remained weak and submissive he only beat me more."[6]

Still, his father continued to pay for his education for another decade or so, for which Mao was never heard to utter a word of gratitude. In this, he resembled his ideological forbearers, Marx and Lenin, both of whom sponged off their families. All his life, instead of thankfulness, he continued to exhibit anger and bitterness toward his father. When his father died in 1920, Mao did not mourn his passing or even attend his funeral.

This estrangement from, even hatred of, his father set the trajectory of his life—his later family relationships as a husband and father were all dysfunctional—but it was par for the course for Mao Zedong. Mao had displayed a rebellious streak from childhood not just toward his father but against all conventions of Confucian propriety, and indeed against all authority. As he grew older, Mao became even more insubordinate and unmanageable, unwilling to accept any authority but his own.

---

5   Snow, *Red Star Over China*, 155.
6   Snow, *Red Star Over China*, 155.

As Lucifer rejected God's headship, so Mao angrily rejected his earthly father's headship and became a law unto himself.

Mao's Assault on the Family

"The family is the 'original cell of social life. . . . Authority, stability, and a life of relationships within the family constitute the foundations for freedom, security, and fraternity within society.'"

—*Catechism of the Catholic Church* 2207

"I think we should regard [a couple who rejected marriage for cohabitation] as our leaders and organize an 'Alliance for the Rejection of Marriage.' Those who have marriage contracts should break them. . . . Those who do not have marriage contracts should not enter into them. . . . I think that all those men and women who live under the marriage system are nothing but a 'rape brigade.' I have long since proclaimed that I would not join this rape brigade."

—Mao Zedong[7]

One of the many blessings that Christianity brought into the world was teaching that men and women were equal in dignity. Mao gave formal assent to this notion of equality, famously announcing that "women hold up half of heaven." But in practice, both as a professional revolutionary and in his personal life, he relentlessly used and abused them.

Marx, in the *Communist Manifesto*, claims that "the bourgeois sees his wife as a mere instrument of production. He hears that the instruments of production are to be exploited in common, and, naturally, can come to no other conclusion than that the lot of being common to all will likewise fall to the women. He has not even a suspicion that the real point aimed at is to do away with the status of women as mere instruments of production."[8]

---

7   Mao Zedong, *Mao's Road to Power*, 608–9.
8   Marx, *Manifesto of the Communist Party*, 45.

This accusation by Marx is, of course, demonstrably false. The natural division of labor from time immemorial in the community of love and life known as the family is one of mutual dependency and support, not exploitation. It was the followers of Marx, including Mao Zedong, who actually saw not just wives but all women as "mere instruments of production."

Mao, like Marx, hated the natural family, consisting of a father, a mother, and their natural or adopted children. Unlike Marx, however, who could only scribble his disgust with this "bourgeois institution" (while fully enjoying its benefits thanks to his faithful and dutiful wife, Jenny), Mao was in a position to act on his beliefs. He may have said that women only hold up "half of heaven," but those who fell under his control often wound up holding up the entire sky, and the earth below as well. Their labor was ruthlessly exploited.

Rural women had traditionally been homemakers, a reserve workforce that helped in the fields only at the critical times of planting and harvest. But in the Communist base areas controlled by Mao, first in the south and later in Yan'an, every able-bodied man was drafted into the military, and many were killed. This created a need for field hands that could only be filled by women. The necessarily self-sufficient economies of these blockaded areas came to depend heavily upon wives and widows for both agricultural and handicraft production as they had to fill the roles vacated by their conscripted or dead husbands.

In setting up the People's Communes in 1957, Mao launched a further attack on the family. Tens of millions of women were ordered out of their homes and into the economy in the Great Leap Forward, when all able-bodied men and women were mobilized to labor in the newly organized communes, on giant construction projects, and in urban street factories. In the Pearl River Delta, where I lived for a time, many villages were emptied out of men in their twenties, thirties, and forties as they were sent to distant coal mines and large-scale labor projects.

The communes, Mao had declared, should have communal kitchens, separate dormitories for men and women, and nurseries where
small children would be cared for. If his program had been fully implemented throughout China, it would have effectively dissolved the family as an institution by handing over all its basic functions—shelter,
food, and the care of children—to the state.

As it happened, only a few so-called model communes were able to
carry out the entire program, but all seized control of the local food
supply and set up communal kitchens. The rule at the time was "no
work, no eat," so the wives of the absent corvée laborers had no choice
but to troop into the fields, dropping off their children to state-run
childcare centers on the way. The communal kitchens closed in 1960
when the food ran out and famine ensued, but the communes lasted
until the early eighties.

Communists have seen employment for women outside the home
as the key to woman's liberation ever since Engels wrote in 1884: "To
emancipate women and make her the equal of man is and remains an
impossibility so long as the woman is shut out from socially productive
labor and restricted to private domestic labor."[9] But it turns out that
forcing women to work outside the home under the supervision of the
male cadres who ran the communes did not elevate their status at all.
Instead, it reduced them to slavery.

At the same time, it did weaken the family—separating husbands
from wives and children from their parents—undermining what the
Catechism calls the "original cell of social life" in what had been one
of the most family-centered civilizations on the planet. Mao, who
himself had rejected the authority of his father and a stable family
life for a life of fleeting sexual relationships, was clearly pleased. It
was what he had intended all along—to strip the individual of the
freedom and security of the family and make him stand, naked and
afraid, before the power of the state. Mere "instruments of production," one might say.

---

9   Engels, *The Origin of the Family, Private Property, and the State,* 137.

The Sixth Commandment: You Shall Not Commit Adultery

"You have heard that it was said, 'You shall not commit adultery.'
But I say to you that everyone who looks at a women lustfully
has already committed adultery with her in his heart."

—Matthew 5:27–28

"I need the waters of Yin to replenish my Yang."

—Mao Zedong[10]

A Christian believes that "adultery, divorce, polygamy, and free union are grave offences against the dignity of marriage."[11] Mao, a grossly immoral man, committed all of these offenses numerous times. The story of his personal life reads like a pornographic novel. A very bad pornographic novel.

Wives, Children, and Other Inconveniences

Despite swearing that he would never join the "rape brigade"—his charming phrase for marriage—Mao did marry, four times, in fact. But he generally treated marriage as nothing more than a slight inconvenience to his sexual impulses. Some argue that we shouldn't count Mao's first bride in this exhibition of serial polygamy, Luo Yixiu, since she was an eighteen-year-old cousin who arrived to live with Mao's family when he was only fourteen years old. He himself rejected the idea that it was a valid marriage, since it had been arranged by his parents and, according to him, was never consummated.

Mao certainly portrays himself as a passive actor in this whole scenario, telling Edger Snow, "My parents had married me."[12] But it wasn't as if his future bride had suddenly shown up on his doorstep.

---

[10] Yin (阴) and Yang (阳) in a philosophical sense refer to the female and male principle in nature, with Yin passive and negative, and Yang active and positive. But Yin can also refer to the vagina, and Yang to the penis. So Mao's statement could also be translated, "I wash my penis in their vaginas." And Mao, ever the crude peasant, would have meant both.
[11] *CCC* 2400.
[12] Snow, *Red Star Over China,* 172.

The business would have begun with an exchange of horoscopes to see if this particular Snake and Ox (Luo Yixiu's animal sign) were compatible, followed by a careful consultation of the Lunar Calendar to pick a propitious day to get married. It would have involved the exchange of gifts between the two families, the most important of which was the payment of the bride price to the bride's family. A two-day feast at Mao's house would have followed, with the bride, dressed in red, arriving on the second day of the feast in a red palanquin. The bride would have poured wine for her husband and his parents; then together, they would have kowtowed to the guests, to the ancestral altar, to the spirits of heaven and earth.[13]

Finally, after much toasting and ribald remarks, the tipsy couple would have been led to the bridal chamber, given instructions on how to proceed, and locked in for the night. The following morning, the bedsheets would have been inspected for bloodstains that would prove (1) that she had been a virgin and (2) they in fact had lain together. It seems unlikely that the young couple had not consummated their marriage. Mao was already sexually active, later bragging to his personal physician about these early encounters, including one with a twelve-year-old girl.[14] Mao seems to have seen the arranged marriage as a kind of "honey trap" that was set by his hated father to seduce him into staying on the farm. Whatever the truth of the matter, Luo Yixiu died of dysentery a couple of years later.[15] The young widower immediately demanded to leave Shaoshan and study at a modern school.

---

[13] Although the kowtow had been replaced by a bow by the 1970s, other parts of the ceremony remained the same in rural China.

[14] Li Zhisui, *The Private Life of Chairman Mao*, 103.

[15] More evidence that Mao and his first wife were in a relationship is suggested by the fact that he was unusually solicitous of the well-being of the Luo family in the years that followed. Returning to Shaoshan in 1925 to organize a local peasant movement, he made a point of calling on Luo Yixiu's father, Luo Helou, and other relatives. He also recruited one of Luo Yixiu's cousins into the CCP. Even more tellingly, because Luo Yixiu had died without offspring, when the Mao clan updated its clan genealogy in 1941, Mao listed one of his sons, Mao Anlong (毛岸龙), as her descendant. This kind of fictive kinship adoption is not something you do

From then on Mao, as he himself once wrote, was "like a sex maniac on heat and prowling for a lover."[16] There seems to have never been a time when he wasn't in multiple relationships, whether or not he was married at the time. In 1920, he seduced a young woman, Yang Kaihui, who was the daughter of one of his professors. By the end of the year, without family ritual or government registration, they announced to their friends that they were married. Kaihui was deeply in love with Mao, but that didn't stop him from bedding her cousin, among others.

Kaihui was initially furious when she found out about Mao's affairs, but she soon reconciled herself to them, writing, "I learnt many more things, and gradually I came to understand him. Not just him, but human nature in all people. Anyone who has no physical handicap must have two attributes. One is sex drive, and the other is the emotional need for love. My attitude was to let him be, and let it be."[17]

Mao continued fomenting revolution over the next six years while Kaihui had three children in quick succession. Then in 1927, seeking a secure base from which to operate, Mao left the provincial capital of Changsha and fled into the mountains of Jinggangshan. He simply abandoned his wife and children, making no effort to rescue them then or later. Kaihui managed to avoid arrest for the next three years, but in October 1930, she was finally captured by the Nationalists. They wanted her to publicly renounce Communism and denounce that notorious "Communist Bandit" Mao Zedong. Loyal to the last, she refused and was executed.

By the time of Kaihui's death, Mao had long since moved on to his next conquest. Not long after arriving in his mountain lair, he began "courting"—if that is the right word—one of the few available females, a girl named He Zizhen. Zizhen, who had just turned eighteen, initially rejected his advances, finding him unattractive and, at thirty, too old. She later revealed that she finally consented to the relationship

---

for a woman with whom you have not had a relationship. Changming Hu, *A Few Historical Facts on Mao Zedong's First Marriage*, 111–14.

[16] Quoted in Chang, *Mao,* 14.
[17] Quoted in Chang, 25.

because she needed "protection politically in that environment."[18] Over the next decade, they had six children together.

Unlike Kaihui, Zizhen was not willing to take Mao's infidelities laying down. On one occasion, finding Mao in bed with his latest conquest, she began screaming hysterically and physically attacking the woman. As these episodes grew more frequent, Mao began contemplating divorce. It was when a beautiful young actress from Shanghai showed up in Yan'an that Mao decided it was time to get Zizhen permanently out of the way. On the pretext of getting her medical treatment for a wound suffered in battle, he sent her to Moscow, where she wound up in an insane asylum.[19]

Jiang Qing, the Shanghai actress who was Mao's fourth and final wife, managed to find her way to Yan'an and into his bed in 1937. Finding her way to the Communist base area through the Nationalist lines was the hard part; after that, all she had to do was let the chairman know she was available. Madame Mao stayed out of politics until the disastrous Cultural Revolution when, at Mao's behest, she played a leading role as one of the most radical of the chairman's supporters. As a result, she was one of the first to be arrested in the political backlash following Mao's death in 1976. Bizarrely accused of being a "counter-revolutionary," she spent the rest of her life in prison, committing suicide in May 1991.

All of Mao's wives came to a bad end, one way or another. His first wife was abandoned and died an early death. His second was not only abandoned but executed as a result of her relationship with him. His third was locked up in a Soviet insane asylum for many years. His fourth was arrested for political activism that she undertook on Mao's behalf, and she later killed herself.

Although all of Mao's wives met unhappy fates, his ten known children fared even worse. Most of them died shortly after birth or were "lost" in the chaos and confusion of civil war. His only surviving son

---

[18]   Chang, 59.
[19]   Terrill, "What Mao Traded for Sex."

died in the Korean War, and he paid little attention to his two surviving daughters, one by He Zizhen and the other by Jiang Qing.

This indifference to the fate of his wives and children starkly illustrates the Third Son of the Monolith's hardness of heart toward others. His capacity for love was stunted, if it existed at all. Of the millions who died under his long reign of terror, a good portion were children who starved to death due to his draconian policies. Mao was unmoved. During the collective farm era, he even toyed with the idea of doing away with names and calling people by a "number." That's what human beings–especially young ones–were to Mao. They were faceless objects, not to nurture and care for, but to serve the interests of the state.

Mao was never able to form bonds of communion with others, even those closest to him. Nor was he ever able to bring his passions, especially in matters of sexuality, under control. In fact, as he grew older, his endless search for intimacy, what Blaise Pascal called "licking the earth," reached a fevered pitch.

The Ninth Commandment: You Shall Not Covet Your Neighbor's Wife

"You shall not covet your neighbor's wife."

—Exodus 20:17

"Everyone who looks at a women lustfully has already committed adultery with her in his heart."

—Matthew 5:28

It seems superfluous to mention the ninth commandment, which requires purifying the heart, purity of intention, and the practice of chastity, where Mao is concerned. There is no record of the Third Son of the Monolith making any effort to rein in his passions or practice temperance, especially where matters of the flesh were concerned. Instead, he was the ugly poster child of the kind of man that Our

Lord was speaking about when He said, "Out of the heart came evil thoughts, murder, adultery, fornication" (Mt 15:19).

Of course, only God can read the human heart. But if ever a man's heart was laid bare by his actions, Mao's was by his carnality. His vices in matters of the flesh were so numerous that they cannot be explained away as youthful indiscretions or by the chaotic circumstances of civil war. For him, the battle for chastity was over before it began. But his abusive war on women continued to intensify as he grew older, and he became ever more obsessed with what Blaise Pascal aptly called "licking the earth."

Enter the Tea Girls.

Tea Girls

Few dictators, Communist or otherwise, have been as insanely lustful as Mao Zedong.

It is generally accepted that Stalin spent his energies in nonsexual pursuits like mass murder, at least while his wife was alive, while Hitler was reportedly faithful to Eva Braun, whom he at last married. Stalin only gave up family life after his wife's suicide, after which he was provided with a constant stream of beautiful "housekeepers" by his security chief, Lavrentiy Beria. Mao, on the other hand, was consistently, even flagrantly, unfaithful from the beginning.

Once victorious in the Chinese Civil War, his activities increased. Mao actually designed for himself a special oversized "sex bed," constructed with one side raised four inches higher than the other. And, as a tortoise is never separated from its shell, so Mao was never separated from this bed. He took it with him wherever he went—on his special train, at his resorts, and so on. He once said he couldn't go "forty days without sex," and that any female would do. Mao's agents made sure that attractive young women were available wherever he went so that he never slept alone, but always had one or more bedmates available for carnal purposes.

There was no romance in these frequent dalliances, no sense in which these women were anything other than masturbatory vessels to be used and discarded. "I need the waters of yin to replenish my yang," he told his personal physician, Li Zhisui. Dr. Li, who later escaped to the United States and wrote a tell-all book about his master, reported that he was "nauseated" by both Mao's behavior and his graphic language. He was a straitlaced man who was shocked by Mao's incessant carnal pursuits.[20]

Anyone who dared to comment on Mao's carnality often came to an unhappy end. A technician happened to mention to one of Mao's bed partners, a young teacher with whom he had spent the night on the train, that he had heard them in the night. "I heard everything," he told the young woman. He disappeared shortly afterward, never to be heard from again. As for Dr. Li himself, who recounted this incident and others in his memoirs, he passed away shortly after they were published. The death was reported as a heart attack.

Underage Tea Girls: The Older Mao Grew, the Younger the Girls

"Connected to incest is any sexual abuse perpetrated by adults on children or adolescents entrusted to their care. The offense is compounded by the scandalous harm done to the physical and moral integrity of the young, who will remain scarred by it all their lives."

—*Catechism of the Catholic Church* 2389

"[Mao] followed the tradition of Chinese emperors. The legendary first emperor of China, the Yellow Emperor, father of the Han race and the man from whom all other Chinese are said to have descended, is reputed to have become immortal by making love with a thousand young virgins. . . . Mao attempted to add years to his life according to the imperial formula."

—Dr. Li Zhisui[21]

---

20   Li Zhisui, *The Private Life of Chairman Mao,* 364.
21   Li Zhisui, 104.

Given that Mao was the ruler of all of China, everyone in the country—old and young, men and women—were in a sense entrusted to his care. It was a trust that he constantly betrayed. He viewed the entire country as a child views his toy box, filled with "people and objects . . . [that] are all there only for me,"[22] especially teenage girls.

One way in which the chairman abused his position was by having his palace guard bring him an endless series of innocent country girls for his amusement. They were told in advance that the chairman was about to do them a great honor and that they should do their best to please him. Before they were actually allowed into the chairman's bedchamber, they were given an ancient Taoist sex manual called the *Classic of the Simple Girl*[23] to read. Mao did not want to waste time explaining.

Although a handful of these girls became semi-permanent "girl-friends" and were given positions on his household staff, the vast majority of these loveless couplings ended almost as soon as they had begun. These victims, after being warned not to talk about their encounter with the Great Helmsman, were simply dropped off in the town or village they had been snatched up from. They were expected to ignore the damage to their physical and moral integrity and simply pick up their old lives again.

Many of Mao's tea girls lost more than their innocence. They also contracted a venereal disease that, at least in some cases, rendered them infertile. According to Dr. Li, Mao suffered from a sexual disease but, because it didn't bother him, absolutely refused to have it treated.[24] His early practice of poisoning his enemies might also have made him leery of prescriptions, even when they came from his most trusted doctor. In any case, his untreated STD did not inhibit his serial polygamy in any way. Without showing the slightest concern for his conquests, he continued to bed one woman after another. He preferred to serially infect women by the hundreds rather than ingest an antibiotic.

---

[22] Chang, *Mao,* 13.

[23] Su Nu Jing, also translated as the *Classic of the Plain Girl.*

[24] From the symptoms, it seems that Mao was suffering from Trichomoniasis.

Mao's girlfriends—the ones who were part of Mao's personal staff—had to be treated for Mao's STD on multiple occasions, but they didn't mind. They were constantly competing with each other for his attention, and being re-infected was a sign that they had once again been invited into his bed. "The illness, transmitted by Mao, was a badge of honor," Dr. Li recalled, "testimony to their close relations with the chairman."[25]

By the time he was in his sixties, Mao was obviously aging. His neurasthenia worsened, he was infertile, and other health problems were cropping up. He was desperate to find a way to reverse the aging process. Turning to traditional Chinese medicine, he convinced himself that his problem was an excess of male energy, or yang, and that he needed the cooling influence of female energy, of yin.

He informed his doctor that he needed the waters of yin to replenish his yang.[26] The best way to go about this, he claimed, was to bed as many women as possible, the younger the better. Dr. Li disagreed as strongly as he dared, but Mao would not take no for an answer. Mao, an avid reader of ancient chronicles, had come across the claim that the legendary Yellow Emperor, as Dr. Li later wrote, "[had] become immortal by making love with a thousand young virgins. . . . Mao attempted to add years to his life according to the imperial formula."[27]

As tens of millions of villagers were starving and dying in the Great Leap Forward famine, Mao began having sex with as many girls as his aging body would allow. For most of the girls, it was a nightmare that would haunt them for the rest of their days. Not only did he carry an untreated sexual disease, he never bathed or brushed his teeth either.

A lucky few got added to his entourage; among them was a young girl named Chen, who was part of what was called a People's Liberation

---

[25]   Li Zhisui, *The Private Life of Chairman Mao,* 363.

[26]   Yin (阴) and Yang (阳) in a philosophical sense refer to the female and male principle in nature, with Yin passive and negative, and Yang active and positive. But Yin can also refer to the vagina, and Yang to the penis. And Mao, ever the crude peasant, would have meant both.

[27]   Li Zhisui, *The Private Life of Chairman Mao,* 104.

Army dancing troupe. In fact, the troupe was organized for the sole enjoyment of the chairman, who would watch the girls dance and then invite some of them into his bedroom—conveniently located next door—to "make him his tea."

Chen, who was only fourteen years old, quickly became one of the sixty-nine-year-old Mao's favorites, both in bed and on the dance floor. Despite the fifty-five-year age difference, he began what was to be a five-year affair with her in 1962. It wasn't until several years later that Chen's parents learned what her dance performances consisted of, and they were outraged. Her father started to write Mao an angry letter but thought better of it. The Cultural Revolution had begun, and to criticize the chairman was to court death.

Word of the long-running affair did reach Mao's wife, however. Jiang Qing, who up to that point had turned a blind eye to her husband's parade of bed partners, apparently feared that she was about to be replaced by wife number five. She demanded that Mao send Chen away, and he did, albeit reluctantly. He even arranged a marriage for his little lover with someone else to ensure that she would be well taken care of, something he had never done before, and would never do again. This episode and others left Mao completely estranged from Jiang Qing. He spent his eightieth birthday not with her but with five of his "girlfriends."

In this area, Mao not only rejected God's laws but rejected conventional Confucian morality as well. A man without a conscience, he had no more concern for conventional Confucian morality than he had for the laws of God. He left a trail of abandoned wives, children, and sexual encounters that were by no means consensual across the length and breadth of China.

Chinese emperors have always felt themselves entitled to a large number of concubines. But the Forbidden City was no Playboy Mansion. There were rules to be followed and relationships to be respected. While the Qianlong Emperor, for example, had forty concubines, each and every one, like the empress herself, enjoyed a recognized legal status in the eyes of the law and the public. Many were there simply to forge alliances and rarely, if ever, enjoyed the emperor's attention.

It is true that the emperors would sometimes violate the rules of propriety by having sex outside of concubinage. In the late nineteenth century, the boy emperor Tongzhi used to slip out of the Forbidden City in disguise. Accompanied by one of his courtiers, he would visit the brothels of Beijing. It is hard to understand why he was driven to do this since at seventeen he already had a wife and two concubines to choose from. He did not force himself on the prostitutes he visited but rather paid for their services like any other customer.

Mao, however, behaved as if he were living in a continent-sized Playboy Mansion, and he took full advantage of the fact that his would-be playmates dared not refuse him. The thousands of girls who passed through Mao's bedchambers received nothing for their troubles except an STD. They did not deserve to be violated in this way, and yet few risked refusing, and fewer still dared to complain afterward.

It seems certain that Mao surpassed all previous Communist dictators in the number of rapes he committed over his last quarter century. He slept with many hundreds, perhaps thousands, of young women. He traveled nearly fifty times to a certain city to party and hook up with young girls. Mao, who knew that he would never face any charges for his criminal behavior, plunged ever deeper into the depths of carnality.

Some may object to the use of the term *rape*, but given the age and power disparities between the all-powerful Mao and the powerless "tea girls" who served him, these relationships cannot be considered consensual. And as he grew older, and the girls grew younger—most in their early-to-mid teens—it was also statutory rape. Recall that Mao himself once wrote a fiery article against arranged marriages, claiming that this was a kind of "indirect rape." But if "Chinese parents are all the time indirectly raping their children,"[28] what does this say about

---

[28]   Cited in Chang, *Mao,* 7.

his own behavior? There was nothing indirect about the kind of rape, statutory and otherwise, that Mao was engaging in. All of his adulterous liaisons were what the *Catechism* calls "intrinsically evil acts."[29]

What was the point of all this endless copulation? Mao was a complete narcissist, incapable of loving anything outside of himself; he felt little or nothing for these young girls who briefly shared his bed. Nor were these acts intended to conceive children. Mao, because of his untreated sexual disease, was sterile. Rather, it was solely for his own pleasure.

Mao was a profoundly disturbed individual who sought to substitute copulation for true human communion. It was a bad bargain for all concerned, but especially for the hundreds of girls barely into puberty who were robbed of their innocence.

We are made in the image and likeness of God. When God created Eve to be Adam's helpmate, the first man was overjoyed: "This one at last is bone of my bone and flesh of my flesh; she shall be called Woman." Genesis goes on to explain, "Therefore a man leaves his father and mother and cleaves to his wife, and they become one flesh" (Gn 2:23–24).

Mao was too attached to his own flesh to ever become truly attached to anyone else.

---

[29]   *CCC* 2356.

CHAPTER 7

THE KILLINGEST MAN IN HISTORY[1]

The Fifth Commandment: You Shall Not Kill

"You have heard that it was said to the men of old, 'You shall not kill: and whoever kills shall be liable to judgment.' But I say to you that every one who is angry with his brother shall be liable to judgment."

—Matthew 5:21–22

"If we were to add up all the landlords, rich peasants, counterrevolutionaries, bad elements and rightists, their number would reach thirty million. . . . Of our total population of six hundred million people, these thirty million are only one out of twenty. So what is there to be afraid of? . . . We have so many people. We can afford to lose a few. What difference does it make?"

—Mao Zedong[2]

The murderous reign of Mao and his successors was a direct result of Communism's doctrine of class struggle. For the ruthless chairman of the Chinese Communist Party (CCP), the need to destroy class enemies collapsed the distinction between war and peace. Until Communism was achieved, Mao declared, China would remain in a state of war. "War is politics," Mao declared. "Politics is

---

[1] You won't find the word *killingest* in the dictionary yet, but you soon will. Paul Kengor used it in the title of his book on Communism, which he called *The Politically Incorrect Guide to Communism: The Killingest Idea Ever.*

[2] Li Zhisui, *The Private Life of Chairman Mao,* 217.

war by other means."[3] It was a recipe for endless war on the Chinese people; paradise was always just one execution away.

Not that Mao had any regrets about unleashing war on the Chinese people. On the contrary, he positively delighted in the attendant deaths and destructiveness that it would wreak, arguing that "long-lasting peace . . . is unendurable to human beings, and tidal waves of disturbance have to be created in this state of peace. . . . When we look at history, we adore the times of [war] when dramas happened one after another . . . which make reading about them great fun. When we get to the periods of peace and prosperity, we are bored. . . . Human nature loves sudden swift changes."

It is a measure of the man's dark character that he even rhapsodized about the deaths that were to come. Referring to himself with a royal "we," he wrote, "We love sailing on a sea of upheavals. To go from life to death is the greatest upheaval. Isn't it magnificent!"[4]

In Mao's endless political wars, just as in the Chinese historical novels he so loved to read, there were no rules. It was kill or be killed or, as the Chinese say, "You die, I live." And kill he did, by the tens of millions, all the while taking evil pleasure in his actions. Mao, like Satan himself, was a murderer from the beginning.

And the pipe dream called Communism, of course, always remained just one execution away.

What Makes the Red Base Red?
Red Terror, of Course

"A revolution is not a dinner party, or writing an essay, or painting a picture, or doing embroidery. It cannot be so refined, so leisurely and gentle, so temperate, kind, courteous, restrained and magnanimous. A revolution is an insurrection, an action of violence by which one class overthrows another."

—Mao Zedong[5]

---

3   Mao Zedong, "On Protracted War," in *Selected Works of Mao Tse-Tung,* vol. 2, 152–53.
4   Chang, *Mao,* 15.
5   Mao Zedong, *Quotations from Chairman Mao Tse-tung,* 13.

As soon as Mao was in control of his first Red base in South China—at a mountain redoubt in "bandit country" called Jinggangshan—the looting and killing started. But Mao was not content to merely eliminate "class enemies," such as landlords, rich peasants, or anyone associated with the Nationalist government. He wanted the execution to be done in the most public way possible in order to strike fear into the hearts of the population at large. He understood how useful terror was as a weapon of political control.

So it was that when Mao captured his very first government official, a county chief, he made a great spectacle of his execution. He personally drafted accusatory couplets, wrote them on the red paper—the carmine color of happiness—in his own hand, and summoned the entire population of the town to watch. The official was tied to wooden posts while Mao whipped up the crowd into a frenzy. On Mao's command, a dozen people rushed at the helpless official, slashing and stabbing him with short spears until he died.

As Chang and Halliday note, "Mao did not invent public execution, but he added to this ghastly tradition a modern dimension, organized rallies, and in this way made killing compulsory viewing for a large part of the population. To be dragooned into a crowd, powerless to walk away, forced to watch people put to death in this bloody and agonizing way, hearing their screams, struck fear deep into those present."[6]

Terrorizing the population into submission was, of course, the entire point of the exercise. Mao always did his best to exacerbate their terror by denouncing his victims loudly while killing them slowly. One of his favorite couplets, used over and over again as the years went by, read as follows:

> Watch us kill the bad landlords today
> Aren't you afraid? It's knife slicing upon knife

If you wonder how a billion people fell under the control of Chairman Mao, the answer is simple: abject terror. He had people hacked

---

6   Chang, *Mao,* 54.

to pieces with knives, stabbed with swords, and shot in the public square. He ordered them buried alive, tortured to insanity, and starved to death without mercy his entire life.

Mao's justification for the ongoing slaughter that characterized his rule was simple: "If we don't kill them, they will kill us." That was probably true. But it was also true, as he told his inner circle, that he enjoyed it.

To Kill with a Borrowed Knife

Although Mao was happy to slaughter unarmed civilians by the millions—as he would later prove—when facing armed troops, he preferred to husband his own troops and, whenever he could, let others do the fighting and dying for him. So it was that, following the Japanese invasion of China in 1938, he refused engagements. He made plenty of warlike noises about Red Army offensives, but in reality, he held his army in check and let the Nationalists do almost all the fighting.

Instead, he spent endless hours plotting the downfall of any potential rivals, which in his paranoia included any of his fellow Communist leaders who were not personally loyal to him. Understanding that "political power grows out of the barrel of a gun," he was especially concerned to destroy, one way or another, all Red Army units that were not under his direct control, to eliminate the power base of potential military rivals.

There was no way that these units could be attacked directly since they were also part of the Red Army. Instead, Mao resorted to an ancient Chinese military strategy called *Jie Dao Sha Ren*, which means "to kill with a borrowed knife." This ploy involved deliberately ordering a unit to undertake a mission into enemy territory so dangerous that it was unlikely to return. The enemy they encountered was the "borrowed knife" that would do Mao's killing for him. Whether the rival general was killed or not was irrelevant. If he did manage to escape complete annihilation, his force would be so shattered that he was in no position to further threaten Mao's rule—and Mao could blame him for the disaster.

Mao used a wide assortment of "borrowed knives" over time to eliminate rivals that included, at various times, Nationalist, Muslim Uyghur, Japanese, and even American forces. One early episode occurred during the Long March.

For a time in the mid-thirties, it appeared that a Communist general by the name of Chang Kuo-tao would emerge as the leader of the Red Army. Chang had commanded a force of eighty thousand well-armed and well-provisioned forces—more than ten times larger than Mao's battered contingent—when they briefly joined forces on the Long March. Then Mao, who was determined to reach the Red base in Yan'an first, went to work. First, he managed to maneuver his rival into attempting to traverse a "black vicious swamp, which sucked in anyone who broke through the thin crust or strayed from the narrow path."[7] Then, to cripple his rival's forces, he betrayed Chang Kuo-tao's position to the Nationalists. From then on, Chiang Kai-shek allowed Mao's forces to pass unmolested through territory he controlled, while continually harassing and attacking Chang Kuo-tao's army as it tried to follow. By the time Chang reached the Red Base a year later, his battered force had been cut in half.

But Mao was only getting started. No sooner had Chang arrived in Yan'an than Mao ordered him to send the bulk of his forces northward to the border with the Soviet Union to open a supply route for arms and ammunition. Once again, there was a Nationalist army lying in wait, and Chang's forces were badly mauled. To make matters worse, the Nationalist forces had also alertly seized the ferry crossings, leaving the twenty-two thousand survivors trapped on the north bank of the Yellow River.

Mao then devised another scheme, one which called upon Chang's forces to link up with the Soviets and collect arms farther west. The only problem was that to reach the rendezvous point, his forces, now renamed the Western Contingent, would have to march across nearly one thousand miles of desert terrain defended by a fiercely

---

[7] Braun, *A Comintern Agent in China,* 136–37.

anti-communist Uyghur army. But the biggest obstacle the force faced was Mao Zedong himself, who was bent on its destruction:

> Mao . . . [issued] a stream of contradictory orders that drove the Contingent from one hellish locale to another, continually plunging it into pitched battles. Its commander recorded bitterly that the task assigned him by Yan'an [that is to say, by Mao] were "elusive and changeable." When the Contingent cabled early in February 1937 from the middle of the desert that it could not hold out much longer, nor go on, and asked for permission to come to Yan'an, Mao ordered it to hold on where it was, telling it to "fight to the last person and the last drop of blood."[8]

Clearly, Mao wanted all of Chang's followers dead. Thanks to the "knife" he had "borrowed" from the ferocious Uyghurs, he got his wish, or nearly so. There remained only the matter of the four hundred or so stragglers who later made their way back to Yan'an, more dead than alive. Mao finished the job. He had them secretly taken out to the hills and executed, but only after they had first dug their own graves.

He had Chang's grave ready as well, politically speaking. The reason the Western Contingent had been lost, Mao said, was because it had been following the "Chang Kuo-tao Line."[9]

Mao resorted to this same strategy of "killing with a borrowed knife" many times in the years following, but perhaps the biggest "knife" that he ever borrowed belonged to the Americans.

On June 25, 1950, the entire North Korean army poured across the border and fell upon the almost defenseless south. But the war soon turned against Korean Communist dictator Kim Il Sung. By late

---

[8]   Chang, *Mao,* 210–11.

[9]   Most accounts of the destruction of the Western Contingent accept the CCP's fictional account, which is that Chang Kuo-tao was entirely to blame for the disasters that befell his troops. Philip Short, for example, writes that "Zhang [Chang Kuo-tao], in his role of General Political Commissar, ordered it to strike out to the west on a suicidal march through the Gansu corridor, where it was cut to ribbons by Muslim cavalry." It begs credulity that Kuo-tao would send his own troops on a death march. But Mao would and did. Short, *Mao: A Life,* 343.

November 1950, American forces under the command of General Douglas MacArthur were approaching the Yalu River, which separates Korea from China. In desperation, Kim appealed to Mao for aid.

Mao promptly responded with a grand imperial gesture, throwing a huge army of so-called volunteers into the fray. Recklessly inviting casualties, the Chinese army advanced by overwhelming the overextended American forces. The poorly armed and equipped Chinese troops were slaughtered in appalling numbers, but they just kept coming in wave after wave.

American commanders were astonished that the People's Liberation Army would throw away its soldiers like that. What they didn't understand at the time was that these weren't, properly speaking, People's Liberation Army units at all. Until a year or two before, they had been units of the Nationalist Army who had surrendered *en masse*, betrayed by their generals. Now, given new uniforms, new insignia, and new Communist commanders, these same units were then deliberately sent into the meat grinder of modern warfare.

As a military tactic, these human wave attacks, as they came to be called, were only partially successful. The American and allied forces were forced to retreat south of the thirty-eighth parallel but quickly regrouped and, after fierce fighting, fought their way back to near the thirty-eighth parallel in October 1951. In a 1958 speech to his generals, Mao claimed that the Korean War was "a big war in which we defeated America and gained valuable experience," but this was mere bluster. Viewed strictly as a military contest, the People's Liberation Army merely held its ground while suffering grievous losses: At least a quarter million or more men were killed compared to America's thirty-four thousand casualties.

But if you see the contest as an example of "killing with a borrowed knife"—which it was—then Mao's assertion makes more sense. America had in fact done the chairman a great favor by eliminating hundreds of thousands of former Nationalist troops whose loyalty was in question. What we called human wave attacks was his way of purging his forces of the largest number of possible reactionaries. Being Mao Zedong, he took a fiendish delight in sending hundreds of thousands of Chang Kai-shek's former troops to their deaths at the hands of none other than their former American allies.

Following the Korean Armistice, nearly all of the captured Chinese soldiers opted to join Chiang Kai-shek and the Nationalists in Taiwan rather than go back to Communist China. Why? Because they had been Nationalist troops all along.

"We Have No Conscience!"

"You'd better have less conscience. Some of our comrades have too much mercy, not enough brutality, which means that they are not so Marxist. On this matter, we indeed have no conscience! Marxism is that brutal."

—Mao Zedong[10]

Mao bragged about having no conscience; the evidence shows that we should take him at his word. When over forty-five million people were starving to death from 1960 to 1962 in a famine caused by forced collectivization, he quipped that the people could live on "tree bark and grass." When some resorted to cannibalism to survive, he not only turned a blind eye to their suffering but also took a series of actions that made the famine worse. He ordered the army into the countryside to collect the last stores of grain from starving peasants so that he could feed his soldiers and the urban population. As millions lay dying, he refused emergency grain shipments from around the world on the grounds that China had a surplus of food and exported grain to Africa and Cuba to prove it.[11]

The first accurate accounting of the number of deaths in Mao's Great Famine did not come until 1989 when a senior party official named Chen Yizi fled to the United States following the Tiananmen Massacre. Chen was a senior party official who had done a close study of how rural China had fared during the Mao years. With the backing

---

10   Chang, *Mao,* 411.
11   Dikötter, *Mao's Great Famine,* 114–15.

of the then-chairman of the CCP, Zhao Ziyang, he and his team were able to gain access to the CCP archives in every province. He arrived at a death toll of between forty-three and forty-six million. I personally interviewed Chen not long after his defection and found him a perfectly credible witness.

Frank Dikötter, the author of *Mao's Great Famine* and a recognized authority on the subject, agrees with Chen Yizi's estimate of 43 to 46 million *as a minimum*: "Some historians speculate that the true figure stands as high as 50 to 60 million people. It is unlikely that we will know the full extent of the disaster until the [CCP] archives are completely opened. But these are the figures informally discussed by a number of Party historians. And these are also, according to Chen Yizi, the figures cited at internal meetings of senior party members under Zhao Ziyang [in the 1980s]."[12]

In 1961, China's population stood at around 640 million. What was the leader of China doing while the vast majority of his fellow Chinese were going hungry in a famine that would end up killing nearly 10 percent of the population? He was shrugging it off as a common occurrence in Chinese history. "When there is not enough to eat, people starve to death," he said nonchalantly. "It is better to let half the people die so that the other half can eat their fill."

At times, Mao almost seemed to welcome the arrival of a famine, a war, or a pestilence that would greatly reduce the population. "Don't make a fuss about a world war," he said. "At most, people die. . . . Half the population wiped out—this happened quite a few times in Chinese history. . . . It's best if half the population is left, next best one-third."

The Church teaches that human life is sacred because man is created in the image and likeness of God and that man is only a little lower than the angels. Mao, on the other hand, ascribed to the standard Marxist view that man is merely an intelligent animal, only a little higher than the apes.

---

12 Dikötter, 333–34.

Now it is possible to hold a Darwinian view of evolution and still have some feeling for one's fellow human beings. Not if you are Mao Zedong, however, who seemed to regard the people of China as no more than a collection of meat machines who in life would serve his purposes, and in death would "fertilize the ground."

The Church teaches that we are not to see our fellow human beings as "units in a human collective" but rather as "someone," individuals each deserving of attention and respect.[13] But Mao not only viewed others as interchangeable units in an otherwise undifferentiated mass but even constructed agricultural collectives to make them so. He taught his followers not to see others as individuals but as members of a class, thus dehumanizing them prior to the slaughter. And that it was sometimes necessary to cull the herd.

Torture, He Wrote

"Torture which uses physical or moral violence to extract confessions, punish the guilty, frighten opponents, or satisfy hatred is contrary to respect for the person and human dignity."

—*Catechism of the Catholic Church* 2297

"Look at World War II, at Hitler's cruelty. The more cruelty, the more enthusiasm for revolution."

—Mao Zedong[14]

"The dog that barks is not cooked well."

—Mao Zedong

As the history of the twentieth century shows, Communist regimes invariably use terror and torture to intimidate the population into obedience. The target—a class, an ethnic or religious group, or even "revisionists" within the party—is first identified and then systematically destroyed. People are arrested, tortured, and killed, oftentimes seemingly at random.

---

13   *CCC* 2212.
14   AZ Quotes, "Mao Zedong Quotes."

The CCP, with Mao at its helm, frequently resorted to such *zheng-zhi yundong*, or "political campaigns." But this was not done just to ensure party discipline, to quell unrest, or to terrorize the population at large. It was also done because Mao—a man with an oversized ego and a stunted conscience—took pleasure in inflicting emotional and physical pain on those who had slighted him or who stood in the way of establishing the despotic utopia of his fever dreams.

In the Sermon on the Mount, Christ set a very high bar for human behavior. It is not enough to avoid killing; you must also reject anger, hatred, and vengeance (see Mt 5:21–22). Later, facing arrest in the Garden of Gethsemane, he told Peter to leave his sword in its sheath (see Mt 26:52).

But clearly, Mao lived out the "anti-beatitudes." He seethed with anger when his decisions were questioned. He taught his followers to hate and despise "class enemies." And he invariably sought vengeance—usually by means of a slow and painful death—against any one or any group who had crossed him or even appeared likely to. Once he had commandeered a military unit and gained the use of swords, they were rarely in their sheathes. Peter's evil twin, he bloodied them on a regular basis.

Mao not only killed vast numbers of people but often did so in the cruelest possible way. For decades following, he and his thugs delighted in inflicting increasingly hideous forms of torture and death on his enemies, and he always seemed to have more of both: new enemies and new ways to torment them. One method by which Mao's real and imagined enemies were punished was called "striking landmines," in which the thumb was gradually forced back until it broke. Another, still in use today, involved burning victims over and over again using a lit candle.

Like so many of Mao's crimes, this is hard to read about and even harder to write about. There were even more cruel and inhuman forms of torture that were, in the words of the *Catechism*, used to "extract confessions, punish the guilty, frighten opponents, or satisfy hatred," but I am not going to describe them here.

Suffice it to say that the CCP frequently resorted to every form of torture developed during China's two-thousand-year history of totalitarian rule—and added some new ones. Virtually nothing in the way of causing excruciating pain to human beings was not used to torment, control, and kill their own people. Most of these torture techniques still occur today, especially against political prisoners, religious believers, and Tibetan, Uyghur, and other minorities—people that Han Chinese Communist officials regard as racially inferior.

Just as Joseph Stalin had his Lavrentiy Beria, so Mao had his secret police chief, Kang Sheng.[15] In fact, there was a direct connection between the two, since Kang had been trained in the Soviet Union by some of the world's greatest experts in breaking down human minds and bodies. The chairman made it clear to his chief henchman that "the dog that barks is not cooked well." It was the job of Kang and his many minions to turn up the heat on those who were "barking" until they stopped. Those who had been tortured into submission and terrorized into making a confession generally did not make so much as a whimper of complaint thereafter, if they still had breath to whimper with.

Mao's hatred and inhumanity not only infected his immediate followers but also trickled down into the population at large as well. That's why they began eating their political enemies.

"A Revolution Is Not a Dinner Party." Really?

Mao deliberately brought out the worst in people, encouraging what he called a "kill culture." He intended this instruction to be taken literally, and it was. Tens of millions of those the chairman accused of being "class enemies" were murdered in his endless campaigns, while tens of millions of others were tortured and scarred for life by his minions.

---

[15] The best biography of Kang Sheng is John Byron and Robert Pack's *The Claws of the Dragon*.

Mao's "kill culture" reached perhaps its fullest and darkest expression during the Great Proletarian Cultural Revolution. Mao's Red Guards all over China, to demonstrate their loyalty to the chairman as well as their revolutionary fervor, proceeded to arrest, torture, and kill "class enemies" by the millions.

Communist revolutions, it has been noted, end up devouring their own children. In some parts of China, this turned out to be literally true; they took Communist savagery to a new level: they began eating their victims.

There had been cannibalism during Mao's great famine, but most of this involved people driven mad by hunger digging up the corpses of those who had died and eating their putrefying flesh. What happened a few years later in China was different and much, much darker.[16]

Dissident writer Zheng Yi, who carried out an in-depth investigation of Cultural Revolution cannibalism in the southern province of Guangxi, discovered that in the beginning, only the most zealous followers of Mao would engage in this heinous practice. They would steal to the execution grounds in the dead of night, cut open the abdomens of the dead class enemies, remove the heart and liver, and cook and consume them in secret. Later, as the frenzy grew, the victims would be disemboweled in the public squares immediately after they were executed. After the killings, the leaders would carry away the best parts— hearts, livers, and genitals—leaving the rest for the public to carve up.

By the end of this Cultural Revolution killing spree—what Zheng calls the "hysterical stage"—unfortunate class enemies were being dragged out to undergo "criticism and struggle" at the hands of a mob. Zheng describes the scene, "As soon as a victim fell to the ground, and even if they were still breathing, a crowd would rush forward, drawing the knives and cleavers they had come equipped with, and slice off parts in a free-for-all fashion. At worst, collective banquets of human flesh would follow."[17]

---

[16]   See Dikötter, *Mao's Great Famine,* 320–23.

[17]   Zheng Yongnian, *The Chinese Communist Party as Organizational Emperor.*

Zheng interviewed one villager who had disemboweled a "class enemy" while he was still alive, ripped out his internal organs, and cut them into pieces to share with a mob of his fellow villagers. "Yes, I killed him," the man said defiantly. "I give the same answer no matter who asks me. So many of the masses were behind me, and the man I killed was a bad man, so what am I afraid of? . . . Am I supposed to be afraid his ghost will get me? Ha, ha! I'm a revolutionary, my heart is red! Didn't Chairman Mao teach us, 'If we don't kill them, they will kill us?' It's life and death. It's class struggle."[18]

In reviewing Zheng Yi's book, dissident intellectual Liu Binyan noted, "After killing the enemy became fairly common, eating the enemy became a way of showing an even higher-class consciousness."[19] It was, he explained, something new in human history, cannibalism not based on hunger but on political hatred.

One of Mao Zedong's most famous remarks begins, "A revolution is not a dinner party."[20] But by siccing his snarling followers on class enemies during the Cultural Revolution, he perversely managed to turn it into one—a "dinner party" in which the main course was the "enemies" themselves.

Life and Death in Mao's China

"Power comes out of the barrel of a gun," Mao noted to one of Stalin's agents in China in 1927.[21] And as soon as he was able to get his hands on some, the killing began. Using guns—as well as every other lethal instrument that fell into the hands of his supporters—he orchestrated the killing of more people than *any man in human history*.

The Third Son of the Monolith didn't care. There is no evidence that he ever suffered a single pang of conscience or felt a moment's regret. Rather, he delighted in the destruction of his enemies and the

---

[18]   Quoted in Liu Binyan, "An Unnatural Disaster." In the article, Liu reviews Zheng Yi's *Lishi de Yibufen* (A Piece of History).

[19]   Liu Binyan, "An Unnatural Disaster."

[20]   Mao Zedong, *Quotations from Chairman Mao Tse-tung*, 13.

[21]   Mao Zedong, *Mao's Road to Power*, vol. 3, 31.

murder of countless innocent human beings, and he goaded his followers into doing the same by falsely claiming, "If we don't kill them, they will kill us."

No one should in any way try and justify this ruthless carnage, much less romanticize it. The deliberate murder of innocents is a grievous violation of God's law, the Golden Rule of the Greeks, and the Silver Rule of Confucius. It is everywhere and always a great crime.

Mao believed that he was the final arbiter of life and death in China, but that role belongs to God alone.

CHAPTER 8

THE ART OF STEALING: ALL THE WEALTH OF CHINA

"You shall not steal. . . . You shall not covet . . .
anything that is your neighbor's."

—Exodus 20:15, 17

"Mao's order to cadres was to 'confiscate every last single thing' from those
picked out as victims. Often whole families were turned out of their homes."

—Mao Zedong[1]

The Seventh and Tenth Commandments

Rules for Thee, but Not for Me

Communism offers the perfect justification for avarice and theft. You are allowed to look greedily at the possessions of your neighbor, the Communists first say, for their very wealth and property are proof that they have exploited the masses. You must help us strip them of their wealth, they then insist, for it has been stolen from you. To further quash any qualms that people may feel about the proposed smash-and-grab operation, they are promised that whatever is confiscated will be used for the good of all.

It is easy to be swept up in a grand enterprise that claims to first liberate man from the bondage of capitalism and then to create a perfectly egalitarian society of perfect charity—from each according to his ability, to each according to his need. It is all a deception, of

---

[1] Chang, *Mao*, 107, citing documents gathered from Mao's first red state.

course, but an exceedingly clever one that in some ways mimics, and in other ways mocks, Christian teaching. After all, *Gaudium et Spes* suggests, "In using them, therefore, man should regard the external things that he legitimately possesses not only as his own but also as common in the sense that they should be able to benefit not only him but also others."[2]

Communists have used their grotesque exaggeration of Christian charity to great effect to mobilize the masses and seize power in a dozen countries, including China. What happens then is all too predictable: a tiny elite consolidates power, using totalitarian means of control to subjugate and virtually enslave the people, expropriating the bulk of their wealth for its own use.

In theory, everything in China belongs to the people, to be distributed—in Marx's famous formulation—according to need. Underneath this fig leaf of equality hides the naked truth: everything in China belongs to the top leaders of the Chinese Communist Party (CCP), who apportion it out to their followers and factions on the basis of formal rank and favoritism. What was portrayed as something akin to "the universal destination of goods"[3] quickly devolves into a kind of new spoils system.

Seventy years after the founding of the "New China," it is estimated that one-sixth of China's total GDP is siphoned off to fund the salaries, banquets, resorts, junkets, and other activities of the ninety-seven million members of the CCP. Another one-sixth is lost to corruption, and most of that also winds up in the hands of corrupt CCP

---

[2]   Vatican Council II, Pastoral Constitution *Gaudium et Spes* (December 7, 1965), no. 69.

[3]   The universal destination of goods, in Catholic theology, refers to the fact that a cornucopia of resources that God pre-deployed on planet earth or produced by the hand and mind of man are intended not just for a select few but for the use of all humanity. At the same time, as the *Catechism* notes, "For the sake of the common good, [the seventh commandment] requires respect for the universal destination of goods *and* respect for the right to private property" (*CCC* 2401, cf. 2424, italics added). Each tends toward extreme forms of socialism or capitalism in the absence of the other.

officials.[4] Former premier Wen Jiabao (2003–2013), for example, reportedly left office a staggering $2.3 *billion* richer.[5]

Taken together, this means that one out of every three dollars of the wealth produced by the toil of the Chinese people finds its way, one way or another, into the stomachs or pockets of party members, who are but a tiny fraction of China's population.

And this rapacious behavior began, of course, with none other than Mao Zedong.

Mao, the "Mountain Lord"

Chairman Mao's self-description as "a lonely monk walking the world with a leaky umbrella," along with his simple, sometimes patched peasant garb, was intended to suggest to the naive—a category that included most visiting foreigners in the early days—that he lived the spartan lifestyle of the true revolutionary. Nothing could have been further from the truth. Mao always reserved the best of everything— housing, food, doctors, and medicine—for himself from the very first. "Of course there are people and objects in the world, but they are all there only for me," Mao had written as a young man. It turns out that he meant this to be taken literally.

As soon as Mao arrived in the Jinggangshan mountains, he commandeered not just a local school to serve as his headquarters but also two of the best homes in the region for his personal use. One of these houses, spacious and built in the distinctive Chinese architectural

---

[4]   For one estimate, see China Power, "How does corruption hinder China's development."

[5]   Senior officials rely primarily on their factional ties to amass wealth and advance to leadership positions in the party, military, and government. By brokering their connections into lucrative—if shady—investment deals, by peddling their influence as silent partners in some of China's biggest enterprises, and by serving as backroom "fixers" when legal, labor, or other problems arise, many have become fabulously wealthy over the course of the past few decades. A *New York Times* investigation revealed that the family of former premier Wen Jiabao, by trading on his name and connections, had managed to accumulate a fortune worth more than $2.7 *billion* during his ten years in office. Barboza, "Billions in Hidden Riches for Family of Chinese Leader."

style, still impresses visitors today. The Octagonal Pavilion, as it is called, sits beside a river and boasts a large courtyard. Its most distinctive feature—the one that gives the house its name—is an octagonal skylight lined with wooden panels and rising two stories to a glass roof.

The house had been owned by a doctor, who had the misfortune of being home when Mao and his guards arrived. Mao found both the house and its occupant very useful. He confiscated the house and virtually enslaved its owner, relocating him to a cowshed in the courtyard where he was forced to serve as Mao's personal physician, treating his many maladies.

Mao lived like an emperor-in-exile. He had his own guard force, a pool of secretaries, and a majordomo to run his household. This included cooks, housekeepers, orderlies, a groom for his horse, and, of course, the unfortunate doctor. And within the region controlled by the Red Army, the chairman helped himself to whatever took his fancy. One orderly's sole task was keeping his master supplied with his favorite brand of cigarettes, while another's was ransacking looted towns and houses for books and newspapers to feed his master's voracious appetite for the printed word. And unbeknownst to anyone except his brother, Mao also secretly kept part of the plunder from the army's looting for himself.

Now it was there at Jinggangshan that Mao drafted the rules of good conduct for the soldiers of the Red Army that were to become famous. Known as "The Three Main Rules of Discipline," they were relentlessly drummed into the ranks. The three rules were:

- Obey orders in all your actions (一切行动听指挥).
- Do not take a single needle or piece of thread from the masses (不拿群众一针一线).
- Everything captured belonged to the collective (一切缴获要归公).

Any Red Army soldier, no matter what his rank, who disobeyed orders, engaged in unauthorized looting, or kept any captured goods for himself was punished.

While Mao may have drafted these rules, he didn't feel the least obligated to follow them himself. He began surreptitiously setting aside some of the looted gold, silver, and jewelry for a rainy day, entrusting his brother to secret it away in a nearby cave to keep it safe from prying eyes.

Mao, who was always looking out for himself, was looking ahead. At the time of the Nationalist-Communist split in 1927, he had had a foot in both camps, and he had agonized for weeks over which way to jump. Now he again decided to hedge his bets. He wanted to have something to fall back on if things went south—if the Communist Party was defeated by the Nationalists, if the party leaders succeeded in expelling him from their ranks, or if he himself decided to split with the party.

But the fact that Mao was a thief mattered far less than what his thievery represented. In stealing from the party, he was not only betraying Communism's collective ideals and disobeying his own orders but also proving beyond doubt his lack of commitment to the cause to which other senior leaders had pledged their lives. The CCP's leaders and Moscow were already alert to Mao's perfidy from the failed Autumn Harvest "Uprising." Had they further discovered that he had been stealing from the party's coffers since arriving in Jinggangshan, they would have instantly expelled him from the party—or worse.

In the end, however, Mao's private stash paid off in a way that even he may not have expected. By 1934, the Nationalist armies were closing in on the Red Base. The CCP leaders, led by Zhou Enlai, decided that it was time to evacuate the majority of their forces to the safety of Yan'an in the far north, where they could be resupplied by Soviet Russia. As they prepared to embark on what would become known as the Long March, Mao learned to his horror that the other leaders had decided to leave him behind: he was to be appointed the commander of the skeleton force that would remain in the Red Base. It is hard to avoid the conclusion that, wearied of Mao the Snake's endless deceptions, Zhou Enlai and the others were hoping that Chiang Kai-shek's forces would finish him off.

Now was the time to cash in his private hoard, Mao decided. He turned it over to the CCP—on condition that he be allowed to join the evacuation.[6] Short of funds for the march, Zhou reluctantly agreed to Mao's terms.

Luxuries for Me, but Not for Thee

The Long March is customarily described in the history books as a grueling journey of some six thousand miles across some of China's most inhospitable terrain. And so it was for nearly all. But it was much less taxing for Mao, who traveled in comparative comfort in a litter—a covered and curtained couch carried on the backs of four bearers. Through deserts and mountains, good weather and bad, he whiled away the days reading or plotting with other similarly ensconced senior leaders.

Once in Yan'an, Mao resumed his accustomed emperor-in-waiting lifestyle, surrounded by an even larger coterie of guards, scribes, and cooks than before. For visiting foreigners, however, Mao donned the guise of an ascetic revolutionary who was living in a cave dwelling and practicing self-denial. He understood the power of the international media, and he was determined to bend it to his purposes.

US diplomat John Stuart Service, visiting Yan'an in 1944, was so taken in by this Chinese shadow play that he wrote in his official reports that Chairman Mao was not a real Communist at all but merely an "agrarian reformer." As for the Red Base itself, he claimed that it had the atmosphere of a "religious summer conference."[7] Service's escorts made sure that he and his team were kept well away from the luxurious mansions that the chairman generally occupied—known as Phoenix Village and Date Hill—as well as from his concentration camp—complete with torture chambers and frequent executions—all of which were not far away.[8]

---

[6]   Salisbury, *The Long March,* 50.
[7]   Quoted in Mosher, *China Misperceived,* 58.
[8]   John Stuart Service and I crossed paths in 1978 when he enrolled in a class called "Chinese Anthropology" that I was teaching at the University of California at

The Chinese Communist revolution was, on paper, being carried out in pursuit of something akin to the Catholic Church's admonition to promote "justice and charity in the care of earthy goods and the fruits of men's labor."[9] But if Mao was good at hoarding the best for himself, where he truly excelled was in stripping others of their earthly goods and the fruits of their labor. As a result, the populations of his growing fiefdoms fared very badly from the beginning.

One problem was that the dividing line between the masses, from whom the Reds were not to steal a single needle or thread, and "reactionaries," whose homes could be looted with impunity, was never very clear. This was not, for Mao, a theoretical question as much as a very practical one. Who could he incite into attacking their better-off neighbors by stoking their envy and appealing to their greed? On the other hand, who would prove immune to his incitements?

In Jinggangshan, the answer to Mao's question often came down to who owned a pig. Those families raising a pig—known to Chinese peasants as the farmer's bank—were usually reluctant to turn on their neighbors and were, therefore, in Mao's view, "reactionary." Those families without a pig, on the other hand, could generally be counted on to covet their neighbors' animals and were, therefore, in Mao's view, "revolutionary." It was these latter who became the foot soldiers of his movement. It was these that he trained as village cadres to ransack the homes of their neighbors and whom he drafted into his army to fight the Nationalists.

But Mao didn't stop there. Once all of the wealth had been looted from those who had managed to, usually by dint of hard labor, get a little ahead, he began squeezing everybody else. Here, too, he was both relentless and remorseless. Of course, all Communists have a

---

Berkeley. He was a mild-mannered man who, sadly, had been completely deceived by the Chinese Communists about their true nature and purpose. For years, this wild-eyed innocent argued on the basis of his Yan'an experience that Mao merely wanted to carry out a land reform and was ultimately committed to democratic rule.

[9]   *CCC* 1807.

ready-made justification for confiscating private property "for the public good," since they believe that "property is theft." But Mao's exactions in terms of food and forced labor were often so severe that they not only left people destitute but sometimes also dead.

The *Catechism of the Catholic Church* notes that occupying oneself with productive work is a salutary thing: "Work is for man, not man for work."[10] And St. Paul, writing about the early Church communities where the believers shared all their goods in common, cautioned against freeloaders: "If anyone will not work, let him not eat" (2 Thes 3:10). But Mao forced peasants in the base areas to work on the meagerest of rations and, on several occasions, by requisitioning what little food they had on hand, in effect sentenced large numbers of people to death by slow starvation.

Theft of Grain from Peasants—Leaving Them to Starve

"How can we not recognize Lazarus, the hungry beggar in the parable (cf. Luke 19:19–31), in the multitude of human beings without bread, a roof or a place to stay."

—Catechism of the Catholic Church 2463

"Let them eat the bark of trees."

—Mao Zedong

The Red Army won the Chinese Civil War with the secret help of Joseph Stalin. At the end of World War II, the Soviet dictator ordered all the Japanese military equipment that his troops had seized in Manchuria, Outer Mongolia, and North Korea—hundreds of aircraft and tanks, thousands of artillery pieces and machine guns—to be turned over to Mao's forces.[11] Not only that, but he ensured that the

---

[10] *CCC* 2427.

[11] The total amount of captured Japanese armaments that Stalin turned over to Mao is staggering. It included "900 Japanese aircraft, 700 tanks, more than 3,700 artillery pieces, mortars and grenade launchers, nearly 12,000 machine guns, plus the Sungari River flotilla [gunboats], as well as numerous armored cars, and anti-aircraft guns, and hundreds of thousands of rifles." Viacheslav Zimonim, "Teheran-Yalta-Potsdam:

200,000 troops of the puppet Manchukuo army, along with tens of thousands of captured Japanese prisoners of war, were dragooned into Mao's army, often under pain of death. Then there were the 200,000 battle-hardened North Korean troops under Kim Il Sung who also entered the fray. With Stalin's help, in other words, Mao's forces doubled overnight and became far more lethal.

At the time, Mao was claiming with a straight face—he was an excellent actor—that his forces were hopelessly outmatched. The Red Army, he said, has "only millet plus rifles to rely on, but history will finally prove that our millet plus rifles is more powerful than Chiang Kai-shek's aeroplanes plus tanks."[12] His story of impoverished guerrillas heroically battling a far superior force elicited sympathy from Western progressives. But it was an utter fabrication. Moscow had in fact provided enough weapons to arm the entire Red Army, not to mention augmenting its ranks with hundreds of thousands of additional soldiers. But Mao knew his Sun Tzu: "When strong feign weakness."[13]

Both parties to the transfer of arms and armies went to extraordinary lengths to conceal it. Moscow called reports that it was aiding the Chinese Communists "fabrications from start to finish," while the CCP hid behind its "millets and rifles" dodge.[14]

Soviet Entry Into the War with Japan," *Far Eastern Affairs*, no. 2, 1995. Cited in Chang, *Mao*, 297. The Soviets also supplied captured German arms and ammo, and some of their own.

[12] Mao Zedong, "Talk with the American Correspondent Anna Louise Strong," August 1946, in Mao Zedong, *Selected Works of Mao Tse-Tung*, vol. 4, 100. The article includes a long note about how "To help Chiang Kai-shek start civil war against the people (sic), U.S. imperialism gave his government a very great amount of aid." Mao neglected to mention the much greater amount of military aid that his forces were even then receiving from the Soviet Union.

[13] Sun Tzu, *The Art of War*.

[14] Even today, when the evidence of Stalin's massive assistance to Mao's forces has been well-known for decades, there are still writers who decry "Stalin's perfidy," as Philip Short did. Short claimed, "Once again the Soviet leader had sold out the CCP for Russia's national interests" by signing a post-war treaty with the Nationalists. In fact, the treaty was merely a ruse, a cover for the transfer of the troops and military equipment that Mao would use to win the war. See Short, *Mao*.

But the aid was real, and it left Mao in something of a quandary. He was in desperate need of arms, but at the same time, he did not want to be indebted to the Soviet dictator. He insisted on paying for the aid in the only currency he had on hand: grain. He promised Stalin that he would send one million tons of grain to Russia each year.

The promise meant famine and death for some of the villagers in the areas controlled by the Communists. Determined to meet their quotas, cadres would kick in the doors of peasant huts looking for contraband food, ignoring the pleas of those they were leaving to starve.

And starve they did, even in the long-established Yan'an base area, where over ten thousand peasants perished from hunger in 1947. Chang and Halliday write, "Mao knew the situation very well, as he was traveling in the region that year, and saw village children hunting for stray peas in the stables of his entourage, for the sake of its driblets of nutrient. . . . In Manchuria itself, civilian deaths from starvation were in the hundreds of thousands in 1948, and even Communist troops were often half-starved."[15]

Even today, historians explain the famine in the areas under Communist control in the late forties as a consequence of the ongoing civil war. But the truth was that it was a direct consequence of Mao's decision to export precious foodstuffs to the Soviet Union—and he didn't care.

Mao was completely insensitive to the human suffering his decision to export food caused the people. He thought of the masses as an inexhaustible resource, and he made free to expend them in whatever way he wished. There is no record of Mao ever mourning those who had died at his hands.

It would not be the last time that Mao stole grain from starving peasants to build his castles in the sky. And the next time, the death toll would be much, much higher.

---

[15]   Chang, *Mao,* 298–99.

Ten Years to Utopia

"First, it is always the human person who is the purpose of work.
It must be said over and over again that work is for man, not man
for work. Man is indeed 'the true purpose of the whole process of
production.' Every consideration of the value of work must begin with
man, and every solution proposed to the problems of the social order
must recognize the primacy of the human person over things."[16]

—Pope Saint John Paul II

"In ten years' time commodities will be abundant, the standard of morale
will be high. We can start Communism with food, clothing, and housing.
With free food in the collective canteen, that's Communism."[17]

—Mao Zedong

In 1958, the Great Leap Forward, the brainchild of Chairman Mao, began. Hundreds of millions of Chinese villagers were herded into huge People's Communes, where it was intended that they would farm the land in common under the watchful eye of Communist Party cadres. Most villagers were unhappy at having their land and livelihoods stripped away from them in this fashion.[18]

Mao, on the other hand, was exuberant. The radical experiment in social engineering that he had dreamed about for decades was finally getting underway. To listen to him talk, utopia was just around the corner—or at most a decade distant. At a conference for the CCP's senior leadership, held at the party's exclusive resort at Beidaihe from August 19 to 21, 1958, he enthused:

> People's Commune are big, and they are public: Lots of people, a
> vast area of land, large scales of production, [and] all activities are
> [performed] in a big way. [They] integrate government [admin-
> istration] with commune [management] to establish collective
> canteens, eliminating private plots. Chickens, ducks, and young

---

16   Long, "St. John Paul II, 'Work is for man, not man for work.'"
17   Quoted in Zhou Xun, *Forgotten Voices of Mao's Great Famine*, 13.
18   See Mosher, *Broken Earth*.

trees in front of, and behind, the houses are still private. This, of
course, will not exist in the future. . . . With a surplus of grain we
can implement the supply system. . . .

In ten years' time commodities will be abundant, the standard
of morale will be high. We can start Communism with food,
clothing, and housing. With free food in the collective canteen,
that's Communism.[19]

The communes didn't last ten years, at least in their original con-
figuration. Neither did many of the villagers forced into them, as it
turned out.

The chickens and ducks went first, hastily consumed by village families before they, too, could be confiscated by the commune leaders.
The trees disappeared next, fed into the gaping maws of the so-called
steel smelters that Mao had ordered built. In some areas, desperate
for fuel, the cadres began tearing down houses as well, leaving people
homeless or sleeping ten to a room.

One of the many reasons the communes failed is because Mao
insisted that the communes adopt agricultural techniques from the
Soviet Union, which was reporting triple-digit increases in food production. Such techniques as deep plowing, close planting, and increased
irrigation, based as they were on Marxist-Leninist pseudoscience, turned
out to be disasters in practice. Deep plowing, for instance, effectively
destroyed the fertility of the soil for years to come, as peasants trenched
the ground to depths of four or five feet. Seedlings planted in extremely
high densities died, while the irrigation projects—mostly small reser-
voirs—were so ill-conceived and executed that they were later dismissed
by the Ministry of Agriculture as "completely worthless."

The communal kitchens folded after a few months as food became
scarce. From 1958 to 1962, Chinese people starved to death by the
tens of millions. But the "three difficult years," as the Beijing regime
still daintily refers to this atrocity, saw not merely death from famine

---

[19]   Quoted in Zhou Xun, *Forgotten Voices of Mao's Great Famine*, 13.

on a massive scale. It was also a period of state terror, during which party officials ransacked villages, torturing and murdering peasants for refusing to hand over secret stores of grain that did not exist.

Mao, in his great vanity, was oblivious to all this. Instead, he believed the reports of sycophantic party officials that food production had sky-rocketed under the commune system and his other innovations. Local cadres went all out to create the impression of a bumper harvest. When he traveled by train, Mao would see miles and miles of thriving crops along the tracks, unaware that they had just been transplanted there by peasants the day before. When Mao visited the model commune of Xushui in 1958, he saw piles of vegetables, turnips, cabbages, and carrots strategically placed along the main road. Officials told him that the peasants had dumped the vegetables there because they had grown so much food they did not know what to do with it.

Buoyed by a flood of such false reports, the Beijing regime encouraged peasants to eat grain. It doubled its grain exports, even giving away grain gratis to its friends in North Korea, North Vietnam, and Albania. Although no one knew it at the time, every ship that left the docks condemned additional tens of thousands to die.

By the winter of 1958–59, the commune granaries were bare, but Mao refused to believe that there was a food shortage. Instead, egged on by officials still boasting of record crops, he became convinced that the peasants were hiding their grain. In places like Henan, where the provincial leadership was fanatically devoted to Mao and his illusions, this led to mass murders that the party would later describe as "a holocaust."

As Jasper Becker writes, "The great terror began in the autumn of 1959 . . . when the prefectural Party committee declared war on the peasants . . . launch[ing] a brutal anti-hiding campaign. . . . 'It is not that there is no food [one local official said]. There is plenty of grain, but 90 percent of the people have ideological problems.'"[20] The result was that virtually all the grain harvested was confiscated by officials who used arrests and torture to achieve their ends.

---

[20]   Becker, *Hungry Ghosts,* 136.

Mao dismissed the suffering of the peasants with a curt, "Let them eat bark." And eat bark they did. "By the start of winter," Becker continues, "it was clear that the peasants had nothing to eat but tree bark, wild grass seeds and wild vegetables. [Local officials] declared that this was merely 'a ruse of rich peasants' and ordered the search for grain to be redoubled. Party cadres were also incited to smash the cooking pots in every household to prevent them from being used at home to cook grass soup."[21]

At the time, some villagers were sometimes reluctant to blame Chairman Mao, having been told for decades that he was the great savior of the Chinese people. Instead, they pointed to rapacious local officials as the cause of the famine. Indeed, some of the starving people believed to the end that Mao would miraculously come to their rescue if they could only somehow make him aware of their suffering. It was said that there were those who hauled themselves up to the top of nearby hills where, facing the direction of Beijing, they cried out in a loud voice for Mao to come and save them.

The man they had been told was a "god" was in fact utterly indifferent to the suffering of the faceless "masses." Had Mao been aware of it, he would have simply echoed Scrooge and said, "If they would rather die, . . . they had better do it, and decrease the surplus population."[22] Indeed, he did say something eerily similar—and equally inhuman—in a secret 1959 speech: "When there is not enough to eat, people starve to death. It is better to let half of the people die so that the other half can eat their fill."[23]

By the winter of 1959, the great thinning had started. One woman later recounted, "All the trees in [my] village had been cut down. Any nearby were all stripped of bark. I peeled off the bark of a locust tree and cooked it as if it were rice soup. It tasted like wood and was sticky."[24]

---

[21] Becker, 136.

[22] Dickens, *A Christmas Carol*.

[23] From a speech Mao gave to party leaders in Gansu, China, on May 25, 1959. Quoted in Dikötter, *Mao's Great Famine*, 134.

[24] Becker, *Hungry Ghosts*, 136.

But man cannot live on tree bark alone. Over the next three years, forty-five million or more villagers died of starvation, many because Mao and his minions were obsessed with the idea that they were somehow hiding and hoarding grain.

The masses could not be allowed to steal from the party under any circumstances. The party, on the other hand, was free to take every last thing that they possessed, even their very lives.

After the Revolution, the Entire Country Was His Plaything

> In Xanadu did Kubla Khan
> a stately pleasure dome decree:
> Where Alph, the sacred river, ran
> Through caverns measureless to man
> Down to a sunless sea. . . .
> And all should cry, Beware! Beware!
> His flashing eyes, his floating hair!
> Weave a circle round him thrice,
> And close your eyes with holy dread,
> For he on honey-dew hath fed,
> And drunk the milk of Paradise.

—Samuel Taylor Coleridge

> "But I had grown to hate the hypocrisy around me, the communist leaders' public carping against the corrupt bourgeois lifestyle of their predecessors, the touting of their high and lofty communist moral principles, while they themselves were living lives of luxury as the masses suffered and toiled and died."

—Dr. Li Zhisui, Mao's personal physician[25]

Once Mao had secured his position as chairman of the CCP in Yan'an, he no longer felt the need to hoard gold, or anything else for that matter. The party owned everything in the Red Bases, and Mao owned the party.

---

[25]   Li Zhisui, *The Private Life of Chairman Mao*, 354.

Mao was even more unrestrained in his pursuits after he had driven the Nationalists off the mainland and founded the People's Republic. He had become the master of more people than any ruler in human history. And he promptly, in pursuit of the perfect Communist paradise, began toying with their lives like a mad god.

Self-denial and sacrifice were for his subjects. Mao's own life was one of perpetual, unrestrained indulgence. According to his longtime doctor and confidant, Dr. Li Zhisui, Mao refused to curb any of his appetites. He ate rich, oily food even as others were starving. He rinsed his mouth with tea, rebuffing entreaties to brush his teeth and heal his infected, oozing gums. He refused to bathe, preferring an occasional rubdown with hot towels as a poor substitute. And he insisted on a steady stream of country girls, even as he would not allow Dr. Li to treat his venereal disease.

Mao was undisciplined in other ways as well. He refused to follow a set schedule, whiling away long hours in his specially designed bed or lazing by the side of private heated pools. But when he summoned anyone, up to and including members of the Politburo, they were expected to hasten to his side regardless of the day or the hour. Since he was habitually on the move, receiving a summons from Mao meant that you sometimes had to travel thousands of miles to wherever the chairman happened to be staying.

Mao was driven to change his whereabouts by long-standing paranoia, no less than by his fear of assassination. "It's not good for me to stay in one place too long," he confided to Dr. Li. A special armored train was designed and built for his peregrinations—and his protection. When it left the station, all other rail traffic was halted and all of the stations along its route were closed and heavily guarded against potential assassins.

Knowing that the chairman would sooner or later be paying them a visit, every provincial party secretary built Mao a luxurious villa, keeping it staffed and ready year-round. Mao's favorite was located on a small islet in the middle of the Pearl River not far from the bustling metropolis of Guangzhou. Regardless of where in China he happened to be, however, Mao's food was always airlifted to him from the same place: a prison camp on the outskirts of Beijing. He who had poisoned others was deathly afraid of being poisoned himself, so every dish was sampled by tasters before it was set before him.

Chairman Mao also needed constant medical attention. Sometimes his intense sense of insecurity would threaten to drive him mad with worry, while other times he would be euphoric over a political victory. Like Hitler and Stalin, Mao suffered multiple ailments, some mental and some physical, and was on multiple medications. Dr. Li had to constantly sedate him with barbiturates so he could sleep. But it wasn't pangs of conscience that kept him awake at night; it was his fear of betrayal, his incessant plotting, and his insatiable appetites.

The cost of allowing Mao to indulge his passions while calming his fears must have been astronomical. What with the train, the travel, the villas, and his huge entourage, he surely ranks as China's most extravagant emperor. He had not one Forbidden City but dozens. All of this excess was forcibly extracted from the masses, who were simultaneously suffering from his get-communism-quick schemes.

Yet why should Mao have doubted that the Communist utopia had truly arrived—when he himself, the mad emperor in the flesh, was drinking the milk of paradise? He was living in the modern-day equivalent of Kublai Khan's "stately pleasure dome," with the people and the resources of all of China at his beck and call.

For all that, the Red Emperor who enjoyed every creature comfort known to man never knew a moment's true peace. Rather, he lived in fear—fear of assassination, fear of poisoning, fear of betrayal, fear of what tomorrow would bring. He was crippled by his inability to love, driven nearly insane by his lust for power and control, and at war with his very humanity. It is in sacrificing for the good of others that we become truly human. Yet Mao, while hoarding all the goods of China for himself, would not continence the slightest inconvenience. In his last years, he behaved more like a wolf guarding its kill, fangs bared and snarling, than a human being.

"Everything that is not given is lost," Saint Teresa of Calcutta taught us. And, in the end, Mao Zedong, having given nothing, lost everything, even his God-given rationality and humanity.

CHAPTER **9**

THERE ARE LIES, DAMNED LIES, AND MAO'S LIES

"You shall not bear false witness against your neighbor."

—Exodus 20:16

*"It was said to the men of old, 'You shall not swear falsely,
but shall perform to the Lord what you have sworn.'"*

—Matthew 5:33

"Politics is war without bloodshed, while war is politics with bloodshed."

—Mao Zedong[1]

The Eighth Commandment

Mao Was the Father of Chinese Communist Lies

In a courtroom setting, one can impeach a witness by catching him in a single lie. "False in one thing, false in all things," as the Latin saying goes. (*Falso in uno, falso in omnibus*.) By this standard, Mao would have convicted himself by simply opening his mouth, for he was decidedly false in all matters of moment.

Indeed, it is no exaggeration to say that the Third Son of the Monolith delighted in deception. This propensity to deceit followed naturally from Mao's beliefs. Not only did he wholeheartedly embrace Sun-Tzu's ancient dictum that "all warfare is deception,"[2] he considered

---

[1]   "On Protracted War," in Mao Zedong, *Selected Works of Mao Zedong*, vol. 2, 153.

[2]   Mao greatly admired China's ancient strategist, writing that "war . . . is mundane process governed by necessity. That is why Sun Wu Tzu's [Sunzi's] axiom,

135

politics—his sole occupation—as a form of warfare. There can be no mistaking this, because he himself affirmed that "politics is war without bloodshed, while war is politics with bloodshed." It is one of his most quoted statements.

You don't have to be a logician to understand that if "all warfare is deception," and if "politics is war," then it must be true that "all politics is deception." In any event, this was the syllogism that Mao lived—and lied—by his entire life.

Mao's lies, and the actions that followed, often went beyond the bounds of political necessity. The record shows that Mao even lied when the truth would have sufficed to win his point. It is hard to avoid the conclusion that, for Mao, deception was not a disagreeable necessity of the political craft but a positive pleasure. It was as if he consciously rejected the truth in favor of falsehood in order to deceive his audience—even when he didn't need to—so he could count himself clever in doing so.

Mao Zedong, in other words, was a faithful son of the Father of Lies. His life, in one sense, was one long story of the betrayal of those closest to him; he cheated on his wives, abandoned his children, and— as I detail below—repeatedly betrayed his erstwhile comrades, even unto death. Mao's political career, especially, may be viewed as an endless series of deceptions in which he betrayed friends and deceived enemies alike to advance himself.

In fact, Mao first rose to prominence in the Chinese Communist Party (CCP)—and first attracted the notice of the man who would become his patron, Soviet dictator Joseph Stalin—by practicing a deception that, even a century later, is breathtaking in its sheer audacity. The history books refer to the episode as a peasant uprising. But it could more accurately be called "Mao hijacks an army," because that's exactly what the young—but very ambitious—political operator did.[3]

'Know the enemy and know yourself, and you can fight a hundred battle's with no danger of defeat,' remains a scientific truth." Mao Zedong, 164.

[3] The following section is based on Jung and Halliday's very detailed account of Mao's maneuverings that enabled him, for the first time, to seize control of an

Mao Hoodwinks His Comrades into Giving Him Control of an Army—Then He Steals It

"You are of your father the devil, and your will is to do your father's desires. He was a murderer from the beginning, and has nothing to do with the truth, because there is no truth in him. When he lies, he speaks according to his own nature, for he is a liar and the father of lies."

—John 8: 44

"[My] little army, leading the peasant uprising, moved southward through Hunan. It had to break its way through thousands of Kuomintang troops and fought many battles, with many reverses."

—Mao Zedong to Edgar Snow[4]

Mao's primordial deceit appears in the CCP history books—and in the writings of naïve Western sinologists—as "the Autumn Harvest Uprising." The claim is that in September 1927, Mao singlehandedly assembled and led a small peasant army against the Nationalists and the landlords of Hunan. According to these accounts, the uprising was successful in setting up something called the "Hunan Soviet," but was eventually defeated two months later by Nationalist forces.

Or, in Mao's own telling, "[My] little army, leading the peasant uprising, moved southward through Hunan. It had to break its way through thousands of Kuomintang troops and fought many battles, with many reverses."[5]

It was only at "this critical juncture," claims Mao hagiographer and all-around Communist lickspittle Han Suyin,[6] that Mao Zedong

---

armed force. See Chang, *Mao,* chapter 5, "Hijacking a Red Force and Taking over Bandit Land," 49–63.

[4]   Snow, *Red Star Over China,* 194. Snow's account, which was carefully curated by Mao, always puts the Red supremo at the center of the action and in the best possible light.

[5]   Snow, 194.

[6]   Han Suyin was a Eurasian who early in life wrote *A Many-Splendoured Thing* and other successful novels. Later in her career, she became a virtual flack for the Chinese Communist regime, writing a series of books about Mao Zedong that were scarcely more reflective of reality than her earlier fiction.

experienced an epiphany: "Instead of disbanding his very reduced forces or marching them to join other levies engaged in city-storming, Mao took the momentous decision to follow his own judgment—to forge a Red Army and to select a base in the countryside for survival."[7]

To hear Han Suyin tell it, Mao's decision to retreat into the Jinggang Mountains in the border region between Hunan and Jiangxi provinces was a stroke of genius. Because it was supposedly there, in this mountain fastness, that he set up the first of what would later become many Red Bases, built up the first Red Army, and crafted the rural strategy and guerrilla tactics that would eventually lead the CCP to victory.

Or so the official story of the "Autumn Harvest Uprising" goes.

This story is the basis of the widely held belief that Mao was a brilliant tactician, a far-seeing strategist, and an inspiring leader of men. But it is all—or nearly all—a complete fabrication. The much-ballyhooed "Hunan Soviet" never really existed. Mao not only did not lead an "uprising" but actively sabotaged it. And he did so out of the basest of motives: he was determined to gain control of his own army, no matter how many "comrades" he had to sacrifice to achieve this ambition.

Two things happened in April 1927 that set the stage for Mao's rise from rural obscurity to a position of leadership in the CCP. The first was that Chiang Kai-shek purged the Communists from the ranks of the Nationalist Party. The second was that Joseph Stalin, in response to Chiang's action, ordered the CCP to take up arms.

Mao enthusiastically seconded this approach, telling the Russian representative—in a saying that later became famous—that "political power grows out of the barrel of a gun." But Mao, as Jung and Halliday note, "harbored his own agenda—to command both the gun and the Party. His plan was to build his own army, carve out his own territory, and deal with Moscow and the [CCP leadership] from a position of strength."[8]

In lieu of undertaking the formidable task of raising, equipping, and training an army himself—a task for which he was woefully

---

[7]   Han Suyin, *The Morning Deluge,* 200.
[8]   Chang, *Mao,* 50.

unsuited—Mao instead began maneuvering to get his hands on an existing army. His first thought was to angle for some of the twenty thousand troops in the neighboring province of Jiangxi who had rebelled following Chiang's crackdown. The only problem was that these mutineers were already under orders to march to the coast, where the Russians had promised to resupply them with arms and ammunition, while Mao was inland, in Hunan.

Mao solved this problem by concocting a ruse. He told the party leadership in Shanghai that South Hunan was ripe for a peasant uprising, and he was just the man to organize and lead it. He promised to wrest away from Nationalist control "at least five counties" and set up a "Hunan Soviet" that would be governed by the CCP. The only thing he required, he wrote, was that some of the Jiangxi troops be diverted to Hunan and that he be given command of them. Excited by the prospect of having a Red Base, and unaware of Mao's real intentions, the party leaders signed on to his scheme.

When the promised troops failed to show up, Mao abruptly changed course. From his refuge in the Russian consulate in Changsha, he demanded of the local Hunan Party committee that the plans for a Hunan Soviet be canceled and that an attack on the city be carried out instead. Mao's proposal was adopted, and he, as the senior representative of the CCP, was put in charge of several local Red units.

Mao then somberly announced that he was going to lead the assault and left the consulate. Instead of joining the troops, however, he decamped to a town some sixty miles distant. There, he promptly countermanded the orders for an attack and ordered the units to retreat to his location.[9]

Both the Russians and the CCP leadership were furious at this betrayal. Moscow called the affair "a joke of an uprising." The secretary of the Soviet

---

[9]   In his own account of the Autumn Harvest Uprising, Mao claims that "while he was organizing the army, he was captured by local militia and narrowly escaped execution." The story, as recounted to Edgar Snow, is notably devoid of specifics of time and place, but it is reasonable to suppose that it occurred while Mao was fleeing Changsha. See Snow, *Red Star Over China,* 193.

consulate in Changsha was even more scathing, calling Mao's actions the "most despicable treachery and cowardice." The CCP leadership in Shanghai, learning of these developments, said that "the . . . army led by comrade Mao Zedong . . . has committed extremely serious errors politically."

Belatedly realizing that Mao had set the whole thing up simply to make off with an army, the party leadership relieved Mao of command on November 14 and expelled him from all of his party posts. The Hunan Party committee, of which Mao was a member, was ordered to enforce the order. Before they could act, however, the entire committee was arrested and executed by the Nationalists. It would not be the last time that Mao would betray his erstwhile comrades.

In the yarn he later spun for Edgar Snow, Mao doesn't mention Changsha at all. Instead, he tells a tale about how his "little army" had led "the peasant uprising . . . and fought many battles, with many reverses." In fact, Mao led no uprising and avoided pitched battles, for he was intent upon absconding with his little army intact. The "reverses" he suffered along the way came chiefly from men going AWOL. By the time he reached Jinggangshan, more than half of his original force of 1,500, including its commanders, had deserted. Most left after learning that Mao intended for them to survive in the mountains by raiding neighboring communities. Mao told them that they were to become "lords of the mountains," but the Nationalists coined a more accurate description of their activities. They called Mao and his followers *Gong Fei*, or "Communist bandits."

As a result of his continued flouting of party orders, the party leadership tried to expel Mao from the party two more times in the years that followed. But they were never able to successfully rid themselves of him. Instead, it was Mao who, by various ruses and betrayals, gradually eliminated his enemies within the party leadership one by one until he stood alone at the top.

But it was stealing an army that was his first big score. His political power grew rapidly out of the barrels of the guns he now controlled, as he knew it would.

Alas, Poor Comrade, I Hardly Knew Ye

*"Cain said to his brother Abel, 'Let us go out to the field.' And
when they were in the field, Cain rose up against his brother Abel,
and killed him. Then the Lord said to Cain, 'Where is Abel your
brother?' He said, 'I do not know; am I my brother's keeper?'"*

—Genesis 4:8–10

*"One of the emperors Mao admired most was the Shang dynasty tyrant
Emperor Zhou, who had reigned during the eleventh century B.C. The
Chinese people have always regarded Emperor Zhou with revulsion, horrified
by his cruelty. The lives of his subjects had meant nothing to Emperor Zhou,
and he was in the habit of displaying the mutilated bodies of his victims
as a warning to potential rebels. . . . He had killed some loyal and able
ministers, to be sure [Mao argued to me] . . . but what emperor had not?"*

—Dr. Li Zhisui[10]

A complete list of the real or imagined party rivals that Mao had
assassinated, poisoned, or sidelined during the long Chinese civil war
would take up an entire chapter. It would include Chang Kuo-tao, a
leading general whose army and reputation were destroyed by Mao's
machinations,[11] as well as Stalin's pick to lead the CCP, Wang Ming,
who, it was widely suspected, was slowly being poisoned by Mao's
doctor using mercury. Both of Mao's intended victims only narrowly
survived: Chang because he went over to the Nationalists; Wang Ming
because Stalin—who happened to be holding Mao's son, Anying, in
Moscow—intervened.

Mao did not often leave his rivals alive, however, believing that in
politics, as in war, it was best to annihilate one's opponents, not leave
them wounded and brooding about revenge. So it was that the popular
leader of the Yan'an Red Base, Liu Chih-tan, met an untimely death
shortly after Mao's arrival in 1936.

---

10   Li Zhisui, *The Private Life of Chairman Mao,* 122.
11   I tell this story in chapter 9.

Chih-tan had offered no resistance when Mao, who outranked him in the party hierarchy, took over the base he had founded. Nor did he object when Mao demoted him to command a small unit on the front lines. It was there that he was killed by a single shot to the heart, said to have been fired by an enemy machine gun from over two hundred yards away. The only witness to his death was the political commissar of Chih-tan's unit who, as it happens, was also a member of the Chinese KGB and one of Mao's trusted minions.

Chairman Mao's determination to eliminate any and all threats to his rule—real or imagined—did not slacken with the success of the revolution in 1949. Nor did the passage of years dampen his passion to wreak vengeance on those who crossed him. But while he never forgot, much less forgave, a slight, he was also not one to move rashly. Like his totem, the snake, he would lie in wait, sometimes for years, for the right political moment to strike. He wanted to be sure he would draw blood.

Peng Dehuai

One of Mao's oldest comrades was a bluff general named Peng Dehuai. Peng had arrived in Jinggangshan in 1928, and more than once had saved Mao's life. In the years that followed, the plain-spoken Peng had frequently annoyed the chairman by questioning his judgment on military matters, usually with good cause.

As the disaster of the Great Leap Forward was unfolding in 1959, however, Peng crossed a line, speaking his mind about the famine spreading across the land. The Communist general had grown up in a poor peasant family and, on a visit to his home village in Hunan, had been heartbroken to see firsthand the suffering of the people under the commune system. Crops were left to rot in the fields, the people were in rags, and there was widespread starvation. He lamented their plight in a sad poem:

> Grain scattered on the ground, potato leaves withered;
> Strong young people have left to make steel;

Only children and old women reap the crops;
How can they pass the coming year?
Allow me to raise my voice for the people![12]

At a 1959 meeting, Peng sent Mao a private letter summarizing the suffering of the Chinese people. The masses were hungrier than they had been in the period between 1933 and 1953, he wrote, and if rations were not improved, there would be riots and uprisings. As for the Great Leap Forward, the people's communes, the steel drive, all these had been done in haste and were wasting resources and manpower. "In the view of some comrades, putting 'politics in command' [one of Mao's slogans] is a substitute for everything, but it is no substitute for economic principles," Peng concluded.

Mao took the attack personally, as well he might, since the Great Leap Forward had been his brainchild. His counterattack was not long in coming. He circulated Peng's letter to all 150 officials present at the meeting, and then, assisted by Zhou Enlai and others, he began relentlessly attacking the general day after day. Peng was soon relieved of command and forced into retirement. But Mao wasn't done with him yet.

Peng didn't know it, but in criticizing Mao's Great Leap Forward, he had unwittingly signed his own death warrant—although the sentence wouldn't be carried out for many years. It wasn't until 1966, with the beginning of the Cultural Revolution, that the chairman had his final revenge.

Peng was one of the first to be arrested by the Red Guards. He was beaten until his ribs were broken in a vain effort to break his will. In the months and years that followed, he was periodically trotted out in chains to be publicly humiliated in struggle sessions, although he never did confess to being a "capitalist roader." Peng's fellow generals did their best to protect him, pleading with Mao that he be rehabilitated. Not only did Mao refuse their entreaties but, as the elderly general's

---

[12]   Domes, *Peng Te-huai,* 83.

health deteriorated, even hastened his death by denying him medical care.[13] Peng died in prison in 1974.

The chairman had a long memory for slights.

Liu Shaoqi

Liu had been at Mao's side for decades, supporting the chairman through power struggles and purges alike. But as the death toll from the Great Famine climbed into the tens of millions, even the first vice chairman of the CCP had had enough.

In January 1962, before seven thousand cadres from all over the country, Liu shocked his audience by saying that the ongoing famine was not primarily a natural disaster but a man-made one (*renhuo*). Mao, who was present, was furious. "He's not addressing the question of whether we are going the capitalist road or the socialist road," he later complained to his doctor. "He talks about natural disasters versus man-made disasters. That kind of talk is a disaster in itself."[14]

Mao had begun to doubt Liu's loyalty, a suspicion that hardened into fact after the two had a heated confrontation later the same year. To boost food production and end the ongoing famine, Liu wanted to dissolve the people's communes and redistribute the land to those who actually tilled it.

Upon hearing this, Mao exploded into a string of earthy curses. The people's communes were his creation, central to his dream of creating the "industrial armies for agriculture" that Marx had written about in his *Communist Manifesto*.

Liu forged ahead, undaunted. "So many people have died of hunger!" he shouted. "History will judge you and me, even cannibalism will go into the books!"

Mao flew into a towering rage. "The Three Red Banners [another name for the Great Leap Forward] have been shot down, now land is

---

13   Domes, 122–24.
14   Li Zhisui, *The Private Life of Chairman Mao*, 386.

being divided up again," he shouted. "What have you done to resist this? What's going to happen after I'm dead?"[15]

From that point forward, Liu was a dead man walking. Like Peng, he was one of the first to be arrested during the Maoist purge known as the Cultural Revolution. But without generals to protect him, he didn't last nearly as long. Labeled China's foremost capitalist roader, he was brutally tortured, incessantly struggled, and then left to die half-naked in a freezing cellar in Kaifeng, Henan, in 1969.

Zhou Enlai

Mao Zedong seized control of the CCP from Zhou Enlai in 1934 during the Long March. After this, Zhou never again challenged the chairman, being content to become his most faithful acolyte. Still, forty years of service was not long enough to erase from Mao's mind the threat to his ambitions that now-Premier Zhou had once posed. There was a price to be paid, and at the end of Zhou's life, Mao made sure that it was paid in full.

Mao's chance to settle this particular score came in November 1972, when Premier Zhou was diagnosed with early-stage bladder cancer. Since Mao had to personally approve all medical treatment for Politburo members—this was one of the ways he controlled them—Zhou's doctors came to Mao. They told him that, given the proper treatment, the premier had an excellent chance of recovery, which they estimated at 80 to 90 percent.

Hearing this, Mao decided it was payback time. Zhou's doctors were first sworn to secrecy: they were not to tell the ailing premier then he was suffering from cancer. Then Mao ordered that no further examinations were to be carried out, no treatment was to be prescribed, and absolutely no surgery was to be performed.[16] Then he sat back to watch Zhou die a painful death.

By the time Mao finally allowed the doctors to act two years later, Zhou's cancer was too advanced for the surgery to halt its spread. Zhou

---

15   Gao Wenqian, *Zhou Enlai,* 97–98.
16   Gao Wenqian, 235–36. See also Chang, *Mao,* 592–94.

had escaped the fate of Peng Dehuai and Liu Shaoqi—he did not die in prison—but Mao had nevertheless found a way to extract his pound of flesh by hastening Zhou's death. The chairman had mastered the art of what the Chinese call "killing without shedding blood" (*Sha ren bu liu xie*).

Chairman Mao may have claimed that "politics is war without bloodshed, while war is politics with bloodshed." But the record shows that he was always ready, in war or peace, to go for the jugular. For him, politics was very much a blood sport—as long as the blood belonged to someone else.

Mao Zedong's Biggest Lie Is the PRC Itself

In 1940, Mao Zedong published an article entitled "On New Democracy," in which he claimed that he was working toward "a China that is politically free." In subsequent articles and speeches, he laid out his vision of the future. Yes, he conceded, he wanted to give land to the peasants and the factories to the workers. At the same time, however, he guaranteed that intellectuals would continue to enjoy intellectual freedom and that the entire government would operate on the Lincolnesque principle of a government of, by, and for the entire Chinese people. He would ensure that everyone enjoyed Roosevelt's four fundamental freedoms—freedom of speech, freedom of religion, freedom from want, and freedom from fear.

Mao's pronouncements convinced many Chinese liberals and intellectuals in the years following that they could work alongside the CCP in pursuit of these common goals. Liberals in the West as well, including many in the State Department and the Truman White House, were also impressed by his supposed moderation. Mao was merely an agrarian reformer, not a Communist, they told the American president.

It was all a hoax. Mao had adopted a moderate pose solely in order to weaken his political adversary, Chiang Kai-shek. And it worked. A number of small democratic parties and intellectuals switched their support to the Communists in response. More importantly, after

World War II ended, Truman was convinced to hold up crucial military and economic aid to the Nationalists to force them into "peace negotiations."

Mao Zedong continued the pretense of "negotiating" with the democratic parties and Nationalist factions to finalize a so-called "common program" until his victory seemed assured. Then, with the Red Army advancing into south China, he dropped the mask. At the opening of the Chinese People's Political Consultative Conference in Beijing in September 1949, he announced that the new Chinese government would be "under the leadership of the Communist Party of China." And, just like that, the People's Republic of China became a one-party dictatorship.

Mao then proceeded to turn each and every one of the promises that he had made earlier on their head. Under the pretense of land reform, China's farmers were soon to lose their land forever. Instead of running their own factories, workers were forbidden from setting up independent labor unions or striking. Instead of enjoying freedom of thought, intellectuals were forced to undergo "thought reform." Instead of a government of the people, by the people, and for the people, the Chinese people found themselves living in a "peoples' republic" in which they weren't allowed to vote.

Mao's grand deception makes no appearance in the official histories of China, which continue to insist that the "Chinese people achieved a democratic revolution under the leadership of Mao Zedong." Neither do any of the other countless plots, deceptions, and betrayals, both personal and political, that Mao the Snake continually engaged in.

Our Lord's words to the Pharisees seem to echo down through history here: "You are of your father the devil, and your will is to do your father's desires. He was a murderer from the beginning, and has nothing to do with the truth, because there is no truth in him. When he lies, he speaks according to his own nature, for he is a liar and the father of lies" (Jn 8:44).

PART 3
CHINESE KNOCKOFFS: THE CHINESE COMMUNIST PARTY SPREADS ITS ERRORS ACROSS ASIA

"It is impossible for any genuine people's revolution in any country to win victory without various forms of help from the international revolutionary forces. . . . Just imagine! If the Soviet Union had not existed. . . . In such circumstances, could we have won victory? Obviously not."

—Mao Zedong[1]

"The principle of subsidiarity is opposed to all forms of collectivism. It sets limits for state intervention. It aims at harmonizing the relationships between individuals and societies. It tends toward the establishment of true international order."

—*Catechism of the Catholic Church* 1885

Our Lady told the children at Fatima that Russia would spread its errors across the world. What she didn't say was that once those errors had taken root in China, the Chinese Communists would then continue to propagate these errors across Asia—or at least try to. But that is exactly what happened. Mao was obsessed with the idea that he could foment a truly global revolutionary movement and that the greatness of Chinese Communism would become a light unto the

---

[1] Mao Zedong, *On People's Democratic Dictatorship.*

nations of the world as he refashioned them in China's image. Using Communist internationalism as an ideological justification, the Chinese Communist Party would support the Third World and "liberate" all of humanity.[2]

So it was that, at the same time that he was spouting anti-imperialist rhetoric aimed at the West, Mao Zedong was busy with his own imperialistic ventures closer to home. His first goal was to reassemble the former Qing Empire, various outlying parts of which—Mongolia, Eastern Turkistan, and Tibet—had won their independence following the dynasty's 1911 collapse. These countries and peoples had been conquered by the Manchus in the late seventeenth century but had never been part of China proper under earlier Chinese dynasties.

Mao sent his Red Army on the march and, through a combination of duplicity and direct military action, managed to recover most of what had been lost nearly a half-century before. All of Manchuria was wrested back from Russian influence. Although the northern half of Mongolia—Inner Mongolia—was permanently lost to Soviet machinations, the southern half was recaptured and renamed the Chinese province of Outer Mongolia. Eastern Turkestan, the ancient homeland of the Uyghurs, was invaded, conquered, and renamed Xinjiang, which means, fittingly, "New Border." As for Tibet, it first agreed—under duress—to become a Chinese protectorate. For a time, it would continue to control its own domestic affairs, albeit under ever-increasing Chinese scrutiny and supervision. But in 1959, it was invaded in force and conquered. The Dalai Lama fled to India with 100,000 of his followers.

By the end of Mao's imperialistic adventures, he had recovered nearly all of the Qing Empire's colonial holdings except the port of Vladivostok and the Russian Far East, parts of Central Asia, and Taiwan—Chiang Kai-shek and the Nationalist's last redoubt.

---

[2]   Liu Xiaobo, "The Roots of Chinese 'Patriotism,'" *No Enemies, No Hatred: Selected Essays and Poems,* 67.

With Mao's appetites whetted, he then turned farther afield to several former Qing tributary states—Korea, Vietnam, and Cambodia. These were kingdoms whose rulers had recognized China's emperor as their superior and periodically sent emissaries bearing tribute to acknowledge this fact. Now, he embarked on an effort to turn these one-time vassal states into despotic utopias modeled on China's own. Over the years, he succeeded in helping to establish "people's democratic dictatorships" in Korea, Vietnam, and Cambodia. It's a tossup as to which of these three best exemplifies the evil of Mao's Chinese Communist regime. In the next three chapters, we will examine each of these three countries in turn and let you decide.

CHAPTER 10

MAO SAVES KIM IL SUNG'S HALF KINGDOM

*"My God is none other than the people. Only the popular
masses are omniscient and omnipotent and almighty on earth.
Therefore my lifetime motto is: 'The people are my God.'"*

—Kim Il Sung[1]

*"Communism is . . . adoration of the State; a glorification of the
human collective through the de-personalization of men; a suffocation
of human personality and its subsequent absorption into the mass."*

—Archbishop Fulton Sheen[2]

The first chance for Chairman Mao to expand Communism's
writ and, not coincidentally, recover one of the Qing dynasty's
lost tributary states came soon after he founded the People's Republic
of China on October 1, 1949.

The end of the Second World War in 1945 brought decades of
brutal Japanese colonialism to a close but left the Korean peninsula
divided. With Soviet troops occupying the north and American troops
in the south, Koreans faced an uncertain future. Little did they know
that they would soon find themselves in the middle of the first armed
conflict of the Cold War between Communism and democracy. The
two sides had originally agreed that their partition of the peninsula
between north and south along the thirty-eighth parallel was only

---

[1] Kim Il-Sung, *With the Century.*
[2] Marlin, *The Quotable Fulton Sheen,* 48.

temporary.[3] Once elections were held, a unified Korea would regain its independence. Soviet dictator Joseph Stalin violated that agreement, setting the stage for the conflict that has left Korea divided between north and south to the present day.

Popular elections were held in the south, and the Republic of Korea was established in 1948. In the north, however, Stalin refused to allow elections. Instead, he promoted loyal Korean communists to lead the nation. Chief among these was Kim Il Sung, a militant Communist and partisan fighter, whom he appointed to head the Provisional People's Committee of North Korea in 1946.[4] Stalin also turned over to Kim's forces, as he had done with Mao's forces in Manchuria, all of the armaments of the surrendered Japanese occupying army.

Following Stalin's example and emboldened by his support, Kim Il Sung ruthlessly purged political rivals from other Communist and nationalist factions and quickly created a one-party state with himself as the unquestioned head of what was called the Korean Worker's Party.

Communist dictator Kim Il Sung was not content to just rule North Korea with an iron hand. As Mao hungered to reconquer all the Qing dynasty's imperial domains, so Kim hungered to control all of the Korean peninsula. He convinced his patron, Stalin, to allow him a "limited offensive."[5] On June 25, 1950, the entire North Korean army, armed and equipped by the Soviet Union, poured across the thirty-eighth parallel and fell upon the nearly defenseless South. The United States quickly rushed in troops to slow the North Korean offensive and then, together with the South Koreans and military units from twenty other nations, quickly pushed them back into the north.

As the US-led forces approached the Yalu River, which separates Korea from China, a desperate Kim Il Sung appealed to Communist

---

[3]   OHCHR, "Report of the Commission of Inquiry on Human Rights in the Democratic People's Republic of Korea."

[4]   OHCHR, "Report of the Commission of Inquiry on Human Rights in the Democratic People's Republic of Korea."

[5]   Mosher, *Bully of Asia,* 81.

China for aid.[6] Mao responded with a grand imperial gesture, sending a huge "volunteer" army of some 300,000 troops across the Yalu to stop the US-South Korean advance.[7] As we discussed in chapter 7, these former Nationalist troops were the ultimate expendables, and Mao was happy to see them slaughtered by the Americans. He was both seizing an opportunity and reacting to a threat. The opportunity that presented itself was the reestablishment of Chinese dominance over a former vassal state, while the threat was that if the Korean peninsula was unified under a US ally, China might find American troops on its border. At a minimum, Mao wanted to preserve North Korea as a buffer state, saying, "If the lips [North Korea] are gone, the teeth [China] will get cold."[8]

After three years of fighting, North and South Korea agreed to cease hostilities in 1953, although no formal peace treaty has ever been signed. Instead, the two sides simply withdrew their armies from the front lines and created a demilitarized zone. The war, which claimed the lives of nearly forty-three thousand Americans, a quarter of a million Chinese, and three million Koreans, had ended in a stalemate roughly where it began, along the thirty-eighth parallel. Although South Korea has tried to avoid war, the North has repeatedly violated the peace. In the years since, hundreds of South Korean soldiers, civilians, and politicians have been killed in North Korean raids, terrorist attacks, and missile strikes on South Korean territory.[9]

---

[6]   Kim, at the urging of the Soviets, had earlier sent 200,000 troops to Manchuria to fight at Mao's side, so he had a reasonable expectation that Mao would reciprocate. See Kim Il Sung, "Let us Provide Active Support for the Revolutionary Struggle of the Chinese People."

[7]   Pierre Rigoulot, "Crimes, Terror, and Secrecy in North Korea," in Courtois, *The Black Book of Communism,* 549.

[8]   This saying is usually mistranslated by those who think it means that China and North Korea are as close as lips and teeth. But what Mao was actually referring to was North Korea's role as a buffer state. "If the lips are missing, the teeth will get cold" meant that Mao did not want a US ally, a unified Korea, on China's border.

[9]   Rigoulot, "Crimes, Terror, and Secrecy in North Korea," 550.

Collectivization Kills—Again

"Comrades, Last year we achieved another brilliant victory in agricultural production. . . . The domestic Korea hens do not lay many eggs because they sit on them through habit, . . .and they gradually degenerated into a meagre-laying species. But hens kept in modern [state] farms do not sit on their eggs. . . . We are building egg farms to provide 100 eggs to every citizen of Pyongyang."

—Kim Il Sung, 1969[10]

"Because the abolition of property is the beginning of slavery, the Church is opposed to . . . Communism which confiscates it all in the name of the collectivity. Being profoundly interested in the liberty of man, the Church takes the practical step of suggesting that which will make him free; namely, give him something he can call his own."

—Archbishop Fulton Sheen[11]

After World War II, South Korea carried out a successful land reform program. Farmland owned by Japanese colonists was redistributed to Koreans, and a new class of free and independent farmers was created. The land reform in North Korea took a different and darker path as Kim Il Sung followed his mentors, first Stalin and then Mao, down the socialist road toward forced collectivization. Soon everyone in the North, not just wealthy landowners, were forced to hand over their farmland to the state to be farmed in common.[12]

This forced collectivization led to ever stricter controls over any and all economic activity as the 1950s progressed, as North Korean farmers lost the right to engage in any kind of private trade.[13] Even selling their own garden produce to others was soon declared a crime. Communism had reduced Korean farmers to little more than slaves of the state.

---

[10] Kim Il Sung, "On Further Accelerating Socialist Rural Construction."
[11] Marlin, *The Quotable Fulton Sheen*, 42.
[12] Rigoulot, "Crimes, Terror, and Secrecy in North Korea," in Courtois, *The Black Book of Communism*, 549.
[13] Natsios, "The Politics of Famine in North Korea."

The failures of North Korean Communism can be seen in the frequent famines and other humanitarian disasters that ravage the country. The most devastating famine occurred between 1994 and 1998. Soviet aid had ended with the collapse of the Soviet Union, and North Korea lacked the cash to buy the machinery, oil, fertilizer, and pesticides it needed from Russia. Without these inputs, the country's already struggling state farms simply could not produce enough food. The Public Distribution System that had controlled the country's food supply soon collapsed and starvation set in.[14]

Kim Jong Il, who took power upon his father's death in 1994, told the people that they simply had to work harder.[15] He urged his people to set out on what he called an "Arduous March," experimenting with different crops to halt the famine. Even though North Korea hid the true extent of the famine from the outside world, the West still came to its aid with shipments of grain. Unfortunately, little of this food wound up on the tables of ordinary North Koreans; instead, it was used to feed the army, party members, and the people in the cities. Millions in more remote areas were simply left to starve to death.[16] Although the exact number is a party secret, it's estimated that between one and three million North Koreans died of hunger from 1994 to 1998.[17]

The destruction of the family farm had tragic consequences for the populations of China and North Korea as food shortages and famine ensued in both countries. But while in China the communes were finally dissolved in 1981, North Korea's system of state farms continues. After Mao's death in 1976, Chinese Communist Party (CCP) leaders, realizing that the people's communes were better at producing famine than food, divided the land back up again into family farms. No such retrenchment has occurred in North Korea, probably because the Kim family dynasty—Kim Il Sung's grandson Kim Jong Un is now

---

14   Natsios, 44.
15   Natsios, 35.
16   Natsios, 8.
17   Ulferts, "North Korean Human Rights Abuses and Their Consequences."

in charge—does not want to admit that the Great Leader could have made such a costly blunder.

It wasn't until a famine in the mid-1990s killed up to three million North Koreans—15 percent of the population—that the highly collectivized state was forced to allow some private trade. The state-run farms continue to struggle today, leaving the North Koreans perpetually on the brink of starvation. The official ideology continues to be Jim Il Sung's *Juche*, or "self-reliance," which in practice means make do or do without.

Of Cults and Camps

"The Communist State, instead of protecting the workers against exploitation, rather protects the State through the exploitation of workers."

—Archbishop Fulton Sheen[18]

After the war, South Korea deepened its ties with the West and developed a market-based economy. Kim Il Sung, on the other hand, modeled himself on Mao and Stalin. The North Korean dictator purged the Communist party of his political enemies while using terror campaigns to crush dissent among the wider population. In 1949, Kim declared himself to be *suryong*, which means "Supreme Leader." As his personality cult grew, he began modeling it on Mao's, even to the point of, later in life, claiming to have written poems and plays. Again like Mao, to befit his godlike status, he began demanding unquestioned obedience from everyone.[19]

To enforce his will, Kim created a vast number of informers and police to spy on and control the population.[20] No one, even inside the party, was safe. During just one of the many purges ordered by Kim during his long reign, over nine thousand party members were

[18]   Marlin, *The Quotable Fulton Sheen*, 41.
[19]   OHCHR, "Report of the Commission of Inquiry on Human Rights in the Democratic People's Republic of Korea."
[20]   OHCHR.

executed between 1958 and 1960.[21] Party members were not the only targets of mass terror campaigns. North Korea's large Christian population was also targeted by the state for arrest and execution.[22] By the close of the twentieth century, it is estimated that the regime had directly executed a minimum of 100,000 North Koreans.[23] The actual death toll is surely many times higher since millions were imprisoned in concentration and labor camps in which they were literally worked to death.

There was no limit to the Communist state's effort to control every aspect of public and family life, even down to the very thoughts of individuals. In 1957, the Workers Party of Korea ruled that it had the right to examine the conscience and political convictions of every adult citizen in the country.[24] Thought control was reinforced by what was called the *Songun* system, which not only put the military first in line for food and other resources but also gave priority to party members and other loyalists.[25] According to a United Nations report, "the entire economic framework of the country, and in particular the Public Distribution System, became an important means of social, economic, and political control."[26] The *Songun* system ensured that suspect individuals and groups, such as Christians, received little or no food—or anything else for that matter.

By the end of the 1950s, Kim Il Sung's reign of terror had transformed his entire country into a prison, and it remains one today. North Koreans are unable to travel freely abroad or even within their own country. They live under the constant threat of arrest for even the most minor

---

[21]   Rigoulot, "Crimes, Terror, and Secrecy in North Korea," in Courtois, *The Black Book of Communism,* 552.

[22]   OHCHR, "Report of the Commission of Inquiry on Human Rights in the Democratic People's Republic of Korea."

[23]   Rigoulot, "Crimes, Terror, and Secrecy in North Korea," in Courtois, *The Black Book of Communism,* 553–64.

[24]   Rigoulot, 553–64.

[25]   Human Rights Watch, *World Report 2020: Events of 2019.*

[26]   OHCHR, "Report of the Commission of Inquiry on Human Rights in the Democratic People's Republic of Korea."

of infractions.[27] The network of concentration camps has continued to expand and today holds 200,000 political prisoners, an incredible number for a country of only twenty-five million.[28] In addition, a much larger number of labor reeducation camps exist for lesser offenders.

Eyewitness accounts tell of endless work, scarce rations, high death rates, and the constant brutality of prison guards. Escape is almost impossible. Not only are the prisoners kept under constant guard, but the camps themselves are surrounded by electric fences that, like those of Auschwitz, are charged to fifty thousand volts and are deadly to the touch.[29]

Life in North Korea's camps is cruel, brutish, and short, with most of the prisoners dying within a few years of their arrival. Those fortunate few who survived their prison terms speak of how violence, starvation, overwork, and sexual abuse are systematically used to dehumanize and control prisoners.[30] Approximately 1.5 million people, or roughly one in ten North Koreans, perished in communist concentration camps during Kim Il Sung's rule from the 1950s until his death in the 1990s.[31]

Several years ago, I sent investigators to Pyongyang to look into that country's bizarre and brutal population policies. They found that pregnancy is considered to be an actual crime under some circumstances and that abortion is legal up to childbirth. They reported that pregnant women are seen as "unsightly" and that women who become pregnant are actually banished from the capital city. Triplets are regarded as inauspicious and are separated at birth from their parents and sent to a special orphanage that specializes in neglect.

---

[27] The best account of daily life in North Korea is by Yeonmi Park, who escaped across the border to China and from there to South Korea. Park, *In Order to Live.*
[28] Ulferts, "North Korean Human Rights Abuses and Their Consequences."
[29] Among the few who have escaped is Shin Dong-Hyuk, whose incredible escape is recounted by Blaine Harden in *Escape From Camp 14.*
[30] Ulferts, "North Korean Human Rights Abuses and Their Consequences." The best account of life in North Korea's political prison camps is Blaine Harden's *Escape from Camp 14.*
[31] Rigoulot, "Crimes, Terror, and Secrecy in North Korea," in Courtois, *The Black Book of Communism,* 558.

The worst thing they found was that women who are imprisoned in North Korea's vast network of concentration camps are absolutely forbidden to get pregnant. If they do, they are simply beaten by the guards until they miscarry, or the guards will do a cesarean-section abortion, leaving the woman to die. Women who do manage to somehow give birth see their babies murdered in front of them. And then they are killed in turn.

It is almost impossible to escape to the south across the DMZ—the demilitarized zone that divides the north and south. It is closely guarded by Kim's million-man army, which has orders to shoot to kill. So those who would flee go north, attempting to cross the Yalu River into the People's Republic of China. The guards in the north are under the same deadly orders, but there are fewer of them and it is sometimes possible to get across.

And the North Koreans keep coming, drawn by the bright lights of China's cities and the desire to escape from grinding poverty. Among them are large numbers of young girls who are being sex-trafficked into China to help make up for the shortage of women there. As the US State Department's 2013 *Trafficking in Persons Report* notes, the "one-child policy" is a "key source of demand" since it has resulted in the killing of baby girls and a huge surplus of men.

Although the North Korean birthrate, like South Korea's, is below replacement, the UN Population Fund—the population control arm of the UN—has an office in Pyongyang from which it promotes contraception, sterilization, and abortion, making a bad problem even worse.

One would think that of all the things that this dying country needs—freedom of conscience, freedom of religion, freedom of speech—that the last would be population control. But the death peddlers, as Fr. Paul Marx famously called them, are here as well, working hand-in-glove with a government that acts as though human lives are worthless, a death cult in all but name.

Of Death Cults and Christianity

All Communist regimes are officially atheistic and generally hostile to religion. But the hatred of the Kim family dynasty for Christianity has few equals. In large part, this is because Kim Il Sung and his descendants, like ancient Chinese emperors, have all claimed to be demigods who can control man and nature alike. This means that in addition to the constant threat of arrest or imprisonment, North Koreans are also forced into a kind of spiritual bondage.[32] The goal is to eliminate all independent thought among Koreans by forcing them to join the Kim dynasty cult that "breathes, moves, and thinks as one, under the leadership of a single man."[33]

Many Christians fled south before the advancing Communists, knowing the brutal fate that awaited them if they remained. Those who did not manage to escape often found themselves placed under arrest and sent to concentration camps. Of North Korea's remaining 100,000 Christians, as many as half may be imprisoned as of this writing. Simply being a believing Christian is grounds for incarceration.

Satellite pictures of the Korean peninsula at night tell a story. The southern half is bathed in light. The major cities of South Korea, Seoul, and Pusan gleam like bright jewels, surrounded by a glowing lacework of smaller cities and towns.

The northern half of the peninsula, on the other hand, is a black hole. Only the dim light of Pyongyang, the capital of the Communist North, breaks the unrelenting darkness.

The picture illustrates the stark contrast between the wealth generated by the free peoples and free markets of the South and the wretched poverty wrought by the Communism practiced by the North. But the picture can stand as a spiritual metaphor as well. The light of Christ shines brightly in South Korea, one of the most Catholic countries

---

[32] United States Commission on International Religious Freedom, 2019 *Annual Report.*

[33] Rigoulot, "Crimes, Terror, and Secrecy in North Korea," in Courtois, *The Black Book of Communism*, 558.

in Asia, but it has been all but extinguished in the north. Decades of harsh persecution and imprisonment of believers have decimated the Church in the north and left it shrouded in darkness.

In August 2014, Pope Francis paid a five-day visit to South Korea on the occasion of the Sixth Asian Youth Day. Upon his arrival, he was greeted by South Korean President Park Geun-hye, and millions gathered for the papal Masses.

The pope had also reached out to North Korea, but the welcome he received from dictator Kim Jong Un was rather different. While no one had expected North Korea to respond positively to the pope's visit, even the secular press was taken aback when Pyongyang fired *five* missiles almost as the pope landed. It was a reminder that not only are the two Koreas still technically at war, but also the North is overtly hostile to Christianity in general and Catholicism in particular.

It is no surprise that Pyongyang did not respond to the pope's peaceful overtures. In fact, the North Korean state-controlled media did not even report on Pope Francis's visit to the South, nor his call for reconciliation between the two Koreas. Few North Koreans would have learned this from other sources, since internet access is restricted, and it is a crime punishable by death to listen to South Korean radio broadcasts.

But North Korea's rejection of Pope Francis should not be solely attributed to its Communist brutality or its knee-jerk atheism. For there *is* a kind of state religion practiced in North Korea, a religion that, strangely enough, was founded on an evil distortion of the Christian faith.

Few people know that Kim Il Sung, the first dictator of North Korea, grew up in a Christian home. He left the faith when he became a Communist, but he carried with him the idea that certain Christian practices—weekly meetings, singing hymns, and devotion to a deity— could become the basis of a state religion.

He called his religion *Juche* and ordered that everyone in North Korea attend regular "self-criticism meetings" to practice it. These meetings resemble nothing so much as Christian worship and praise meetings. Those present sing hymns of praise to the Kim dynasty, listen to "sermons" about the writings of Kim Il Sung and his son and now grandson, and recite his "10 Principles," which are a variation of the Ten Commandments. In its essence, *Juche* is essentially the worship of the Kim family, who have thereby claimed for themselves the status of deities.

There is no room for the Son of God in the Kim family pantheon. Nor for any invitation to, or even acknowledgment of, his vicar on earth. For poor North Korean Catholics—who struggle on without priests, without the sacraments—the pope is still worlds away, while the latest Kim looks down godlike from posters plastered on every street corner.

Lost in the Sixties Again

While China remains a tyrannical one-party dictatorship and one of the worst violators of human rights in the world, it has made considerable economic progress in recent years. The reforms undertaken following Mao's death, combined with the willingness of the United States to provide capital and technology, along with access to its domestic markets, have allowed China to develop rapidly.

North Korea runs its economy on the principle of *Juche*, which means "self-reliance," an ideology that has remained unchanged since Kim Il Sung first introduced it over sixty years ago. North Koreans are told that they cannot look outside of their country's borders for aid of any kind but must labor unceasingly to develop the nation's natural resources. As a result, its economy has remained backward and isolated from the rest of the world, even from other Communist states, such as the Soviet Union and China.[34]

Under *Juche*, the supreme leader is responsible for all economic and industrial policy, and he wields absolute control over how and where

---

[34] OHCHR, "Report of the Commission of Inquiry on Human Rights in the Democratic People's Republic of Korea."

resources are allocated, acting through a massive bureaucracy.[35] This gives the state enormous power over the people, who are its virtual slaves, but it also ensures the economy will remain backward and the people poor. It remains in place today.[36] To admit the failures of the centrally controlled economy would damage the prestige of the Kim family dynasty and is not allowed. Instead, North Korea continues to suffer widespread poverty while South Korea has become one of the wealthiest countries in Asia.

The reality of life in North Korea is kept from the world by the secrecy and censorship of this modern Communist state. In fact, North Korea is most often in the news because of a missile launch or a nuclear weapons test and only rarely because of its human rights abuses. Yet all of the problems mentioned above, from widespread hunger and famine to the arrest and imprisonment of people for thought crimes, continue in today's North Korea. According to recent UN and Human Rights Watch reports, the North Korean government commits "crimes against humanity, including extermination, murder, enslavement, torture, imprisonment, rape, and other forms of sexual violence, and forced abortion."[37]

Many of the world's once-captive nations have been able to throw off their chains, but North Korea remains an oppressive Communist regime. The system of terror instituted by Kim Il Sung almost eighty years ago remains in place today, carried on by his son, Kim Jong Il (1994–2011), and his grandson, Kim Jong Un, who succeeded his father in 2011. Courageous refugees and dissidents continue to speak out about the suffering of their people, but the world will not learn the full truth of the Kim dynasty's crimes until the North Koreans win their freedom.

---

35 OHCHR, "Report of the Commission of Inquiry on Human Rights in the Democratic People's Republic of Korea."
36 Silberstein, "Let Them Eat Potatoes: Communism, Famine and the Case of North Korea."
37 Human Rights Watch, *World Report 2020: Events of 2019.*

The brutal state that Chairman Mao helped to create and preserve in North Korea carries on his legacy of terror and oppression down to the present day. But there is hope for North Korea, south of the DMZ. There is a large Christian presence in South Korea, with Catholics and other Christians together comprising about 30 percent of the population. Successive Seoul governments have been sympathetic to Christianity, seeing it rightly as a counterbalancing force to Communism. Pope Pius XI's famous statement that one cannot be a good Catholic and a good socialist remains true today. If the enslaved population of North Korea is one day liberated from captivity, it will surely come about because of the prayers and works of the good Catholics of South Korea.

CHAPTER 11
VIETNAM FALLS TO COMMUNISM

Anti-Vietnam-War college students in the 1960s used to chant "Ho, Ho, Ho Chi Minh," the name of the leader of Communist North Vietnam. But they should have given Chairman Mao equal time since he had sent a huge secret army of some 300,000 men into North Vietnam to help defeat South Vietnam and its American allies. As in North Korea, Communist China was once again spreading "Russia's errors" to another Asian country, with predictably disastrous consequences for the people who lived there.

France Sets the Stage

"We would rather sacrifice everything than lose our country, than return to slavery."

—Ho Chi Minh[1]

"Because the abolition of property is the beginning of slavery, the Church is opposed to [that kind of] Capitalism that concentrates property in the hands of the few, and to Communism which confiscates it all in the name of the collectivity."

—Archbishop Fulton Sheen[2]

The original homeland of the Vietnamese people was South China, but over the centuries, they were driven ever southward by the ever-expanding Chinese empire. For a thousand years, they were ruled

---

[1] Truong Nhu Tanh, *A Viet Cong Memoir.*
[2] Marlin, *The Quotable Fulton Sheen*, 42.

directly by imperial China, and for the next thousand, they preserved their independence by paying tribute to the Chinese emperor. Like the Koreans, the Vietnamese had, over the centuries, adopted many Chinese customs, including the use of Chinese characters. But they simultaneously remained wary of their giant aggressive neighbor and fiercely guarded their independence.

Napoleon III of France launched a piecemeal invasion of Vietnam in 1857 that, because of Vietnamese resistance, did not completely succeed until 1883. For the next seventy years, Vietnam and the neighboring countries of Cambodia and Laos, known as French Indochina, were under French rule. French missionaries were active in all three countries, founding schools and hospitals and making many converts to the Catholic Faith.

The French colonial authorities, on the other hand, were almost solely interested in exploiting the countries' rich resources of rice, rubber, and coal, as well as developing a protected market for French goods. The Vietnamese emperor was reduced to a figurehead, and his officials were rendered powerless. As if it were possible to cause any more resentment of French rule, during World War II, the Vichy French officials collaborated with the Japanese invaders. The forces of Imperial Japan occupied Vietnam's major ports and bases but allowed the Vichy French officials to continue to run the country for Japan's benefit. They were happy to do so.

After the defeat of the Axis powers in 1945, the Vietnamese were understandably eager to gain their independence from the French. Because so few Vietnamese benefited from French rule, the educated population equated free market economics with colonial exploitation. Moreover, because the French had kept the population impoverished by concentrating property in the hands of a tiny minority, many were open to the idea that Communism would allow a more equitable sharing of the economic pie. They didn't realize, as Archbishop Fulton Sheen once wrote, that "the abolition of property is the beginning of slavery."[3]

---

[3]   Marlin, 42.

Seeking an alternative, many were attracted by the false promise of Communism that it would create a worker's paradise on Earth. One of the earliest Vietnamese Communists was a young man named Ho Chi Minh. Born in 1890 and raised under French colonial rule, Ho came to believe that only the revolutionary path laid out by Marx and Lenin could bring his country both independence and prosperity. Like many young revolutionaries of his time, Ho spent time in the intellectual cesspool that was 1917 Paris. This confirmed his Communist sympathies, and in 1920, he became a founding member of the French Communist Party. He later spent many years in Russia, became an agent of the Communist International (Comintern), and served in China before returning to Vietnam.[4]

Ho founded the Indochinese Communist Party (ICP) in 1930 and dedicated it to ending French rule. Following the Japanese invasion in 1941, he created a front group for the ICP called the "League for the Independence of Vietnam" to attract Vietnamese nationalists of all stripes. The *Viet Minh*, as they were called, carried out a campaign of guerrilla warfare and terrorist attacks against both the Vichy French and the Japanese occupiers.

Following Japan's defeat in 1945, France sought to regain control of its colony from its base in the south, while in the north, Ho Chi Minh declared that Vietnam was now an independent country, setting up a separate Communist government.[5] A nine-year war between the French army and the *Viet Minh* fighters followed. It ended with the defeat of the French at the northern town of Dien Bien Phu.[6]

In 1954, peace talks were held in Geneva, Switzerland, and a peace agreement was reached to divide the country in half. The South became the Republic of Vietnam, supported by the United States, France, and other democracies. The north became the Socialist Republic of Vietnam under Ho Chi Minh, backed by Mao's China and Stalin's

---

[4] Fischer, "Ho Chi Minh: Disciplined Communist."
[5] The Democratic Republic of Vietnam, *Declaration of Independence of the Democratic Republic of Vietnam.*
[6] Stanley, "Dien Bien Phu in Retrospect."

Soviet Union. Over a million North Vietnamese, rightly fearful of the coming Communist rule, fled southward toward freedom.[7] Few moved north.

Ho Chi Minh, following the standard Communist playbook, wasted no time in carrying out a series of purges in the North to eliminate his regime's political enemies. The land reform, which likewise slavishly followed Chairman Mao's practice of targeting anyone with more land than they could farm themselves, was estimated to have resulted in up to 100,000 deaths. Far from achieving equality, the collective farms that resulted constituted the functional equivalent of slave plantations since, similar to China, the peasants had few rights and were not free to leave.

Endless War

"You will kill ten of us, we will kill one of you,
but in the end you will tire of it first."

—Ho Chi Minh

"Let every nation know, whether it wishes us well or ill, that we shall
pay any price, bear any burden, meet any hardship, support any friend,
oppose any foe to assure the survival and the success of liberty."

—John F. Kennedy, 1961 Inaugural Address[8]

Communism itself is based on a series of deceptions about the nature of man, God, and the state—that man is a soulless animal, that God is a fiction, and that the state will wither away. Therefore, it is not surprising that the adherents of this diabolical faith also deceive, especially when they are dealing with those they consider to be reactionaries or counterrevolutionaries, and count themselves clever for doing so.

Communist leader Ho never had any intention of abiding by the 1954 peace agreement. Supported by both Communist China and

---

[7]   Olson, *Mansfield and Vietnam.*
[8]   Kennedy, "Inaugural Address."

the Soviet Union, North Vietnam never ceased to wage war on South Vietnam. It armed and supplied a Communist guerrilla movement in the South known as the Viet Cong.[9] It supported Communist organizations inside the cities that organized demonstrations and strikes against the US-backed leader, President Ngo Dinh Diem.[10] Hanoi insisted that these were indigenous movements that it had no connection with, keeping up this pretense until the final open onslaught against South Vietnam in 1975.

At the time, American presidents, determined to preserve freedom in South Vietnam, began increasing their support for the country. They were concerned that if South Vietnam was overrun, then other countries in the region would fall like dominoes. President John F. Kennedy subscribed to this "domino theory" and sent thousands of US military advisers to train South Vietnamese army units and stop the Viet Cong's advance.[11] Following the assassination of President Kennedy, Lyndon Johnson became president. Johnson decided to send in regular US Army and Marine Corps units so that hundreds of thousands of American soldiers were fighting in Vietnam by 1966.[12]

On the other side were the Viet Cong guerrillas supported by North Vietnamese regular army units. And backing them both—although rarely engaging in direct combat for fear of discovery—were 300,000 men of the People's Liberation Army. The war, which by then had spilled over into the neighboring countries of Cambodia and Laos, lasted another seven years.

President Richard Nixon came into office in 1969 determined to end the war in Vietnam. The war had become very unpopular at home. The number of US casualties was mounting—nearly fifty-eight thousand US servicemen gave their lives in the war—and Communist

---

[9] Wiest, *Rolling Thunder in a Gentle Land,* 59.
[10] BBC News, "Vietnam Profile – Timeline."
[11] Global Security, "The Domino Theory." Giglio, *The Presidency of John F. Kennedy,* 256–61.
[12] BBC News, "Vietnam Profile – Timeline."

propaganda was eroding America's will to fight.[13] The anti-war movement in the United States, led by activists like Jane Fonda and Tom
Hayden, endlessly repeated North Vietnamese propaganda about US
troops committing war crimes.[14]

At the time, there appeared to be little chance of a clear-cut victory
on the ground in South Vietnam. Ho Chi Minh died in 1969, but his
successors shared the general Communist view that the people under
their control were disposable. As Ho once said, "You will kill ten of us,
we will kill one of you, but in the end you will tire of it first." North
Vietnam, which had universal conscription, continued to pour new
regular army units into the south in their war of attrition.

In the United States, the Democrats were fighting their own war
of attrition against Richard Nixon. Nixon had humiliated their
candidate, George McGovern, at the polls in the 1972 presidential
election, defeating McGovern by the biggest margin in US history.
They seized upon the pretext of the Watergate break-in to threaten
impeachment.

Nixon withdrew all American forces from South Vietnam by
1973, but he promised the Saigon government that the United States
would continue to supply arms and aid. Nixon was forced to resign
on August 9, 1974, however, and the US Congress suspended all aid
to the embattled nation. Once Hanoi realized that the United States
had abandoned its one-time ally, the entire North Vietnamese Army
was mobilized in a full-scale invasion. South Vietnam's troops fought
bravely to the end, but by April 30, 1975, Saigon had fallen, bringing
the entire country under communist rule.[15]

---

[13]   National Archives and Records Administration, "Vietnam War U.S. Military
Fatal Casualty Statistics."

[14]   In 1972, when I was a student at the University of Washington and enrolled in
the Naval ROTC program there, John Kerry came to our campus to falsely accuse
American soldiers of committing war crimes. A short time later, an anti-war ac-
tivist tried to blow up the NROTC building on campus where I and other cadets
frequently gathered. Needless to say, when Kerry ran for the presidency in 2004,
he did not get my vote.

[15]   BBC News, "Vietnam Profile – Timeline."

American Prisoners of War Are
Starved, Beaten, and Tortured

Hundreds of American soldiers, seamen, and airmen were captured by the Communists during the course of the war. These prisoners of war, or POWs as they were called, were sent to prison camps in North Vietnam. The most infamous of these camps was sarcastically referred to by its American inmates as the "Hanoi Hilton," but it was more like a medieval torture chamber.

The Geneva Accords that mandated captured soldiers should be treated humanely were honored by the North Vietnamese only in the breach.[16] Communist regimes are not known for respecting international agreements. In fact, the prison guards did everything in their power to try and break the prisoners' will to resist and force them to confess to imaginary war crimes. Sam Johnson, an American pilot who was imprisoned in the Hanoi Hilton for seven long years, recalled that "starvation, isolation and torture were constant companions. There was no news from home, and the enemy worked hard to make us feel alone and forgotten. . . . The Hanoi Hilton is no Trump Hotel."[17]

The North Vietnamese, in lies that were repeated by anti-war activists in the United States, denied that American POWs were being tortured. But American prisoners found ways of communicating their suffering. Admiral Jeremiah Denton, for example, was forced to appear on television for a North Vietnamese propaganda campaign. He seized the opportunity to blink out the word *torture* in Morse code.[18] This confirmed to US officials, for the first time, that American POWs were being brutally mistreated.[19]

Many prisoners were fed so little that they literally starved to death. One POW testified that his daily diet consisted of nothing but "rice

---

[16] Pribbenow, "Treatment of American POWs in North Vietnam."
[17] Johnson, "I Spent Seven Years as a Vietnam POW. The Hanoi Hilton is No Trump Hotel."
[18] Military.com, "POW Blinks 'Torture' in Morse Code."
[19] The National Archives, "Scenes from Hell: Commander Jeremiah A. Denton, Jr. -Report from Inside a Hanoi Prison, 1966."

or a third of a loaf of French bread, bland bamboo or cabbage soup, maybe squash on the side."[20] Of the 766 American prisoners held in Vietnam throughout the war, 114 died in captivity as a direct result of these horrific conditions.[21] Those who survived all suffered from lifelong injuries resulting from torture, crippling post-traumatic stress disorder, and haunting memories.

At the same time, however, the Communists were not able to break the American spirit, no matter how hard they tried. Many former POWs tell moving stories of the bravery of their companions and the sense of companionship and mutual support they experienced in the camps.

Collectivization Kills Yet Again

Once South Vietnam had been invaded and conquered, the earlier promise of Ho Chi Minh that the Vietnamese people would enjoy a life "free of imperialist oppression and inequality" was cast aside. Instead, the Communist regime delivered violence, repression, and poverty.

In a reprise of what had earlier happened in the North, the new regime determined to carry out a "land reform" program. But instead of the promised parcels of land, the villagers soon found themselves caught up in a cruel collectivization program. Tens of thousands of landowners were executed as all land was confiscated by the state.[22] Similar to Mao's China, several other killing campaigns followed, variously eliminating political dissidents, crushing rebellions, and slaughtering would-be refugees as they tried to escape across the border.[23] In one typically gruesome event in the city of Hue, nearly three thousand people were massacred by the Communists.[24] The situation quickly began to mirror Stalin's Great Purge or Mao's Cultural Revolution, in

[20]   Yoanna, "From Torture to Freedom, Colorado Vietnam POW Recounts Captivity."
[21]   Marsh, "POWs in American History: A Synopsis."
[22]   Tuong Vu, "Vietnam's Misunderstood Revolution."
[23]   Rummel, "Statistics of Vietnamese Democide."
[24]   Courtois, *The Black Book of Communism*, 572.

which family members turned against each other and innocent people were falsely accused of thought crimes, imprisoned, and executed.[25]

Up to one million South Vietnamese were sent to a newly established network of reeducation camps. Those imprisoned in this new Gulag included students, intellectuals, and just about anyone who was suspected of sympathizing with the South's previous government. Conditions in these remote camps carved out of the jungle were brutal; they were overcrowded, disease-ridden hellholes—by design.[26] Many who were sent to the camps never came back.

These purges and persecutions led a million or more South Vietnamese to attempt to flee the country after the Communist takeover. The risks were considerable, since the Communist authorities had declared anyone attempting to leave was a "traitor" and should be shot on sight. Out of an estimated 200,000 refugees who tried to make their way across Vietnam's Central Highlands into Laos in 1975, for example, only 45,000 successfully crossed the border.[27] The rest died in a hail of bullets.[28]

A China-Style Population Campaign

"China has every reason to feel proud of and pleased with its remarkable achievements made in its family planning policy and control of its population growth over the past 10 years. Now the country could offer its experiences and special experts to help other countries."

—Nafis Sadik, United Nations Population Fund[29]

"Children are the supreme gift of marriage and contribute greatly to the good of the parents themselves. . . . Wishing to associate them in a special way with his own creative work, God blessed man and

---

[25] Courtois, 569.
[26] Courtois, 571–72.
[27] Courtois, 571.
[28] Rummel, "Statistics of Vietnamese Democide."
[29] XINHUA-English, Beijing, 11 April 1991, Foreign Broadcast Information Service (FBIS), *Daily Report: China,* no. 91-071, 12 April 1991, 8-9; See also John Aird, "The China Model," 1.

*women with the words: 'Be fruitful and multiply.' . . . Hence, true
married love . . . cooperate[s] valiantly with the love of the Creator and
Savior, who through them will enrich his family from day to day."*

—*Gaudium et Spes*[30]

It did not take much time—it never does—for the Communists to
wreck the economy of South Vietnam. The former market economy of
the south was soon just a memory, as the bodies of the entrepreneurs
who had run it rotted away in quickly dug graves. The state-planned
economy that was imposed in its place was, once again, a dismal failure. When the Vietnam War ended, 70 percent of the Vietnamese
population lived below the poverty line. Twenty years later, according
to rosy government statistics, 58 percent still did.[31]

Since Communists—followers of the Father of Lies—never take
responsibility for their own failures, they looked about for a scapegoat
to blame. Taking a leaf out of China's book, they decided that the
problem was that Vietnam simply had too many people. The reason
that Vietnam remained poor, the party announced, was because there
were too many people having too many babies. If only *you* would stop
having so many children, Communist officials accused the Vietnamese
people, *we* could develop the country.

The idea to mimic their giant neighbor and declare war on their
own people came from the UN Population Fund (UNFPA), whose
executive director, Nafis Sadik, was touting the "success" of China-
style population control to any official who would listen by the late
eighties. Sadik made headlines in 1989 when she falsely claimed to a
CBS reporter that "the implementation of the policy [in China] and
the acceptance of the policy is *purely voluntary.* There is *no such thing*
as, you know, a license to have a birth and so on."[32]

---

[30] Vatican Council II, Pastoral Constitution *Gaudium et Spes* (December 7, 1965), no. 50.
[31] Davies, "Vietnam 40 Years On: How a Communist Victory Gave Way to Cap-italist Corruption."
[32] Quoted in Smith, "Judging a Civilization," 8, italics added.

Two years later, Sadik made an equally breathtaking claim, gushing to a Chinese reporter that "China has every reason to feel proud of and pleased with its remarkable achievements made in its family planning policy and control of its population growth over the past 10 years." But then she went even further, saying, "Now the country could offer its experiences and special experts to help other countries. . . . UNFPA is going to employ some of [China's family planning experts] to work in other countries and popularize China's experiences in population growth control and family planning."[33]

Exporting the Chinese model to most countries would have been difficult since it requires state planning of targets for birth and quotas for sterilizations, a massive organization to enforce these, and a huge propaganda campaign to soften up the opposition. But not for Vietnam, whose Communist system is almost identical to China's. While most governments are either unwilling or unable to bring all the childbearing within their borders under state control, Hanoi had both the will and the means to embark on a no-holds-barred population control program. It was child's play for the UNFPA, which was serving as the "technical secretary" of the Planned Birth campaign, to fly in Chinese experts to, for example, train the local surgical teams how to tie a woman's tubes assembly-line style.

Hanoi, with assistance from both the UNFPA and China, designed and carried out a population control policy virtually identical to China's earlier program. Beijing's Planned Birth regulations were translated into Vietnamese, with only minor modifications. Only a few details about the specific targets, quotas, and coercive measures used to limit every couple to two children needed to be changed.

"Communist Party members who have more than two [children] face automatic expulsion and parents are often asked to pay the health and education costs of a third child," reported the BBC about such

---

[33] XINHUA-English, Beijing, 11 April 1991, Foreign Broadcast Information Service (FBIS), *Daily Report: China,* no. 91-071, 12 April 1991, 8-9; See also John Aird, "The China Model," 1.

measures. "More serious sanctions include having land confiscated."[34] Serious, indeed. For in a peasant society such as Vietnam's, a family's plot of land is often all that stands between it and starvation.

As a result of following in China's tyrannical footsteps, Vietnam has joined China in having one of the world's highest rates of abortion.[35] Even the *Population and Development Review*, which was, as a rule, no critic of family planning, reports that "women have been forced to use IUDs and have been forced to have abortions."[36]

This familiar litany of abuses has elicited nothing but praise from the UNFPA, which remains unabashedly eager to take credit for the forced reduction in fertility that has resulted. According to one UN document, "although government policy bears the main responsibility for this achievement [Vietnam's falling birthrate], UNFPA's assistance in preparing for and supporting the policy reform provided necessary capacity and support for implementing it."[37] Omar Ertur, a UNFPA country representative in Hanoi, gushed that "they [Vietnam's National Committee for Population and Family Planning] have been very successful. . . . They have achieved a tremendous reduction in a very short period of time."[38]

How a highly regimented regime like Hanoi's was able to drive down the birth rate so quickly is really no mystery. It was simply a purge by another name. In this case, the class of "counterrevolutionaries" to be arrested were women of childbearing age with two children. Instead of being tortured and executed, the women were to be forcibly sterilized, and if pregnant, they were to have their unborn children aborted. The "torture" was a tubal ligation, and while they survived the "execution," their unborn children didn't.

[34] Bennett-Jones, "Vietnam's Two-Child Policy."
[35] *Reuters,* "Vietnam Plans Law to Ban Tests on Sex of Fetus."
[36] "Capacity Building for Eradicating Poverty, an Impact Evaluation of U.N. System Activities in Vietnam 1985-1997," *Population and Development Review.*
[37] "Vietnam Plans Law to Ban Tests on Sex of Fetus," *Reuters,* November 16, 2001.
[38] Bennett-Jones, "Vietnam's Two-Child Policy."

Dealing out death in one fashion or another is the one thing that all Communist regimes excel at. After all, Marx had made it clear from the beginning that Communism was no respecter of individual rights. And did he not warn that shepherding the herd of humanity toward paradise would require constant coercion and frequent culling? But what does it say about the UN Population Fund that it thought it was a good idea to honor Vietnam's population purge with its 1999 "United Nations Population Award"?

Vietnam in Recent Years

Following the collapse of the Soviet Union, Hanoi moved away from state farms back to family farms and allowed private businesses to reopen. It also opened its doors to foreign investment so that the country today is dotted with foreign-owned factories producing goods for export. The lives of the Vietnamese people have begun to improve, at least in purely materialistic terms.

Despite all this, Vietnam remains a one-party dictatorship in which freedom of speech, association, assembly, and religion does not exist. The Vietnamese Communist Party imprisons dissidents, censors criticism, and maintains tight totalitarian control over the population.[39] Lengthy prison sentences are handed down to those citizens who publicly disagree with the party.[40] In 2019, at least 128 people were imprisoned for purely political crimes.[41]

Communist dictatorships are by definition lawless, criminal enterprises—whatever advances the revolution is ethical, Lenin said—and many Vietnamese officials are corrupt.[42] Similar to China, up to 70 percent of the state budget finds its way, one way or another, into the pockets of party and government officials.[43]

---

[39] Human Rights Watch, *World Report 2020: Events of 2019,* 635–38.
[40] Human Rights Watch, "Vietnam: Dozens of Rights Activists Detained, Tried."
[41] Amnesty International, "Vietnam: Surge in Number of Prisoners of Conscience, New Research Shows."
[42] Amnesty International, "Vietnam 2020."
[43] Amnesty International, "Vietnam 2020."

The Vietnamese Communist Party promised that, with independence, everyone would enjoy the liberties and equality denied them under colonial rule. The reality is that Communist overlords have simply taken the place of the earlier Chinese and French overlords. Instead of eliminating class divisions, these new overlords have exacerbated them.

Vietnamese society today is starkly divided between the rich—Communist party officials and their supporters—and the vast majority of the population, which remains poor. The highest-ranking party officials and government ministers constitute a kind of new aristocracy, who live in a rarefied world of luxuries and privileges all but unknown to ordinary people. Apartheid based on position rather than pigmentation is still apartheid.

The only true guarantee of equality is the understanding that we are all children of God. Whenever God is denied as the ultimate source of our rights, there is always a hellish price to pay.

CHAPTER 12
POL POT AND THE TRAGEDY OF CAMBODIA

"Every practical application of Marxist theory has led not merely to tyranny, but to social and economic collapse."

—Sir Roger Scruton, British philosopher (1944–2020)[1]

"Better to kill an innocent by mistake than spare an enemy by mistake. . . . He who protests is an enemy, he who opposes is a corpse."

—Pol Pot[2]

A High-Water Mark in Blood

In the 1970s, Cambodia went further down the socialist road to ruin than any country had ever gone, even China. And the tiny country, located in Southeast Asia between Vietnam and Thailand, did so with Chairman Mao's backing, which included a billion dollars' worth of arms.

The country's first Communist leader, Pol Pot, was an unhinged Maoist who espoused a radical agrarian ideology based on strict one-party rule, rejection of urban and Western ideas, and abolition of private property. Like Mao, he dreamed of remaking human nature and creating a new socialist man. He also wanted to establish a perfectly egalitarian society—with himself in absolute control, of course. He channeled Mao's darker side as well, in that he consciously and

---

[1]   Roger Scruton Quotes, "Every practical application."
[2]   AZ Quotes, "Pol Pot Quotes."

methodically set out to eliminate any hint of opposition, real or imagined, by summary execution in most cases.

But Pol Pot also went where no Maoist had ever gone before. Seeing cities as corrupt, evil places inhabited by the irredeemable bourgeoisie, Pol Pot charted a new and deadly course. Emptying the cities out overnight, he drove the residents into remote, uninhabited parts of the jungle, where he told them to carve out settlements and plant crops—on starvation rations. Few survived.

By the time the Vietnamese intervened four years later and brought his reign of terror to an end, he had unleashed the worst Communist cornucopia of death the world had ever seen. *The Black Book of Communism* conservatively estimates the death toll at two million, but the actual number may be closer to three million.[3]

But it is not the absolute number of people murdered that makes Pol Pot and his Khmer Rouge a real standout among Communist killers; rather, it is the *percentage*. Cambodia's population numbered five to seven million before the Khmer Rouge rampage, which means that Pol Pot's black-garbed soldiers starved, tortured, shot, or bludgeoned to death somewhere between a third to half of the country's population in four short years. It is a high-water mark in blood unmatched in the whole of Communism's already bloody century.

From Peaceful Backwater to Communist Carnage

"If you have a disease of the old society, take
a dose of Lenin as medication."

—Pol Pot[4]

"In order to discover the character of people we
have only to observe what they love."

—St. Augustine[5]

---

[3]   Courtois, *The Black Book of Communism*, 4. For his part, R. J. Rummel uses a figure of 2,035,000. See Rummel, "Death by Government."
[4]   AZ Quotes, "Pol Pot Quotes."
[5]   Augustine of Hippo, *The City of God*, 903.

Back in 1863, under threat from Cambodia's two larger neighbors, Vietnam and Thailand, the king of the small, landlocked country turned to France for protection. The French gladly sent troops, and the country, still nominally governed by its king, became a protectorate of France for most of the next century. The French directed affairs in Cambodia with a light touch, a stark contrast with their heavy-handed rule in neighboring Vietnam, which it finally conquered in 1888 after a violent war of conquest that lasted for twenty years.

After Cambodia won its independence in 1953, it enjoyed a period of peace and prosperity. King Sihanouk, Cambodia's ruler, sought to remain neutral in the conflict between North and South Vietnam. But China, along with the Soviet Union, was eager to spread its own brand of evil into other Southeast Asian countries and, by the sixties, was funneling arms and ammunition to a Maoist guerrilla movement in Cambodia.

The leader of the Communists in Cambodia was a man named Pol Pot. Born Saloth Sar in the 1920s into a prosperous farming family, he was one of a small number of Cambodians selected to study in Paris. He was supposed to study electrical engineering but, like many of his fellow students, fell under the influence of the leftwing radical intellectuals who infested that city. These were so many Wormtongues whispering into the ears of their naïve, Buddhist-educated acolytes from rural Cambodia that their country could be a paradise if only they would ruthlessly implement the ideas of Lenin, Stalin, and, especially, Mao Zedong.

Many of the students, including Pol Pot himself, were radicalized and joined the French Communist Party. And when they returned home, as Pol Pot did in 1953, they arrived determined to start a revolution.[6] Their teachers—immoral, godless pagans all—would never suffer any real-world consequences from the evil, destructive ideas they had planted into the minds of their students, but the Cambodian people would not be nearly so fortunate.

---

[6]   Chandler, *Brother Number One.* See also *Cambodia Tribunal Monitor,* "Chronology of the Khmer Rouge Movement."

For the next nine years, Pol Pot led a double life. By day, he was a respectable teacher in a government school, but by night, he was a Communist revolutionary recruiting followers and organizing party cells. In 1962, however, his activities came to the attention of the Sihanouk government, and he was forced to flee the capital of Phnom Penh. He and his followers set up a base camp in the jungle near the Vietnamese border. From then on, aided by North Vietnam and China, Pol Pot was a full-time revolutionary.[7] The Khmer Rouge, or "Red Cambodian," movement was born.

King Sihanouk himself was overthrown in 1970 by a US-supported coup, and the country descended into a full-scale civil war. Up until that time, the North Vietnamese army had used Cambodia as a safe haven, escaping across the border whenever they were being pursued by South Vietnamese or American forces.

Now, seeking to overthrow the pro-American government of Lon Nol in Phnom Penh, the North Vietnamese army invaded Cambodia in force, drawing that country into the Vietnam War. The United States responded with an aggressive bombing campaign targeting scattered Khmer Rouge and North Vietnamese bases. But many civilians were killed, injured, or left homeless by the bombing as well, which greatly helped Pol Pot to recruit new fighters for his army.[8]

Because of growing anti-war sentiment in the United States, the pro-American government received very little of the military aid it had been promised, even as both Communist China and North Vietnam ramped up their arms shipments to the Khmer Rouge. Surrounded and under siege, the capital city of Phnom Penh fell on April 17, 1975. The Khmer Rouge was now in control of the entire country.[9] The United States had "abandoned Cambodia and handed it over to the butcher," the last US Ambassador complained.[10]

---

[7]   Chandler, *Brother Number One*, 67.
[8]   Owen, "Bombs Over Cambodia."
[9]   Cambodia Tribunal Monitor, "Chronology of the Khmer Rouge Movement."
[10]   Associated Press, "United States 'abondoned Cambodia and handed it over to the butcher' during pullout 40 years ago: ex-ambassador."

Chairman Mao, on the other hand, was ecstatic. When Pol Pot visited Beijing two months later, Mao praised the Khmer Rouge leader for his victory and urged him to carry on the class struggle to the end even if it took fifty or one hundred years. The CCP and the Khmer Rouge shared a common mission: continuing the revolution and preventing the restoration of capitalism in their respective countries.[11]

That butcher—Pol Pot—more than lived up to Mao's hopes and the US ambassador's fears. He renamed the nation Democratic Kampuchea—despite its total lack of any democratic values. Enamored of Mao's Cultural Revolution, he announced that he was determined to make a total break with Cambodia's past. "Two thousand years of history" have come to an end, his spokesman ominously declared. Pol Pot's stated goal was to achieve the Communist dream of perfect equality. Yet the first thing he did was divide the population into three classes: the Khmer Rouge, the Ancients (villagers), and the New People (everyone else). Then he sought to turn his fantasy of perfect egalitarianism into reality in the only way he knew how: by killing everyone he suspected of being opposed to it, which turned out to be most of those he had designated as New People.

Saint Augustine wrote, "In order to discover the character of people we have only to observe what they love."[12] And it turns out that what Pol Pot loved above all else was mass terror. This was the "dose of Lenin" that he prescribed as the medication to cure the "disease of the old society."

A Blank Slate . . .
Or, We Will Rub You Out

"They will begin by taking the State and the manners of men, from which, as from a tablet, they will rub out the picture, and leave a clean surface. This is no easy task. But whether easy or not, herein will lie the difference between them and every other

---

[11]   Wang, "The Chinese Communist Party's Relationship with the Khmer Rouge in the 1970s: An Ideological Victory and a Strategic failure." See also Byron, *The Claws of the Dragon,* 356–57.

[12]   Augustine of Hippo, *The City of God,* 903.

legislator,—they will have nothing to do either with individual or State, and will inscribe no laws, until they have either found, or themselves made, a clean surface. . . . Let there be one man who has a city obedient to his will, and he might bring into existence the ideal polity about which the world is so incredulous."

—Plato, *The Republic*, Book VI

"China's 600 million people have two peculiarities; they are, first of all, poor, and secondly, blank. That may seem like a bad thing, but it is really a good thing. Poor people want change, want to do things, want a revolution. A clean sheet of paper has no blotches, and so the newest and most beautiful pictures can be painted on it."

—Mao Zedong, 1958[13]

Pol Pot admired the way that prior Communist leaders had used mass terror to instill fear in the population and ensure obedience.[14] So as soon as he took control of a city, he ordered the execution of all those associated with the old regime. Anyone who had served in the government, army, or police was systematically tracked down and executed on the spot.[15] He told his followers not to worry about overkill: "Better to kill an innocent by mistake than spare an enemy by mistake. . . . He who protests is an enemy, he who opposes is a corpse."

In summarily executing officials of the old regime, Pol Pot was following standard Communist practice. But these mass executions were just the beginning. In his impatience to eradicate traditional Cambodian culture—to rub out the picture and leave a clean surface, to use Plato's metaphor—Pol Pot skipped over the slow, intermediate steps of propaganda, struggle sessions, and brainwashing that Mao had used to create the new socialist man. Instead, he went straight to mass liquidation. Within the first few months of the Khmer Rouge's reign

---

[13]   Mao Zedong, "Introducing a Co-operative" (April 15, 1958), in *Selected Works of Mao Tse-Tung,* vol. 8.

[14]   Chindawongse, "Pol Pot's Strategy of Survival."

[15]   Gough, "Roots of the Pol Pot Regime in Kampuchea."

of terror, almost all of those who had even a high school education, or who were practicing Buddhists or Catholics, had been slaughtered.[16]

Similar to earlier Communist regimes, the Khmer Rouge set up hundreds of detention centers and prisons, such as the fearsome Prison S-21.[17] Of the estimated seventeen thousand prisoners that were brought into this former high school—which of course was closed down by the Khmer Rouge—only twelve came out alive. The guards at S-21 brutally tortured prisoners until they were willing to confess to anything in order to escape their torment by execution and death.[18] The prison kept detailed records of every man, woman, and child who suffered at S-21, including their mugshots and confessions, which makes for grim reading.[19]

But Pol Pot was far from done. He had been convinced by Mao's writings that a successful cultural revolution required more than just the destruction of individual "bad classes." It was necessary, he thought, to completely eradicate the whole of the "old society" so that a new one could be built from scratch on the ruins. He would create what Mao had rhapsodized about, "A clean sheet of paper has no blotches, and so the newest and most beautiful pictures can be painted on it."

So it was that Pol Pot decided to go where even Mao himself had not dared go. He decided to turn the entire country, and everyone in it, into one giant people's commune where all class differences would be wiped away. This is why when the capital, Phnom Penh, fell to his forces, he ordered the entire population of two and a half million to immediately evacuate the city.[20] Schools were closed, churches were shut down, and families were torn apart.[21] They were going to be forcibly communized and homogenized, whether they wanted to be or not.

---

[16]   Gough, "Roots of the Pol Pot Regime in Kampuchea"

[17]   United States Holocaust Memorial Museum, "S-21, Tuol Sleng."

[18]   Brewer, "How Two Men Survived a Prison Where 12,000 Were Killed."

[19]   Chandler, *Terror and History in Pol Pot's Secret Prison.*

[20]   Courtois, *The Black Book of Communism,* 585.

[21]   Clayton, "Building the New Cambodia: Educational Destruction and Construction under the Khmer Rouge, 1975-1979."

Everyone was sent into the countryside with little more than the clothes on their backs, ordered to work clearing jungle and planting crops under armed guard. By forcing relatively well-off city dwellers to live like peasants, Pol Pot argued that the status of the peasants themselves would be raised, and a society of perfect equality would be created.[22] In order to eliminate differences in wealth, the use of money was banned.

The newcomers were resented by the Ancients, who were encouraged to denounce the city folk they were forced to live near.[23] The New People themselves were treated like expendables by the Khmer Rouge—which they in fact were—and death by starvation was a common fate. They were beaten and tortured for the slightest violation of the rules. Others received one-way tickets to reeducation camps from which few returned.[24] Those who complained were quietly taken into the jungle and bludgeoned to death to save a bullet.

The murderous actions of the Khmer Rouge were a perfect reflection of the inhumanity of their leader. "Since he is of no use anymore, there is no gain if he lives and no loss if he dies," he once remarked of an ill comrade.

Stay Alive, My Son

Perhaps the best autobiography ever written by a survivor of Pol Pot's murderous reign is Pin Yathay's *Stay Alive, My Son*.[25] Yathay, as an engineer *and* a government employee, had twin targets on his back from the moment that the Khmer Rouge took Phnom Penh. He didn't know it at the time, however, thinking that Cambodia's new rulers were patriots first and Communists second. He shrugged off his father's warnings that he had the order reversed.

Yathay was taken aback when the entire population of the capital, which had swollen to three million people as refugees poured in, was ordered out of the capital and into the countryside. An American air

---

[22]   Chindawongse, "Pol Pot's Strategy of Survival."
[23]   Short, *Pol Pot,* 257, 272, 310, 315.
[24]   Gough, "Roots of the Pol Pot Regime in Kampuchea."
[25]   Dith Pran's account of his flight from Pol Pot's genocide in Cambodia is another excellent description of life and death in the camps.

strike was coming, they were told, and they were being evacuated for their own safety. Taking only what they could carry, he and his extended family, numbering some seventeen people, joined the river of humanity streaming out of the city toward an unknown destination.

The noose only gradually tightened. The Khmer Rouge soldiers herding the travelers along were generally polite, even when stealing money and jewelry from them, unless they met resistance. Then masks were dropped, guns were unslung, and the name of "Anghar"—the "organization"—was invoked. And what Anghar wanted, Anghar took.

Yathay's family, along with a couple of thousand others, was eventually trucked into a remote stretch of jungle, given hand tools and an armed guard, and told to make a new life for themselves. They were New People, they were informed, who must reform themselves through labor. It was only then that they realized that the entire evacuation had simply been a pretext by Anghar to put them in reeducation through labor camps.

Turning the jungle into farmland was grueling work, but before the exhausted laborers could eat, they were forced to engage in Maoist-style self-criticism sessions. This was a soul-crushing exercise in which each person had to recount every thought, word, and act of their day that reflected less than total devotion to Anghar. This was a delicate balancing act: confess too little and one would be punished with a beating for not being candid. Confess too much and the Khmer Rouge would decide you were unredeemable and execute you.

The food was never plentiful, but as the weeks went by, the rations were cut, and then cut again, until all a family of six received was a single can of rice a day. A black market in rice sprang up in which Yathay was able to trade gold and dollars for just enough to stave off starvation, even as others in the camp began dying of hunger.

Their own Khmer Rouge guards were behind the black market, Yathay soon realized. They were holding back part of the rice allotment provided by Anghar for the prisoners and selling it on the side. This racket got more and more lucrative over time because, although prisoners were dying every day, the allotment stayed the same. The Khmer

Rouge ensured that it would by the simple expedient of not reporting deaths up the chain of command.

Since more deaths equaled more rice for them, the guards had a perverse incentive to treat the prisoners as brutally as possible. Not that they needed much encouragement since they were already eager to turn as many prisoners into human compost as possible. Work harder, slackers were told by the Khmer Rouge, or we will turn you into "fertilizer." The bodies of those who died of starvation or disease were buried at the edge of the fields for exactly this reason.

Most of the political killings, however, occurred in secret. Neighbors, friends, and family members simply disappeared from the camp in the dark of night, never to be seen again. Or they were led away during the day after some chance remark raised the suspicions of the guards. These were taken a mile or two into the jungle and then, rather than being shot, were simply clubbed to death. Gathering food in the jungle—the inmates had every tenth day off—Yathay would occasionally stumble across a rotting corpse on the ground.

The Khmer Rouge boys had been taught to loathe the New People, and they would execute them on the slightest of pretexts. Yathay had a friend who worked in the communal kitchen who, as a cook, would occasionally use a French expression. He also sported a new gold Omega watch. The cook disappeared one day, but his watch soon reappeared—on the wrist of one of their captors. It had belonged to "that traitor who always used imperialist French words," Yathay overheard him telling his friends.

Anyone who was educated or who had worked in a senior position in the government was a particular target, so Yathay, who was guilty of both, had two strikes against him from the outset. He came close to being liquidated—or should I say composted—several times himself, but he kept his wits about him and managed to grovel sufficiently to appease his captors.

This was not easy. They had been instructed by Pol Pot that it was "better to kill an innocent by mistake than spare an enemy by mistake. . . . He who protests is an enemy, he who opposes is a corpse." So they were not inclined to mercy.

But, although it seems scarcely credible, Anghar's program was even more murderous than the above would suggest. The "final solution" involved the wholesale butchery of the population. As one officer explained to Yathay, "In the new Kampuchea, one million is all we need to continue the revolution. We don't need the rest. We prefer to kill ten friends rather than keep one enemy alive."

At the rate the Khmer Rouge were killing, there is no doubt that, given another decade in power, they would have achieved their goal. Some members of Yathay's extended family were "disappeared."[26] Others died of starvation and disease—this despite his best efforts to buy, barter, and scavenge enough food to keep them alive. He bought rice on the black market with his dwindling hoard of dollars, and he once paid one hundred dollars for a single chicken. Anything that flew, walked, or crawled would be thrown in the pot, cooked, and quickly eaten. Yet it was not enough, and he had to watch his son die in his arms.

Some of his fellow New People turned to cannibalism in their desperation, as the victims of Mao's Great Famine had nearly twenty years before. A neighbor of his was executed for eating part of her sister's corpse.

In the end, only Yathay and his wife were left—sick, starving, and fearful. Yet, as if to complete their utter humiliation, they were afraid even to mourn the loss of their families. They knew that if they cried out their anguish, or wept openly, it would bring their black-clothed captors down on them, and that meant death. All they could do was sit on the floor of their hut and stare brokenly at each other, with tears running down their cheeks.

The title of the book comes from the last words Yathay's father spoke to him: "Stay alive, my son." By then, of course, Yathay had long since realized how right his father had been in warning that the coming of

---

[26] In Communist countries, "to disappear someone" means to arrest a perceived enemy of the regime in secret; e.g., "Wang Ming was disappeared after he criticized Mao."

the Communists would be a disaster for the country. Before he closed his eyes for the last time, his father also promised, "When I die, if my soul endures, I will help you."

But it was his dying sister, Vuoch, who offered the best critique of what had happened. Summoning her last bit of strength, she told Yathay, "The ideology sounded so good. But it just became an excuse for destruction and oppression. Those fanatics . . . now we know what they are. Communists. . . . Do you really believe that, if Marx, Lenin and Mao had not been born, that we would be in this hell?"[27]

The End of the Khmer Rouge

Communist revolutions always devour their own, and Pol Pot's was no exception. It wasn't long before Pol Pot, like every Communist dictator before him, began seeing conspiracies everywhere and suspecting others of disloyalty, including some of those who had been with him from the beginning.[28] By 1978, he had ordered the execution of five out of his dozen closest comrades.

His murderous reign came to an abrupt end in 1979 when Communist Vietnam invaded Cambodia. As Vietnamese units made their way up the Mekong River to Phnom Penh, they found ample evidence of the slaughter carried out by the Khmer Rouge: empty cities, torture chambers, and mass graves.[29] The Communist Chinese tried to come to the aid of their Cambodian allies by attacking Vietnam in turn, but the Vietnamese army turned back the attempted invasion, inflicting serious losses on the invaders.

Pol Pot and his followers retreated into the jungle. They carried out guerrilla warfare against the new government for the next twenty years but without success. Pol Pot died in 1998, and the last remnants of the Khmer Rouge defected or were captured the following year.[30] Most of

27   Yathay, *Stay Alive, My Son,* 128.
28   Courtois, *The Black Book of Communism,* 586.
29   Chandler, *Terror and History in Pol Pot's Secret Prison.*
30   *Cambodia Tribunal Monitor,* "Chronology of the Khmer Rouge Movement."

the other leaders of Khmer Rouge, like Pol Pot, died before they could face criminal charges.[31]

Communist regimes inevitably kill large numbers of people in an attempt to terrorize the population into compliance, but no Communist party has ever engaged in a killing spree like that of the Khmer Rouge. In just four years, Pol Pot and his Communists managed to kill between two and three million people, or a third or more of Cambodia's population.[32] Other Communist countries have killed a greater number of people, but none has killed a larger proportion of its population over a shorter period of time.

Cambodia remains a one-party dictatorship today. Its governing political party, the Cambodian People's Party, is Communist in all but name.[33] And it is, once again, a vassal state of Communist China.

A Specter Is Haunting Asia, the Specter of Mao Zedong

If there is a wearisome sameness about these three Communist regimes in Asia—North Korea, Vietnam, and Cambodia—it's because they owe their existence to the CCP and their extremism to Mao Zedong himself. Whether it's the Kim dynasty cult, North Vietnam's thirty-year war on the south, or Pol Pot's cultural revolution, behind them lurks the figure of Chairman Mao, the greatest mass murderer of all time.

Might we see in Mao a prefiguring of the antichrist? In his loveless narcissism, in his God-hating megalomania, in his absolute indifference to the suffering of others, does he not seem something more—or less—than human? Recall his words: "I do not agree with the view that to be moral, the motive of one's action has to be benefiting others. Morality

---

[31] Human Rights Watch, "Cambodia: Khmer Rouge Convictions, 'Too Little, Too Late.'"
[32] Courtois, *The Black Book of Communism,* 590.
[33] Ellis-Petersen, "Cambodia: Hun Sen re-elected in landslide victory after brutal crackdown."

does not have to be defined in relation to others. . . . *Of course there are people and objects in the world, but they are all there only for me.*"[34]

The people of several surrounding countries never volunteered to be bit players in Mao's cosmic drama, but they were—to their great pain and suffering—drawn into it, nonetheless.

---

[34] Chang, *Mao,* 13, italics added.

PART 4

SCIONS OF A LESSER GOD: MAO'S SUCCESSORS CONTINUE HIS CAMPAIGNS

"Just as there are not two suns in the sky, so there cannot be two emperors on earth."

—Confucius[1]

Mao died in 1976, but all of his successors, from Deng Xiaoping onwards, have been just as committed to the continued rule of the Chinese Communist Party, and they have responded to challenges or threats to its stranglehold on power with political campaigns and brutal crackdowns. And each one, with the exception of Deng himself, has self-consciously modeled himself after the founding emperor of the Red dynasty, Mao Zedong, and maneuvered to become the only sun in the Chinese sky. The present ruler of China, Xi Jinping, succeeded.

Mao's excesses led a chastened Deng Xiaoping, who had seen many of his longtime comrades tortured and killed, such as Liu Xiaoqi and Peng Dehuai, to try and impose a ten-year term limit on the top party office. This attempt to stop the emergence of another Maoist monster failed, as he surely knew it would.

---

[1]   One of Confucius's most quoted sayings, this appears twice in *Li Ji* (*Book of Rites*), in chapters 7 and 30, and once in Mencius, *Mengzi* (*Book of Mencius*), in chapter 5a.4. Easily accessible online versions of these Chinese classics include Confucius, *The Book of Rites*, ed., Dai Sheng (A.D. 80), translated by James Legge (Boston: Intercultural Press, 2013) 249, 320, and *Mencius*, translated by James Legge (Pantianos Classics, 2016), 80.

Communist parties breed such monsters just as darkness breeds cockroaches.

Yet Deng, who passed away in 1997, was no moderate. In 1980, he put in place China's draconian one-child policy to ward off what he saw as the threat of "overpopulation." And at the end of the decade, it was he who ordered the People's Liberation Army to "shed a little blood" to put down student demonstrations in Tiananmen Square. The result was the June 4, 1989, Tiananmen Massacre in which thousands, perhaps tens of thousands, were killed.

Jiang Zemin (1926–2022), chosen by Deng to lead the party, did his best to emulate Mao as well. He had his "thought" written into the Chinese Communist Party Constitution in 2002, alongside that of Marxism-Leninism, Mao Zedong, and Deng Xiaoping. Further cementing his Maoist bona fides, this committed atheist launched a Maoist-style campaign against a peaceful, nonpolitical Buddhist sect called the Falun Gong in 1999. The brutal persecution he unleashed resulted in hundreds of thousands, perhaps millions, of Falun Gong practitioners detained in labor camps. Many were tortured and killed in what was seen as a continuation of Mao's effort to eradicate all religious sentiment in China.

With the ascension of Xi Jinping to power in 2012, all of Mao's campaigns—against political dissent, religious expression, and the private sector—were intensified. It was as if the chairman himself had come back from the grave to infest China again with his demonic presence.

CHAPTER 13
CHILDREN OF A LESSER GOD: THE ONE-CHILD POLICY (1981–2016)

Births Must Be Planned

"Reproduction needs to be planned. In my opinion, mankind is completely incapable of managing itself. We have plans for production in factories, for producing cloth, tables and chairs, and steel, but no plan for producing humans. It is anarchism, with no control, no organization and no rules. We need to have a special government ministry—what about a Planned Birth ministry?"

—Mao Zedong, 1957[1]

"The state has a responsibility for its citizens' well-being. In this capacity it is legitimate for it to intervene to orient the demography of the population. This can be done by means of objective and respectful information, but certainly not by authoritarian, coercive measures."

—*Catechism of the Catholic Church*[2]

It was perhaps inevitable that a man and a political party so bent on total control would seek to control not just production but reproduction. Simply allowing couples to decide for themselves how many children to have and when to have them was inconceivable. The masses—for their own good—must be controlled. For that reason,

---

[1] Zedong, "On the Correct Handling of Contradictions among the People," in *Mao Zedong zhuzuo zhuanti zhaibian*, 970. The translation is my own.
[2] *CCC* 2372.

not long after the founding of the People's Republic of China, the party-state put a national Planned Birth program in place to control the fertility of the Chinese people.

This program went far beyond merely educating women about various means of family planning and then allowing them to use— or not use—the drugs, devices, and surgeries of their choice. True to form, the Chinese Communist Party (CCP) did not allow the people freedom of choice in such matters. The party would address the population problem, and everyone would be expected to follow its dictates.

This was exactly the point that Chairman Mao made in a famous 1957 speech, "On the Correct Handling of Contradictions among the People." "Reproduction needs to be planned," Mao thundered. "In my opinion, mankind is completely incapable of managing itself. We have plans for production in factories, for producing cloth, tables and chairs, and steel, but no plan for producing humans. It is anarchism, with no control, no organization and no rules. We need to have a special government ministry—what about a Planned Birth ministry?"

When Chairman Mao proposed a political campaign, party cadres were expected to ensure that the masses followed in lockstep. They were allowed to use coercive measures to ensure compliance. Opponents of the campaign were labeled class enemies, or even counterrevolutionaries, and punished. The Planned Birth campaign, under which the state would regulate the number of babies born in the country, was no exception.

After a rocky start, the campaign got underway in earnest in 1970.[3] New rules came down: young people were not allowed to marry until their mid-twenties, not allowed to have a second child within four years of the birth of the first, and not allowed to have more than two children. The slogan of the time summarized these rules: "Later, longer, fewer."

---

[3]   The Planned Birth campaign was twice derailed, first by the Great Leap Forward and second by the Cultural Revolution.

The party began by having its propaganda outlets attack the "feudal custom" of early marriage and repudiate what it called "the reactionary theory on marriage" that had supposedly been "advocated by Confucius and Mencius,"[4] who were all-purpose whipping boys in those late Cultural Revolution days. Late marriage, on the other hand, was exalted as part of the "thought of Mao Zedong" and an important aspect of the "class struggle."[5]

As always, this harsh "class struggle" campaign rhetoric inspired equally harsh measures on the part of lower-level officials to control births. The Shanghai Party Committee, for instance, designated the week of January 25, 1970 as "shock week" for the promotion of birth control and late marriage. During this week, the committee ordered, the masses were to be "mobilized," every family was to be visited by officials "in a penetrating and vigorous manner," and "remedial measures" were to be taken "whenever problems are discovered."[6] In plain English, "remedial measures" meant that local cadres were free to use force on women who resisted the new rules, sterilizing or implanting them with IUDs against their will.[7]

In Junan Commune,[8] located in the Pearl River Delta of Guangdong province, these were the years in which virtually every woman of childbearing age with three or more living children was forcefully implated with an IUD or given a tubal ligation. Interviews with local women who had been sterilized under duress convinced me that local cadres had followed their orders to the letter. They had indeed "firmly grasped the struggle between the two lines" and ensured that "the

[4] Shanghai radio, December 27, 1969, FBIS, No. 4, January 7, 1970, pp. C 12–13; and Shanghai radio, December 29, 1969, FBIS, No. 3, January 6, 1970, pp. C 23–24.

[5] *RMRB,* "Firmly Destroy Old Habits, Insisting on Late Marriage," 5.

[6] Shanghai radio, January 24, 1970, FBIS, No. 17, January 26, 1970, p. C 5.

[7] Personal communication to the author, Xingcha Production Brigade Women's Federation.

[8] Junan commune was the site of my original field research in China, which I carried out from 1979 to 1980 under the auspices of the US State Department's scholarly exchange program with China.

dictatorship of the proletariat" had carried the day. The "reactionary fallacy"—as it was called—that couples could have as many children as they wanted was in retreat, replaced by the new party line. The CCP, and the state apparatus that it controlled, would henceforth be in charge of regulating births under a state plan.[9]

By August 1974, the CCP announced that the country's Planned Birth policy had "achieved initial success" and was being carried out "on a voluntary basis under state guidance."[10] How the Planned Birth policy could be "voluntary" when couples were expected to follow "state guidance" in bearing children was not explained. Women who became pregnant with "over-quota children" were pressured into abortions and, often, subsequent sterilization. I later became an eyewitness to the party's "voluntarism" in action as groups of three or four officials would escort distraught and crying pregnant mothers to a local clinic for "voluntary" second- and third-trimester abortions that were anything but.

The end result was that between 1971 and 1979, the annual number of abortions in China increased from 3.91 million to 7.86 million, while the number of sterilizations rose from 1.74 million to 5.29 million.[11] As the decade progressed, the Chinese birth rate plummeted.

The worst, however, was yet to come. The war on China's population was about to go scorched earth.

The Birth of the One-Child Policy

"Of course birth control is still necessary, and I am not for encouraging more births. There should be a ten-year program for promoting Planned Births: three years for pilot programs and publicity, three years for promotion and expansion, and four years

---

[9]   Personal communication to the author, Xingcha Production Brigade Women's Federation.
[10]   XINHUA-English, Beijing, August 23, 1974, FBIS, No. 74-166, August 26, 1974, pp. E 3-4; and XINHUA-English, Beijing, August 31, 1974, FBIS, No. 74-174, September 6, 1974, pp. E 2-5.
[11]   Whyte, "Challenging Myths About China's One-Child Policy."

for universal implementation. . . . I think Planned Birth should be part of the middle school curriculum. It's not OK to have human reproduction in a state of total anarchy—we need to plan births."

—Mao Zedong, 1957[12]

"The state may not legitimately usurp the initiative of spouses, who have the primary responsibility for the procreation and education of their children. It is not authorized to promote demographic regulation by means contrary to the moral law."

—Catechism of the Catholic Church[13]

The rationale behind the one-child policy came from an unlikely source. In the early seventies, a group of MIT-based systems engineers developed a computer model that predicted—I do not exaggerate—the end of the world by 2070 if population growth was not checked.[14] In the book that followed, *The Limits to Growth*, these same scientists declared that there was "no other avenue to survival" than population control, which was "the only feasible solution" to mankind's dilemma.[15]

The stage was now set for Song Jian, a systems control specialist for China's state-owned defense industry, to visit Europe in 1978. He might as well have come from another planet. Like other Chinese intellectuals, he had been isolated from the outside world for decades and was desperately eager to catch up on developments. During his trip, as he later wrote, he "happened to learn about the application of systems analysis theory by European scientists to the study of population problems with a great success." In his baggage when he returned to China was a copy of *The Limits to Growth*.

---

[12] Mao Zedong, "Speech Concluding the Enlarged Third Plenary Session of the Eighth Central Committee of the Chinese Communist Party," in *Mao Zedong wenji*, 308.

[13] *CCC* 2372.

[14] Meadows, *The Limits to Growth*.

[15] Meadows et al., "The Only Feasible Solution" in Mesarovic, *Mankind at the Turning Point*, 196.

What Song thought was cutting-edge systems analysis was little more than a scientific hoax. The data it used in reaching its conclusions was incomplete and sometimes inaccurate, its methodology was flawed, and it assumed—wrongly—that scientific and technical advances would cease. In Julian Simon's words, "*The Limits to Growth* has been blasted as foolishness or fraud by almost every economist who has read it closely or reviewed it in print."[16] Song, however, was so convinced by what he read that he began to make hysterical claims that China must further reduce its birthrate without delay or face catastrophe.[17] China's leaders, led by Vice Premier Deng Xiaoping, began to pay attention.

Deng himself was soon saying things like, "All China's troubles derive from the population being too great"[18] and "Our biggest problem is our huge population. . . . We have not done well enough in controlling population growth."[19]

Borrowing the strident rhetoric of the Club of Rome report, Song hammered home the notion of a world in crisis: "Facing the rapid increase in population, countries everywhere are watching developments with grave concern." He regurgitated its scary scenarios of ecological devastation, applying these specifically to China:

> As population increases, forests are chopped down. Now forest coverage is about 30 percent worldwide; in China that figure is only 12 percent. . . . In our country there is only 1.5 mu [one-sixth of an acre] per person. . . . The decrease in forest area, arable land per person, lack of food supplies, lack of protein, increase in pollution, and the use of natural resources are growing with

---

[16]　Simon, *The Ultimate Resource,* 286.

[17]　Greenhalgh, Just One Child contains the most detailed description of Song Jian's conversion to radical population controller and godfather of the one-child policy. Earlier articles suggesting Song's key role appeared in the *Guangming ribao* "Article Analyses Population Situation," March 6, 1989.

[18]　Sun Huilan, "Population Burden: Root of All China's 'Troubles'—Factual Account of the Population Experts' Warnings on 'Population 1.2 .Billion Day.'"

[19]　Fan You, "Tian Jiyun Addresses Population Meeting," 53.

the increase in population. . . . However, the expendable power of nature's stability is limited. To guarantee future generations adequate or good survival conditions, we cannot exceed our limit on taking natural resources or use a method that destroys the balance and stability of the ecosystem.[20]

He reinforced his rhetoric with eye-catching charts showing China's population remaining low for four thousand years then exploding to one billion by 1980.[21] No mention was made of recent, dramatic declines in the birth rate.

Seeing which way the political winds were blowing, other experts jumped into the debate, arguing that not only China's ecology but also its economy was collapsing under the weight of its gargantuan population. Population growth was said to be responsible for every conceivable economic ill, from rising levels of unemployment and poverty to falling levels of labor productivity and investment. China, it seemed, faced a population crisis of enormous proportions that, if left unchecked, would shatter any hope of ever joining the ranks of the developed nations. They were joined by Vice Premier Chen Muhua, who warned in the pages of the *People's Daily* that nothing less was at stake than the country's drive for wealth and global power: "In order to realize the Four Modernizations, we must control population growth in a planned way."[22]

Once the Chinese leadership had accepted the idea that population growth was sabotaging the nation's modernization, they were ripe for a radical solution. After all, the future of the Chinese nation hung

---

[20]   Song Jian, "Population Development—Goals and Plans," 26. See also Song Jian, "Cong xiandai kexue kan renkou wenti" [Population problems from the perspective of modern science], in Song Jian, *Song Jian kexue lunwen xuanji,* 552–53. Originally published in *Guangming Ribao,* 3 October 1980. Quoted in Greenhalgh, *Just One Child,* 174–75.

[21]   Song Jian, *Population Control in China,* 2.

[22]   Muhua, "In order to Realize the Four Modernizations, We Must Control Population Growth in a Planned Way," 2. The "Four Modernizations" was Deng Xiaoping's plan to modernize China's science and technology, military, industry, and agriculture by the end of the century.

in the balance. It was again Song Jian, armed with a computer simulation right out of the pages of *The Limits to Growth*, who offered a sinister plan. Song first purported to calculate what China's "optimal" population would be and wound up bizarrely claiming that somewhere between 650 and 700 million people would be perfect. He proposed this figure, which was roughly two-thirds of China's 1980 population, as the goal of any birth control program.[23] Borrowing the strident *Limits* language, Song declared that China only had a century to reduce the population down to this level. There was simply "no other way."

Song initially opposed restricting every couple to one child, arguing that under that scenario, China's population would plummet to only 370 million by 2080, or well below his "optimum." He told Chinese leader Deng Xiaoping that limiting women to an average of 1.5 children would produce the kind of population reduction they were looking for. Under this scenario, he explained, the number of Chinese would decline to 777 million by 2080, within striking distance of the "optimum population" of 650–700 million.

Deng and the other Communist leaders had no qualms about regulating the fertility of their subjects—they had done much worse things over the previous three decades—but Song's insistence that Western "science" left them "no other choice" made the decision easy. The only question was whether to adopt the 1.5-child-per-family policy proposed by Song or to impose an even more restrictive one-child-per-family policy. The Communist leaders, never wont to resist a totalitarian impulse, decided to impose a one-child policy on their captive population. They rejected Song's 1.5 children option on the grounds that those pesky peasants would then push for two or more.[24]

To explain the coming fertility crackdown to the masses—"It's for your own good. We're just following 'the science'"—the CCP ordered

---

[23] Song Jian, "Population Development—Goals and Plans," in Liu Zhen, Song Jian et al, eds., *China's Population,* 25–31.
[24] Chen Muhua, "In order to Realize the Four Modernizations."

Song's study published in the pages of the *People's Daily* on March 7, 1980. It still had his name on it, at any rate, but it was no longer the same study. Heavily edited, it had Song dismissing the possibility of a 1.5-child-per-family policy on the grounds that it would be "disadvantageous to our country's four modernizations . . . and to the raising of the people's standard of living." Instead, it insisted that a one-child-per-couple policy was "a comparatively ideal scheme for solving our country's population problem."[25]

Publication in the official party organ, the *People's Daily*, meant that the policy had received the imprimatur of the Communist Party and that no further discussion would be allowed. Six months later, in mid-September 1980, the one-child policy was formally ratified by the third session of the Fifth National People's Congress. From then on, the most brutal population control policy the world had ever seen was set in stone. On this terrible altar, hundreds of millions of mothers were to suffer and children were to die, sacrificed for scientific fraud.

Like Communism itself, unfortunately.

"Use Whatever Means You Must."

"Use whatever means you must [to enforce the one-child policy], just do it. With the support of the Chinese Communist Party, you have nothing to fear."

—Deng Xiaoping[26]

"Human life must be respected and protected absolutely from the moment of conception. From the first moment of existence, a human being must be recognized as having the rights of a person—among which is the inviolable rights of every innocent being to life."

—Catechism of the Catholic Church[27]

---

[25]   Song Jian, "Concerning the Issue of Our Country's Objective in Population Development." Also cited in Greenhalgh, *Just One Child,* 181.

[26]   Aird, *Slaughter of the Innocents,* 92.

[27]   *CCC* 2270. Cf. Congregation for the Doctrine of the Faith, *Donum Vitae* I, 1.

With the adoption of the one-child policy, the CCP went to war against its own people. I was living in a village in the southern province of Guangdong when this war was declared and was an eyewitness to the abuses that followed almost immediately. In March 1980, the Guangdong provincial government secretly ordered a 1 percent cap on population growth for the year. Local officials complied the only way they could: by launching a Planned Birth "high tide"—a political campaign—to terminate as many pregnancies as possible. The rules governing this high tide were simple: No woman was to be allowed to bear a second child within four years of her first, and third children were strictly forbidden. Furthermore, all women who had borne three or more children by November 1, 1979, were to be sterilized without exception.[28]

Over the next few weeks, I became an eyewitness to every aspect of this draconian campaign. I went with young mothers to family planning "study sessions" where they were browbeaten by senior party officials for getting pregnant. I followed them as they were unwillingly taken under escort to the commune clinic. I watched—with the permission of local officials who were eager to demonstrate their prowess in planning births to a visiting foreigner—as they were aborted and sterilized against their will. I will never forget the pain and suffering etched on the faces of these women as their unborn children, some only days from birth, were brutally killed with chemical weapons—poison shots—and then dismembered with surgical knives. There were even cases of out-and-out infanticide, as babies were killed at birth by lethal injection.

The demands of China's family planners escalated as the eighties unfolded. The one-child policy was in place nationwide by 1981, while the "technical policy on family planning" followed two years later. Still in force today, the "technical policy" requires IUDs for women of childbearing age with one child, sterilization for couples with two children—almost invariably performed on the woman—and abortions

---

[28]   Mosher, *Broken Earth,* esp. chapter 9, "A Grim Game of Numbers."

for women pregnant without authorization. By the mid-eighties, according to Chinese government statistics, birth control surgeries— abortions, sterilizations, and IUD insertions—were averaging more than thirty *million* a year. Many, if not most, of these procedures were forced on women by Communist officials who would not take "no" for an answer.

The CCP backed down from the one-child policy—but only a little—when hundreds of thousands of baby girls began being abandoned or killed shortly after birth. Rural families desperate for sons were sacrificing their daughters for another chance at having a son. So the party announced in 1986 that it would allow rural couples whose first child was a girl to have another child.[29] But only after they had waited for four years first. That policy would not change for the next thirty years.

Over the years, I, along with other investigators I had sent to China, interviewed countless victims of the one-child policy. Here is the story of one woman's fight to save her child from the party's minions, and the extraordinary pressure they put on her to abort.

Li Aihai's Story

Li Aihai, happily married and the mother of a two-and-a-half-year-old girl, had a problem. She was four months pregnant with her second child. The Planned Birth officials had come to her home and told her what she already knew: She had gotten pregnant too soon. She hadn't waited until her daughter was four years old, as the CCP required of rural couples. The officials assured her that because her first child had been a girl, she would eventually be allowed a second child. But they were equally insistent that she would have to abort this one. It was January 2000.

She pleaded that she had not intended to get pregnant. She told them that she was still wearing the IUD that they had implanted in her after the birth of her first child, as the law required. They were

---

29   Mosher, "Female Infanticide in China," 110–12.

unsympathetic. Report to the Planned Birth clinic tomorrow morning, they told her as they left, we'll be expecting you.

Aihai had other plans. Leaving her two-year-old daughter in the care of her husband, she quietly packed her things and went to stay with relatives in a neighboring county. She would hide until she brought her baby safely into the world. Childbirth-on-the-run, it was called.

When the county's Planned Birth officials discovered that Aihai had disappeared, they began arresting her relatives. While her father-in-law managed to escape with Aihai's infant daughter, her mother-in-law and brother-in-law were arrested. Her own mother, father, brother, sister, and three other relatives were also imprisoned over the next few weeks. In all, nine members of her extended family were arrested, hostages to the abortion that was being demanded of her, and held in the local Planned Birth jail.

But Aihai knew that her family supported her pregnancy, so she stayed in hiding. And each and every one of her relatives refused to tell the officials where she had gone to ground, despite being told they would be jailed until they did.

Three months later, the Planned Birth officials struck again. The date they chose, April 5, was an important one on the Chinese traditional calendar. It was the festival of Qingming, or "bright and clear," a day on which rural Chinese men, by ancient custom, "sweep the graves" of their ancestors. Starting with the grave of their own deceased parents, they visit in turn the graves of grandparents, great-grandparents, and ancestors even further removed. At each stop, they first clean off the headstones and weed the plot, and then set out a feast for the deceased, complete with bowls of rice, cups of rice liquor, and sticks of incense.

Why did the Planned Birth officials pick this day of all days? Was it a further insult to the Li family, several of whom were languishing in their jail? Or was the day chosen for a very practical reason? With most of the men and boys away in the hills feting their ancestors, the village would be half-deserted, and they could carry out their plan without opposition.

The Planned Birth officials came to the village in the company of a wrecking crew armed with crowbars and jackhammers. These fell upon Aihai's home like a horde of angry locusts. They shattered her living room and bedroom furniture into pieces. They ripped window frames out of walls and doors off hinges. Then the jackhammers began to pound, shattering the brick walls and knocking great holes in the cement roof and floors. By the time they completed their work of destruction, you could stand on the first floor of Aihai's home and look up through two stories and the roof to the blue sky above. The wrecking crew then moved on to her parents' house, and then to her in-laws' house. At day's end, three homes lay in ruins. The Planned Birth officials finished their work of destruction by pillaging the family's livestock and poultry, and then they disappeared.

Still, Aihai remained in hiding, out of reach of the officials, for two more months. It wasn't until her child was actually born, she knew, that he would be safe. Abortions in China are performed up to the very point of parturition, and it is not uncommon for babies to be killed by lethal injection even as they descend the birth canal. Only after she had given birth—to a beautiful baby boy—did she make plans to return home.

Aihai came back to find her family in prison, her home destroyed, and Planned Birth officials furious that she had thwarted their will. Underlying their anger was hard calculation: Every "illegal" child born in their county was a black mark on their performance, depressing annual bonuses and threatening future promotions. But Planned Birth officials, like most Chinese officials, were corrupt, and so set about extorting as much money as they could from the Li family. If you want your relatives released, they now told Aihai, you must pay a fine of seventeen thousand Renminbi (about two thousand dollars). This was a huge sum by the Chinese standards of the day, the equivalent of two or three years' income. It was many days before she was able to beg and borrow enough from family and friends to satisfy the officials' greed and win her family's release.

But no sooner had she paid one fine than she was told she owed another. The Planned Birth officials now explained to Aihai that because her son was born in violation of the Planned Birth law, he was a nonperson. The party does not recognize the existence of this "black child," they warned her. He would be turned away from the government clinic if he fell ill, barred from attending a government school of any kind, and not considered for any kind of government employment later in life. He would not even be allowed to marry or start a family of his own, they said, because the government had decreed that "black children" would not be allowed to reproduce. One generation of illegals was enough. There was an out, however. If she were able to pay another fine of seventeen thousand Renminbi, her son would be issued a national identity number and treated like everyone else—almost. She would still be required to pay double the fees for his school supplies.

She was not surprised when she was ordered to report for sterilization. The Planned Birth regulations, she knew, were unyielding in this regard. Two children and your tubes were tied. This time, she made no effort to resist the authorities. Having a second child had bankrupted her family. Having a third was out of the question. Her newborn son would have no younger siblings.

Even so, Aihai considered herself far more fortunate than Ah Fang, the wife of a neighboring villager, whom we also interviewed. Married at nineteen to an older man in a time-honored village ceremony in front of dozens of relatives and friends, Ah Fang was considered by everyone she knows to be his wife. Everyone, that is, but the local Communist authorities, whose unbending Planned Birth regulations prohibited women from marrying until they reached the age of twenty-three.

When Ah Fang became pregnant, there was no chance that she would be allowed to carry her child to term, even though it would have been her first. The one-child policy did not apply to couples who were, in the view of the CCP, merely cohabiting. For them—and for single mothers of all ages—there was a *zero*-child policy. Ah Fang was ordered to present herself at the local clinic for an abortion. She went in as instructed on September 27, 2001. She had been careful not to criticize the authorities, but her friends were less reticent. "She wanted to keep her baby," they complained openly, "but the law forbade it."[30]

For almost a half-century after the Chinese Communists got deadly serious about controlling births in the late 1960s, millions of Planned Birth police violated the reproductive rights of women, men, and families by a wide variety of coercive measures. The CCP officials in charge always claimed, especially to foreigners, that the program was "voluntary." In speaking to the cadres in charge of enforcing it, however, they emphasize compliance at all costs. The only form of coercion ever mildly criticized is the actual use of physical force—such as tying down pregnant women on operating tables and performing abortions—but it is never, ever punished. Arrest, incarceration, home-wrecking, holding relatives hostage, heavily punitive fines, and like measures were always the whip hand of the program.

Women were psychologically and physically pressured to abort unauthorized children to the point of being dragged to the abortion mill. Networks of paid informants were used to report on unauthorized pregnancies of neighbors, family, and friends. Entire villages were punished for out-of-plan births. Officials conducted nighttime raids on couples suspected of having unauthorized children, and they kept detailed records on the sexual activity of every woman in their jurisdiction—so much for privacy. To make the coercive regime complete, the "Planned Birth centers" had prison cells—complete with guards and bars—to detain those who resisted forced abortion or sterilization. Forced sterilization was used not only as a means of population birth control but sometimes as *punishment* for men and women who disobeyed the rules.[31] The result

---

[30]   Quoted in Guy, "Women and Child Abuse in China," 3.

[31]   See the testimony of Gao Xiaoduan who, as a senior population control official in Fujian province, had systematically committed these and other abuses of human rights with the encouragement and support of her superiors. Following her escape

of this systematic and relentless coercion is that tens of millions of IUD insertions, sterilizations, and abortions were performed each year for decades on end. From the beginning of the Planned Birth program in the PRC until its end, some 400 million preborn and newborn children perished.

The party's marching orders for the one-child policy came from Deng Xiaoping: "Use whatever means you must [to enforce the one-child policy]." China's paramount leader ordered party officials back in 1979, "Just do it."[32] But of course, this kind of no-holds-barred approach is not limited to Deng, nor to the one-child policy, but was characteristic of CCP leaders and their political campaigns from the beginning. Going all the way back to Mao.

The End of the One-Child Policy

The CCP, for its part, was happy to have the Western theory of "overpopulation" to blame for China's backwardness. Otherwise, the people it controlled might begin to question its own rule. For decades, population growth became an all-purpose villain in the official press, blamed for everything from declines in labor productivity to sagging economic growth. If only *you* wouldn't have so many children, the CCP harangued its captive population, *we* could achieve wealth, power, and glory for China in a few years. The victims of Communism are always blamed by the Communists who victimize them.

But you can't kill off 400 million people without consequences.

from China, Mrs. Gao was invited by Congressman Christopher Smith (R-NJ) to testify before the Subcommittee on International Operations and Human Rights of the International Relations Committee. Gao Xiaoduan, "Forced Abortion and Sterilization in China: The View from the Inside," Subcommittee on International Operations and Human Rights, 10 June 1998 Human Rights in China: Improving or Deteriorating Conditions, Hearing before the Subcommittee on Africa, Global Human Rights and International Operations of the Committee on International Relations House of Representatives, http://commdocs.house.gov/committees/intlrel/hfa27067.000/hfa27067_0.HTM#132. Also see Mosher, *A Mother's Ordeal* for similar abuses.
[32] Aird, *Slaughter of the Innocents,* 92.

By 2015, China's National Bureau of Statistics was reporting that Chinese women were averaging only 1.05 children.[33] This was the second lowest fertility rate in the world—only tiny Singapore was lower—and a recipe for demographic suicide. Crushing the birth rate in the world's most populous country had produced a cascade of other crises as well, ranging from tens of millions of excess males to an equal shortage of marriageable women. The most populous country in the world, by the mid-teens of this century, was aging more rapidly than any human population had ever aged. But it was the looming labor shortage that finally got the CCP's attention.

The leaders of the CCP, who had been untroubled by the butchery of the previous decades, now—at long last—began to worry about the impact that continuing the one-child policy would have on economic growth. In 2016, they announced that couples would be free to have a second child.[34]

The years following, however, saw the number of births continue to fall. In 2020, only 12 million babies were born, down from 14.65 million the year before. This was the lowest number of births since China's great famine of 1961 when, coincidentally, some 42.5 million people starved to death. This was also the year when the Grim Reaper beckoned in another way. By my calculations, China went into absolute population decline in 2020, filling more coffins than cradles. COVID-19 only made matters worse.

In May 2021, a three-child policy was announced. The new policy was necessary, China state media Xinhua brusquely explained, "to actively respond to the aging of the population."[35] That's putting it mildly since China today is literally dying. Chinese Communist leaders are increasingly worried about having enough workers and soldiers for the factories and armies of the future.

---

[33] Mosher, "Are Chinese communists lying about number of babies born? They've got every reason to."
[34] Phillips, "China ends one-child policy after 35 years."
[35] https://s.weibo.com/weibo?q=%23三孩生育政策来了%23.

I doubt that the three-child policy will succeed—at least as long as it remains voluntary. The problem is that the ranks of young women were decimated during the decades of the one-child policy. Baby girls were aborted and abandoned to die by the millions by Chinese parents who were desperate for a son. There are simply too few young women of childbearing age remaining to offset the coming population crash—unless every single one marries and has three children.

I can't imagine any combination of carrots that would induce China's young, urban, working women to devote themselves to motherhood in this way. Of course, if persuasion doesn't work, I can easily imagine that the CCP leaders might resort to compulsion. In fact, local party officials are already suggesting that people need to be strong-armed into the baby-making business.

"Only the strong leadership of the Party can solve this problem . . . of a catastrophic population decline," wrote Professor Nie Shengzhe in 2018.[36] His proposals, which have since been echoed by others, include:

- Party cadres should take the lead in having two, three, or four children, and give priority to promoting party cadres who have more children.
- The Party Central Committee should establish strict control over the sale of condoms and contraceptives and forbid hospitals from performing abortions.
- The party's propaganda department should vigorously propagandize the ideas that "more children bring many blessings" and "one is too few, two is not enough, three is good, four is the best."
- Those party members of childbearing age who use contraceptives when having sex should be punished.

Would Chinese Communist leaders balk at imposing such measures on the Chinese population, or even force Chinese women to bear

---

[36] https://web.archive.org/web/20210601144520/https:/net.blogchina.com/bl og/article/530342432.

children? Not if they remember their Mao. The late chairman—who is current CCP leader Xi Jinping's model in all things—said in a famous 1957 speech that "reproduction needs to be planned. In my opinion, mankind is completely incapable of managing itself. We have plans for production in factories, for producing cloth, tables and chairs, and steel, but no plan for producing humans."[37]

The Chinese Communists have now made it clear that they want to "produce more humans," and no one should doubt that they have both the will and the means to enforce a new Planned Birth campaign, this one directed at increasing the birth rate.

Molech Revisited

The CCP's deliberate slaughter of the innocents, which occurred on an almost unimaginable scale, is another sign of the evil that Communism has visited upon China. It was a modern form of human sacrifice practiced by the party in the belief that if they eliminated enough children from their population, they could achieve wealth and power.

It is, in that sense, not all that different from other forms of human sacrifice described in the Old Testament. The ancient Canaanites worshipped Molech, a pagan deity who demanded child sacrifice in return for his diabolical favor. The idol was constructed of bronze in the shape of a bull, with a furnace located in the belly of the beast. The Canaanites, who like modern-day Communists did not view life as a gift from God, would throw their children into the furnace while praying for favorable weather or crops.

The Bible warns against this evil practice: "You shall not give any of your children to devote them by fire to Molech, and so profane the name of your God: I am the Lord" (Lv 18:21). Later, King Josiah razed the "hilled site" not far from Jerusalem on which one of his predecessors had erected another beastly idol, "that no one might burn his son or his daughter as an offering to Molech" (2 Kgs 23:10).

---

[37] Mao Zedong, "On the Correct Handling of Contradictions among the People," in *Mao Zedong zhuzuo zhuanti zhaibian,* 970. The translation is my own.

The CCP leaders, like the ancient Canaanites, did not understand that a nation in the service of Molech is doomed to extinction. Even if they had not consciously rejected the ideas that human life is sacred and that everyone, from the first moment of existence, has an inviolable right to life—but like all leftists, they had—they should still have understood that driving the birth rate down to half the 2.1 births per woman necessary to sustain the population would be, over time, a death sentence.

But, of course, reveling in their control over what they thought of as the endless masses of Chinese humanity, that thought never occurred to them.

CHAPTER 14

THE CHINESE COMMUNIST PARTY'S WAR ON CATHOLICS (AND ALL RELIGIONS)

"[Religion is] the embodiment of the whole feudal-patriarchal system and ideology, and [one of] the four thick ropes binding the Chinese people, especially the peasants."

—Mao Zedong[1]

"If by interfering in politics is meant judging or condemning a philosophy of life which makes the party, or the state, or the class, or the race the source of all rights, and which usurps the soul and enthrones party over conscience. . . . The Church does judge such a philosophy. But when it does this it is not interfering with politics, for such politics is no longer politics but Theology. When a State sets itself up as absolute as God, when it claims sovereignty over the soul, when it destroys freedom of conscience and freedom of religion, then the State has ceased to be political and has begun to be a counter-Church."

—Archbishop Fulton J. Sheen[2]

Chairman Mao's War on Religion

Not long after he joined the Chinese Communist Party (CCP) in 1921, Mao also realized that belief in God was incompatible with the totalitarian ambitions of Communism. As Archbishop

---

[1]   Zedong, "Investigation of the Peasant Movement in Hunan," in *Selected Works of Chairman Mao*, vol. 1, 44.
[2]   Marlin, *The Quotable Fulton Sheen*, 41.

Fulton Sheen noted, "When a State sets itself up as absolute as God, when it claims sovereignty over the soul, when it destroys freedom of conscience and freedom of religion, then the State has ceased to be political and has begun to be a counter-Church." Setting up just such a "counter-Church" was precisely what Mao—and Marx and Lenin before him—took for their life's work. They lusted to command the complete and utter loyalty of the masses to the exclusion of all else. There was no room for God in their calculations because they were going to take His place—or try to.

Mao had abandoned the Buddhist faith of his mother around the age of twelve, but now he became stridently hostile to any mention of the afterlife. In his 1927 "Investigation of the Peasant Movement in Hunan," Mao denounced all religious authority as "the embodiment of the whole feudal-patriarchal system and ideology, and [one of] the four thick ropes binding the Chinese people, especially the peasants." He mocked the Chinese folk belief that there was an "Emperor of Heaven" reigning over the angels of the celestial world or that there was a "King of Hell" presiding over the demons of the netherworld.[3]

But Mao reserved particular rancor for Christianity, which he regarded as the ideological arm of nineteenth-century Western imperialism. As for the Vatican, he regarded it as a hostile foreign power. In truth, it was anything but a recent import, having been first brought to China by Nestorian Christians over one thousand years ago. Later, during the sixteenth century, the Jesuits arrived and won the acceptance of the last Ming emperors to build churches and spread Catholicism throughout the empire. What Mao found objectionable was the huge uptick in missionary activity in the decades surrounding his birth and the large numbers of conversions that followed.

There was a practical side to Mao's objections as well. Christians naturally find Communism abhorrent, and they constituted an important

---

[3]   Mao Zedong, "Investigation of the Peasant Movement in Hunan," in *Selected Works of Chairman Mao*, vol. 1, 44. The Catholic translation of God into China is *Tianzhu*, which means "Lord of Heaven," while the Protestants use *Shangdi*, which means "Heavenly Emperor." King of Hell strikes me as an apt appellation for Satan.

part of the anti-Communist opposition. This point was further driven home when Nationalist head Chiang Kai-shek himself converted to Christianity in 1930,[4] subsequently filled many of the senior positions in his government with Christians, and regularly attended church on Sundays. The only use that Mao had for churches was as local military or party headquarters during the Chinese civil war, since they were invariably the best-constructed building in the village or town his troops were occupying.

The armed conflict with the Nationalists may have ended in 1950 when Chiang Kai-shek withdrew his armies to Taiwan, but Chairman Mao's war on religion was only just getting started. For the next eight years, he brutally suppressed the practice of the Christian faith. Foreign Catholic and Protestant missionaries were, to a man, accused of being spies for whatever country they hailed from. Most were simply arrested and deported, but others were sent to prison, where they were tortured into writing confessions. A few, like Maryknoll Bishop Francis Ford, were tortured to death.

There was no easy escape for the millions of Chinese Catholics, who fared much worse. Some fled to Hong Kong or Taiwan in advance of the coming persecution, but most had no choice but to remain behind. These saw their churches closed down and their bishops and priests arrested and sentenced to long prison terms or executed. The crackdown in Shanghai came on September 8, 1955, when the bishop of Shanghai, Bishop Ignatius Kung Pin-Mei, along with several hundred priests and Church leaders, was arrested and imprisoned. Bishop Kung was later sentenced to life imprisonment for so-called counterrevolutionary activities, which is Communist-speak for his refusal to break with Rome.

Neither were the laity spared. Those who had taken an active role in their congregations, as choir directors, perhaps, or as volunteer youth group leaders, were forced to write self-criticisms. Others fared even worse. The members of the Legion of Mary, an international apostolic

---

4   *Time,* "Religion: Chiang's Testimony."

organization of lay people engaged in doing corporeal and spiritual works of mercy, were accused of belonging to a "paramilitary organization." But even the most innocuous pew sitter was considered to be a member of a "bad class" and prohibited from joining the party or serving in the military or government.

Yet, by 1957, it was evident that, despite the chairman's determination to stamp out all faiths other than his own Communist one, he had failed. No one told him that Christians, especially Catholics, understand that they will often be persecuted by the world for practicing their faith. After all, Christ Himself had forewarned them: "If they persecuted me, they will persecute you" (Jn 15:20). No one told him that Christianity, even under the vicious persecution of emperors like Diocletian and Nero, continued to spread throughout the Roman Empire.

Mao decided it was time to resort to one of the tactics that he used so effectively during the civil war: he would set up front groups. A decade of persecution (1949–57) was about to be followed by a decade of control.

That Which the CCP Cannot Crush It Must Control (1957–1966)

Mao often bragged that the CCP had what he called "three magic weapons." These were, he said, propaganda, united front tactics, and the People's Liberation Army. And they were deployed—in this precise order—to control the population. Propaganda was the weapon of first resort. The masses were constantly being hectored by the party in the press, on television, and in public meetings to accept the current party line without question.

When such political indoctrination wasn't enough to control unruly elements, the party would use united front tactics. It would set up a front group—or even take over an existing organization if there was one—in an attempt to manipulate the resisters. For example, China has labor unions, but these were set up by the party not to represent the workers but to control them from behind the scenes.

The third magic weapon, the People's Liberation Army (PLA), was usually kept hidden after the end of the civil war. Although the Chinese Communist system is, in essence, a military dictatorship, the party is at pains not to undermine the pretense of public support. Only if all else failed—as during the 1989 demonstrations for democracy—would the military be called upon, at least in Han Chinese areas. The PLA has always had a much stronger presence in restive minority areas like Tibet and Xinjiang, and the troops have often been called out of their barracks to deal with the restive population.

By 1957, it was apparent to Mao that his decade-long effort to crush the Catholic Church in China had failed and that it was time to deploy his second magic weapon, united front tactics. He set up a front organization called the Catholic Patriotic Association and coerced some (but far from all) bishops and priests into joining it. His goal was to seize control of the Catholic Church in China, sever all ties between the Vatican and Chinese Catholics, and attempt to make the now-domesticated Church serve the interests of the CCP.[5]

While some bishops, priests, and laity joined the Catholic Patriotic Association, often under duress, others refused to have anything to do with it, seeing it—quite correctly—as a Communist front group. Instead, these brave souls refused the party's demands and went into the catacombs, risking arrest and imprisonment, and all too often torture and death. They wanted to remain faithful to the Church founded by Christ, not a political party founded by men.

And it was about to get worse.

The Great Proletarian Cultural Revolution and Its Aftermath (1966–79)

The wanton destruction of all religious edifices during the Cultural Revolution has been captured in photos and film: maniacal Red Guards smashing statues and stained glass windows with sledgehammers,

---

[5]   The Protestant version, called the "Three-Self Patriotic Movement," had been set up in 1954.

priests and nuns being paraded down the streets by angry mobs, buildings being turned into piles of rubble. From the desecration of churches to the imprisonment of believers, it was a return to a no-holds-barred effort to eradicate not just Christianity but all religions from China.

At least in the cities, all public religious services were shut down. Even the Catholic Patriotic Association and its Protestant counterpart ceased operation. The Red Guards made sure of that. Still, the underground Church survived, led by bishops loyal to the Universal Church. And many Catholics who had joined the Patriotic Church found themselves joining underground services as their own churches were locked, desecrated, or destroyed over the years of the Cultural Revolution.

When Mao, the Nero of modern-day China, died in 1976, the Cultural Revolution came to an end. Yet the Church lived on.

The Respite (1979–2005)

"It is no secret that the Holy See, in the name of the whole Catholic Church and, I believe, for the benefit of the whole human family, hopes for the opening of some form of dialogue with the Authorities of the People's Republic of China. . . . Once the misunderstandings of the past have been overcome, such a dialogue would make it possible for us to work together for the good of the Chinese people and for peace in the world." [6]

—Pope St. John Paul II, 2001

It wasn't until 1979—three years after Mao's death—that a general amnesty for those convicted of political and ideological crimes was declared. Hundreds of thousands of political prisoners of all stripes were released from the prisons and labor camps. Included in the amnesty were a number of priests who had been first arrested in 1958 for refusing to join the Catholic Patriotic Association, chief among them the now-Cardinal Kung Pin-Mei.

---

[6] John Paul II, "Message of Pope John Paul II to the Participants in the International Conference Commemorating the Fourth Centenary of the Arrival in Beijing of Father Matteo Ricci" (October 24, 2001), no. 6.

In the years following, it became possible for the first time since the Communist takeover to build new churches and restore old ones, to open new seminaries and ordain new priests, and to start orphanages.

It was in the early nineties, not long after I entered the Catholic Church, that I went to China seeking to learn more about the fate of my fellow believers under Communism. They were divided into two opposing camps, or so I believed at the time, with some belonging to the state-controlled church—the so-called Chinese Patriotic Catholic Association—while others belonged to the Catholic Church in communion with Rome. We referred to it as the "underground church," given that it was operating outside the purview of the authorities.

Truth be told, I did not think much of those who attended the "patriotic churches." I believed that these were small-*c* Catholics who had compromised with, or entirely capitulated to, the CCP's demands to sever ties with the Universal Church and its head, the bishop of Rome.

My sympathy was reserved for the Catholics of the Underground Church. In short, I believed that the members of the underground church were heroic, while the pew sitters in the patriotic church were more or less craven.

Monsignor Filoni, the unofficial nuncio of the Vatican to China who lived and worked in Hong Kong, was in close contact with the bishops of both the underground and the patriotic churches. He had a surprising and encouraging story to tell about the relationship between these two churches, and with Rome.

As far as the patriotic church was concerned, Monsignor Filoni surprised me by saying 100 percent of the laity, and nearly all its priests and bishops, had remained loyal to the Magisterium. "Nearly all the illicitly ordained bishops have asked the Holy Father to be recognized as legitimate," he told me. "And nearly all, after we examine their character and behavior, have been so recognized. The only exceptions are the patriotic bishops of Beijing, Shanghai, and a couple of other major cities. They have made too many compromises."

He summed up by saying, "The Church is more unified now than at any time since the Communist Revolution. Churches are being rebuilt, and seminaries are being reopened. Although it may appear from the outside that there are still two churches in China, inside of China, there is only one."

I was overjoyed to learn that the underground church was increasingly able to come out of the catacombs and was, in many parts of China, openly preaching the Gospel and making converts. Even more surprising to me was that the patriotic church, which had begun as a Communist front organization intended to co-opt and gradually extinguish Catholicism throughout China, had been transformed from within by faithful Catholics who saw themselves as part of the Universal Church. By the end of Pope John Paul's pontificate, the break between the underground and patriotic churches was almost healed, with patriotic bishops renouncing schism and joining their brother bishops in the Universal Church.

The newfound unity of Catholics in China that Monsignor Filoni described had nothing to do with either political pressure from the party or political overtures to Beijing by Vatican diplomats. It had come about from the bottom up, not from the top down.

It was not a perfect solution—decades of deep wounds from politically fomented division still remained—but it was a workable one. It had, after all, been worked out at the parish and diocesan levels by the real stakeholders—Chinese Catholics themselves—with the quiet encouragement and support of the then-Holy Father, Pope John Paul II.

Beginning in the mid-nineties and continuing until the mid-teens of the twenty-first century, I worked closely with faithful Catholics in China on a number of projects, building and restoring churches, funding safe houses for women fleeing forced abortion, and helping to set up orphanages for babies abandoned under the one-child policy. It was a period of relative openness in China. But it was not to last.

A Pact with the Devil Always Ends Badly (2000 to Present)

"Religion must support the party, the state, and its leaders. . . .
Sinicization means that all religious communities should be led
by the Party, controlled by the Party, and support the Party."

—Xi Jinping[7]

"Every human person, created in the image of God, has the natural
right to be recognized as a free and responsible human being. . . .
The right to the exercise of freedom, especially in moral and religious
matters, is an inalienable requirement of the dignity of the human
person. This right must be recognized and protected by civil authority
with the limits of the common good and public order."

—Catechism of the Catholic Church[8]

The period of relative—and it was only relative—openness lasted roughly two decades. The doors began to close when then-Communist Party leader Jiang Zemin launched a crackdown on a Buddhist sect called the Falun Gong in 1999. This had a chilling effect on all religious practice in China. It is no coincidence that it was around this time that Cardinal Joseph Zen, who had been teaching in both patriotic and underground seminaries, was blacklisted by the CCP and forbidden from reentering China.

Even then, the officially atheistic Communist Party and its agents remained a brooding, hostile presence over both church communities, but by common agreement between the two, it was kept out of the local arrangements that allowed Catholics from both to coexist, even cooperate. Underground bishops, with the permission of the Vatican, named their own successors. The Patriotic Association named its own bishops, but these then almost always sought, and almost always got, consecration by the pope.

---

[7]   Hu Zimo, "China: First CCP National Conference on Religion Held Since 2016."
[8]   *CCC* 1738.

The Vatican Secretariat of State, apparently unhappy with the ambiguity of the situation, decided to enter into formal talks with the People's Republic of China. It established direct contact with Beijing in 2005 and opened negotiations over the appointment of bishops. Then, to make matters worse, it began insisting, after the fashion in Western diplomatic circles, on the need for a formal written agreement on the matter.

That demand brought the negotiations to a speedy end. No Communist official is ever going to put his John Hancock on a document ceding to a foreign power—which is how Beijing regards the Vatican—the authority to appoint anyone in China to any position of authority. Period. Some kind of informal understanding might have eventually been reached, but never a formal agreement. The CCP continued to illegally "ordain" bishops in the years following, eventually bringing the total number of illicit bishops in China to eight.

Cardinal Bergoglio Becomes Pope; Xi Jinping Takes Power

"With God's help, before He calls me home, I will help to bring you China and the great dream of Matteo Ricci will begin to be realized once again."

—Ex-Cardinal Theodore McCarrick[9]

Following the elevation of Cardinal Bergoglio to the papacy on March 13, 2013, the Vatican once again became eager to engage with China. The new pope may not have realized that with the rise of Xi Jinping to power in late 2012, he was now dealing with a Chinese leader who was at least as hostile to Christianity in general, and to Catholicism in particular, as Mao had ever been. In any event, he picked an odd emissary.

Cardinal Theodore McCarrick had already been removed from public ministry by Pope Benedict when Pope Francis tapped him to deal with the Chinese authorities. Because of his sexual abuse of minors, Pope Benedict XVI placed restrictions on McCarrick's ministry and

---

9   Souza, "Figueiredo Report the First of Many to Come?"

travel. Why a notorious homosexual predator was given such a sensitive assignment, one which would affect the fate of millions of souls, is a mystery. Now that the extent of the disgraced ex-Cardinal McCarrick's corruption is widely-known—both sexual and financial—it seems even more incredible that he was ever allowed to negotiate with China, but he played a leading role. More corrupt politician than Catholic prelate, it is perhaps not surprising that the deal that McCarrick helped to negotiate is so deeply flawed.[10]

According to McCarrick's longtime secretary, Monsignor Anthony Figueiredo, McCarrick simply ignored the restrictions placed on his ministry and travel by Pope Benedict. He continued to make visits to Beijing on the Vatican's behalf. As Monsignor Figueiredo reports, McCarrick wrote to Pope Francis, "When you greeted me so cheerfully in Washington as an adjunct member of the foreign service, I received this as a challenge to continue as an amateur in the very noble work of the foreign relations of the Holy See. I have maintained on a quiet level our relationship with China and have been developing new relationships with the Arab countries of the Middle East. . . . With God's help, before He calls me home, I will help to bring you China and the great dream of Matteo Ricci will begin to be realized once again."[11]

This continued effort by the Vatican had another downside. It drew the attention of the Chinese party-state to the activities of the Catholic Church in China. Scattered in communities throughout the length and breadth of the country, Catholics form a small minority of the Chinese population. As such, they were able to evangelize, build churches, and even open seminaries, all while attracting relatively little hostile attention from the central government. "The mountains are high, and the emperor is far away," as the Chinese are wont to say.

Once Vatican officials entered into discussions with Beijing officials, however, the party-state began to pay more attention to the activities

---

[10]   Mosher, "The Sino-Vatican Agreement—One Year Later."

[11]   Souza, "Figueiredo Report the First of Many to Come?"

of the domestic followers of this hostile foreign power. In other words, the mere fact of opening negotiations put a target on the backs of Chinese Catholics. The "space" in which it had operated began to shrink under the unblinking eye of state surveillance.

Vatican diplomats seem not to have realized—and McCarrick may not have cared—that they were dealing with a one-party dictatorship that was far more brutal, and far less tolerant of any expressions of religious faith, than Mexico in the 1990s or Vietnam in the first decade of the twenty-first century. Moreover, since the time of Mao and continuing down to the present day, all belief in transcendental religions, especially those with foreign connections like Catholicism, are suspect, even treasonous, in the eyes of the CCP.

Since the CCP's own religion—Communism—has been unable to win very many adherents among the Chinese population of late, the party has reverted to a national narcissism that has deep roots in Chinese history. Since the 1989 Tiananmen Massacre, the CCP has been promoting an extremely toxic form of race-based nationalism very much akin to fascism. The Chinese people are constantly being told that they, their culture, and their country are naturally superior to any other people, culture, or country that has ever existed. To be numbered among the descendants of the dragon, party propaganda insists, is to be part of the greatest phenomenon in human history. It means that you are part of the Middle Kingdom and that you have a natural right to rule the lesser folk from the fringes.

The state religion of China, in other words, has become China itself. "Socialism with Chinese characteristics" is its catechism, the members of the party are its priesthood, and the head of the party serves as its high priest. The whole of China serves as its temple, within whose sacred precincts its people are encouraged to worship their own collective greatness—and the party, of course.

But whether the CCP is promoting Communism or a kind of xenophobic nationalism or a combination of both as its state religion,

Xi Jinping is its head, and he wants to keep Catholicism under strict control.

That's why China seized upon the Vatican's eagerness to reach an agreement to lay down two conditions that had to be met.

- First, the Holy Father must, without exception, consecrate all the patriotic bishops that he and Pope Benedict, for very good reasons, had previously rejected.
- Second, he must eliminate the underground church, starting with its bishops. Elderly underground bishops must be forcibly retired and replaced with patriotic bishops of Beijing's choosing, while younger underground bishops must be reassigned to subordinate roles in the patriotic church. This process must continue until the last of the thirty or so underground bishops have been sidelined and silenced, one way or another.

It was the prospect of this "sellout" of the underground church, as Hong Kong's Cardinal Joseph Zen characterized it, that sent him to Rome in early 2018 to plead the cause of his Chinese co-believers to the Holy Father himself.[12] He also wanted to alert the Vatican to the fact that under Xi Jinping's dictatorial rule, the CCP was becoming ever more hostile to religious belief and expression.

At the October 2017 Party Congress, Xi demanded tighter controls over religious activity, insisting that the party "exercise overall leadership over all areas of endeavor in every part of the country." As a result, new regulations banning unauthorized religious activity were issued on February 1, 2018. According to a priest of the underground church, the new rules state that "all religious sites must be registered, no religious activities can be held beyond registered venues, non-registered clergymen are forbidden to host religious liturgies, and that minors and party members are forbidden from entering churches. . . . The living space for the Church is getting less and less."[13]

---

12   Mosher, "Parolin and the China Negotiations: First, Do No Harm."
13   UCA News, "China Church further squeezed by revised regulations."

Xi Jinping's Enforcers: The United Front Department of the CCP

Less than two months later, on March 22, 2018, the CCP announced that all "religious affairs" in China would henceforth be supervised by a shadowy party office called the United Front Department. The former government agency responsible for Catholics and other believers—the State Administration of Religious Affairs bureau (SARA)—was summarily abolished.

United Front officials, zealous Communists all, have ever since been enforcing the new restrictions on religious activity that were issued on February 1, 2018. These make it illegal to take one's own children to Mass, require all Catholics to register with the government, and forbid illegal religious assemblies, including catechism and Sunday school classes. The ultimate goal of these new regulations was to stamp out Catholicism.

To understand why the CCP's United Front Department spelled disaster for Catholics, one must understand its purpose. The United Front Department was created by Chairman Mao Zedong to co-opt and control non-Communist organizations and individuals during the Chinese civil war. Its efforts were so successful, as I mentioned earlier, that Mao called it one of the three "magic weapons" that helped the revolution succeed.

Putting the United Front Department in charge of religious affairs meant that the party leadership was determined to make the Patriotic Catholic Church an active "agent of control" for the regime with one goal: to subvert and undermine the faith of China's millions of Catholics and to prevent them from spreading the Faith to others, including their own children. It was nothing less than a hostile takeover—an expropriation if you will—of the Catholic Church in China, an attempt to turn it into a zombie controlled by the CCP.

There is an irreconcilable contradiction between the demands of the United Front Department and the demands of the Catholic Faith. The very creation of the Patriotic Catholic Church in 1957 was a

United Front tactic that was intended to subvert the Chinese church and turn it into an agent of the state. Chinese Catholics understood this, which is why they went underground in large numbers. After the signing of the Sino-Vatican Agreement, however, many felt like they had no choice but to join the patriotic church. The CCP was determined to complete its work of subversion by annihilating the underground church.

Once the underground church is no more—and the work of destruction is well underway as I write—the Patriotic Catholic Church can redouble its efforts to ideologically assimilate all Chinese Catholics into the political order—the people's democratic dictatorship—that Xi Jinping controls. Xi's ultimate goal is the same as Mao's—namely, the total eradication of this "foreign" religion from Chinese soil.

The agents of this subversion were Patriotic Catholic bishops like Bishop Peter Fang Jianping of Tangshan, one of three compromised bishops who, in 2020, were members of China's rubberstamp parliament, the National People's Congress. Bishop Fang eagerly promotes Xi Jinping's call for the "sinicization of religion," which is the idea that religion should chiefly serve the interests of the CCP that Xi himself leads.

Faced with a similar choice between secular and sacred authority, Saint Thomas More famously said, "I am the King's good servant, but I am God's first." Bishop Fang would turn More's affirmation of the Faith on its head. He is saying, in effect, "I am God's good servant, but I am Emperor Xi's first."[14]

In May 2018, a few months before the Sino-Vatican Agreement was signed, I had the opportunity to sit down with Cardinal Parolin, who as the secretary of state is generally regarded as the number two man in the Vatican. I laid out reasons why signing any agreement with the CCP—notorious for having violated nearly every agreement it had

---

[14] Mosher, "Xi Jinping Places Catholic Church in China Under Direct Party Control."

signed—would be a mistake. However, Cardinal Parolin indicated to me that the terms of the agreement had already been negotiated and, as he put it, "We are simply waiting on the Chinese side to sign the agreement."

I specifically briefed His Eminence on the new regulations governing religious activity that had come into effect on February 1, 2018. These called for underground bishops and priests to submit to the Communist authorities as a condition of staying in ministry. He dismissed my concern, saying, "We have no objection to the requirement that everyone register with the authorities."

But this was no simple "registration." In the hands of the Communist Party, it was twisted into a requirement that all clergy join the schismatic Chinese Patriotic Catholic Association and profess that their first loyalty was to the officially atheistic party-state. Those who refused were subject to even more intense persecution than before. "What should we do?" Underground clergy cried out in anguish and confusion, feeling that they had been abandoned by the Universal Church.[15]

In order to reach an agreement, the Vatican would make two further concessions. First, the Vatican promised that the pope would lift the excommunication of the eight illicit "bishops" of the Chinese Patriotic Catholic Association even before the new agreement was signed.[16] It is hard to avoid the conclusion that this entire group of bishops was given a kind of blanket amnesty. Second, the pope ordered two bishops of the underground church, who had faithfully served in their offices for decades under intense persecution, to hand over their dioceses to bishops appointed by the Communist authorities.

The Sino-Vatican Agreement

When the Sino-Vatican agreement was signed in the fall of 2018, Cardinal Joseph Zen, the retired archbishop of Hong Kong, questioned

---

15   Clubb, "Steve Mosher on the Sino-Vatican Agreement."
16   Mosher, "Vatican to Allow Beijing to Name Bishops."

whether the authority to appoint bishops had been ceded to the CCP. The CCP intended for the agreement itself to serve as a tool to be used to force bishops and clergy in the underground church to join the Patriotic Association. It has since become evident that it is being used as cover for intensifying persecution of the Catholic Church as a whole.[17]

After the signing, Father Bernardo Cervellera, a missionary of the Pontifical Institute for Foreign Missions and head of Asia News wrote, "Until now there was talk of a temporary power of veto of the pontiff: the Pope would be able to give the reasons for his refusal within three months, but if the government found the papal motivations inconsistent, it would continue with the appointment and the ordination of the chosen candidate. Not having the text of the agreement, we do not know if this clause has been maintained, if indeed the pontiff will have the last word on the appointments and ordinations, or if instead his authority is only formally recognized."[18]

In the actual Sino-Vatican agreement, Beijing insisted upon using what it called a "Chinese model" for the appointment of bishops. Under the terms of this model, the Communist authorities alone will nominate a potential candidate for bishop. The pope will then have a certain period of time to either approve or reject this candidate. If he vetoes the first candidate, Beijing will nominate another.

As Father Cervellera feared, the pope's "veto power" is not unlimited. As a Chinese official familiar with the negotiations was quoted as saying, "We cannot submit endless candidate lists to the Vatican if the pontiff keeps saying no. We may have to appoint bishops unapproved by the pontiff after a set number of rounds of negotiations. Such bishops may not be legitimate under the Church doctrine, but they can still give Church services to Chinese Catholics."

---

[17] Williams, "China Expert: Communist Party Determined to 'Extinguish the Catholic Faith.'"

[18] Cervellera, "China-Vatican agreement: some positive steps, but without forgetting the martyrs."

In other words, the pope may veto an obviously unsuitable candidate or two, but Beijing has made it clear that there is a limit to the number of times a papal veto can be used. It has also limited the amount of time that the Vatican has to respond once a candidate's name is submitted by the CCP authorities.

These stipulations mean that it is the Communist authorities, and not Pope Francis, who will have the final say over who becomes a bishop in the Chinese Catholic Church.

Aside from the critical question of who is really in charge of appointing bishops, the secret Sino-Vatican agreement has raised other concerns. While this agreement was supposed to provide some protection for the Catholic Church in China, it has instead been turned on its head. It is perversely being used by the Communist authorities to crush the long-suffering but faithful underground Catholic Church while the Vatican stands silently by.

Catholics in China and around the world remain in the dark about any promises—or compromises—the Vatican has made. Even worse, the Communist authorities have been misrepresenting the agreement to the Chinese faithful in different ways, in effect using the borrowed authority of the Vatican to undermine the faith of believers in China in their own Church.

If the Vatican was relying on the trustworthiness of Chinese Communist officials, they were very wrong. Beijing has signed many agreements over the years—agreements whose terms are publicly known—only to violate them before the ink is dry on the paper.

The agreement, as I predicted, has benefited the Chinese party-state, which has used it to assert its control over the underground church in China. It suggests to the faithful that the pope himself has recognized the Communist-run and openly schismatic Chinese Patriotic Catholic Association, and that each and every one of China's twelve million Catholics must worship only in its churches. It has allowed the CCP to greatly intensify its attack on the underground church, using the borrowed authority of the Vatican itself as an ideological assault weapon.

The Communist Party has long been determined to force underground Chinese Catholics out of the catacombs so they can be brought under strict party control. The agreement has given the CCP leverage to do exactly this. It was negotiated by clerics who have little personal understanding of China's recent history of brutally suppressing religion. Why anyone in the Vatican, up to and including the current secretary of state, Cardinal Pietro Parolin, would think it's a good idea to allow the CCP to use the borrowed authority of the Supreme Pontiff remains a mystery.[19]

The agreement is seen as a betrayal by many. They argue that it betrays the authority of the papacy by giving the CCP the right to name bishops. It betrays the underground church in China, a church that not only has survived decades of persecution at the hands of the authorities but is now, once again, under siege. And because it is a secret agreement, it betrays the Truth by allowing both sides to misrepresent it.

Pope Francis seems to have ceded a great deal—if not all—of his God-given authority to appoint bishops to Beijing. In return, China's Communist authorities have reportedly promised him symbolic recognition as the titular head of all Catholics in China.[20]

"I now invite all Chinese Catholics to work towards reconciliation," Pope Francis would later write,[21] as if it were the Catholics themselves who were sowing division. But the division between Catholics in the underground and patriotic churches was not caused by the Catholics themselves. Rather, it arose in reaction to actions by the CCP, which has been viciously persecuting believers since it was nothing but a ragtag guerrilla group in the Chinese hinterland. And it was the CCP

---

[19] Mosher, "Expert condemns Vatican for 'betrayal' in secret agreement with Communist China."

[20] Mosher, "Vatican to Allow Beijing to Name Bishops."

[21] Castelfranco, "Pope Calls for Chinese Catholics to Work Toward Reconciliation."

that, in 1957, set up a party-controlled church called the Catholic Patriotic Association. Those Catholics who were not willing to compromise their faith went underground.

This division cannot be healed by Catholics themselves, because they were not the cause of it. The CCP was the cause of the original division, and it remains today a dominating and controlling presence over all Catholics in China.

The entire exercise seems somehow backward because historically it was the underground church that remained loyal to the Magisterium, while the patriotic church accepted the authority of the CCP to govern its affairs.

Now their roles are seemingly reversed. The pope's secret agreement apparently recognizes the Catholic Patriotic Church as the only licit Catholic organization in the country and puts the onus on the long-persecuted underground church to accept supervision and control by its authorities. That is to say, it lends the authority of the Magisterium to the CCP itself, which will be able to claim—rightly—that the pope has ordered underground bishops, priests, and laity to cooperate with the religious authorities anointed by the CCP.[22]

The Vatican-China agreement almost seems deliberately designed to be nonbinding on the Chinese party-state since its terms have been kept secret from the world in general and from Chinese Catholics in particular.

The Chinese party-state, on the other hand, has cleverly used the pretext of a Vatican-China agreement to increase its persecution of the underground church in China. It has insisted that each and every one of China's twelve million Catholics worship only in churches approved by the Chinese Patriotic Catholic Association. It has used the borrowed authority of the Vatican to further clamp down on unregistered churches in so-called underground communities led by bishops loyal only to Rome.

---

[22] Mosher, "Pope Francis empowered Communists with Magisterial authority in Vatican/China deal."

The Persecution of Catholics Intensifies

"For you, a new age of the catacombs will begin. It will be winter. It will be hard on you. The government will seize your churches. The priests will no longer be able to administer the sacraments. All that will be left for you to do is to go home to farm the land. But you will always be priests."

—Cardinal Joseph Zen[23]

"When, before the signing of the [Sino-Vatican] Agreement we remained fearless and maintained our faith no matter how much we were coerced, the Holy See would have supported us, too. But now, we're really helpless. To be frank, whoever persists [in refusing to sign] will suffer greater suppression and persecution from the CCP."

—Bishop Vincent Guo[24]

By 2020, it was clear to everyone—even Vatican diplomats, presumably—that things had gone from bad to worse for Catholics in China. Until 2018 or so, Catholic churches in China used to boldly proclaim their existence. External signs and statues have all been torn down now to hide their existence.

The Communist authorities were telling underground bishops, priests, and laity that the new agreement not only requires them to register with the government but also to join the so-called Catholic Patriotic Association. Nearly all of them refused to do this since they know that the Patriotic Association is not in communion with Rome. As punishment, the Communists began arresting resisters and demolishing their churches and shrines. The underground Diocese of Fengxiang, Shaanxi province, was particularly hard hit. On April 4, 2019, a newly built church in the diocese, still under construction, was leveled by wrecking balls and bulldozers as its parishioners looked on in horror.

The Vatican seemed to turn a blind eye to the pressure on bishops and priests to join the schismatic Catholic Patriotic Association, perhaps

23   Zen, *For Love of My People I will not Remain Silent*, 141.
24   Mosher, "Faithful Chinese bishop on the run from communists highlights Vatican/China deal disaster."

thinking that the association might provide a safe haven for Catholics in China. But it was mistaken. Being a "patriotic" bishop did not provide automatic immunity from persecution. Nor did being a "patriotic" parish necessarily protect the parish church from the wrecking ball.

In the face of such ongoing persecution and destruction, the silence from the proponents of the agreement that was signed in 2018 was deafening. Cardinal Parolin, the Vatican's secretary of state, who by all accounts was the author of the accord, continued to counsel patience throughout 2019 and 2020, and at the end of that year, he renewed it for another two years.

Yet, judging by the benchmarks that he himself set at the outset, the agreement had failed to deliver. In the two years since its signing, the agreement was used by Beijing as an excuse to limit—not expand—the religious freedom of Catholics in China. If anything, the authorities intensified their efforts to restrict all the activities of all religions, and they remain intent on driving religions out of public life altogether.

When Catholics questioned why they were being forced to study the works of Xi Jinping, an official bluntly told them, "It is because you believe in God that you are required to study and answer the questions. This is to change your thinking." The official added that because they thanked God instead of the party, they needed to "study Xi" more. The goal is to brainwash everyone into believing only in Communist leader Xi and his party while rejecting God and His Church.

Communism has always been a total ideology, one that seeks to control not only the acts and words of those under its power but their very thoughts as well. Those who refuse to submit are enemies of the revolution—counterrevolutionaries—who must be identified, targeted, and destroyed. This is a political system that feeds off the destruction of an endless series of "enemies," real and imagined.[25]

It is hard to say what the Vatican has received in return for an agreement that Cardinal Zen openly calls a "sellout" of the underground

---

[25] Mosher, "After Vatican agreement, China's Communist leader is still trying to stamp out religion."

church. It is perhaps easier to say what it has not received. It has not gotten China to consent to the ordination of the roughly twenty bishop candidates identified by the Holy See within the patriotic church, some of whom have already been secretly ordained. Communist authorities have yet to accept a significant number of the underground church's bishops. In fact, of the forty or so underground bishops, only a couple received official recognition from the Communists.

The only thing that the Vatican and the Chinese authorities seem to have in common is a belief that there should only be one Catholic Church in China. For General Secretary Xi Jinping and his minions, that means eliminating the underground church. For the Vatican, it means encouraging everyone (without explicitly saying so) to join the Chinese Patriotic Catholic Association, which it seems to believe offers a safe, legal haven for Catholics to practice their faith.

But it doesn't. The Chinese Patriotic Catholic Association is merely an instrument that the CCP is using to bring all Catholics under its control. The ultimate goal of the atheistic Communists who run China remains the same: to destroy all religious faith within China's borders.

"When, before the signing of the Agreement we remained fearless and maintained our faith no matter how much we were coerced, the Holy See would have supported us, too," noted Underground Bishop Vincent Guo, who was removed from his diocese at the CCP's request. "But now, we're really helpless. To be frank, whoever persists [in not joining the PCA] will suffer greater suppression and persecution from the CCP."[26]

The road of persecution is still very long, Bishop Guo added, and Catholics must use it to strengthen their faith. Bishop Guo is living out his words on his own long via dolorosa as he tries to keep one step ahead of the Communist authorities.[27]

---

[26]   Mosher, "Faithful Chinese bishop on the run from communists highlights Vatican/China deal disaster." Bishop Guo, the underground bishop of a diocese in Fujian province, was forced by the Vatican to give up his see after the CCP demanded his resignation.

[27]   Mosher, "Faithful Chinese bishop on the run from communists highlights Vatican/China deal disaster."

Faith Forbidden, Churches Shut Down

"Religious groups must propagandize the principles and policies of the Chinese Communist Party . . . to all of their religious staff and followers; [they must] educate and guide all religious staff and followers to embrace the Chinese Communist Party's leadership, to embrace the socialist system, to uphold the path of 'Socialism with Chinese Characteristics.'"

—*Control Measures for Religious Groups*, Chinese Communist Party[28]

"Your Eminence, can we passively witness the murder of the Church in China by those who should protect and defend her from her enemies? Begging on my knees, your brother."

—Cardinal Joseph Zen[29]

In China, Catholic churches are being torn down or denuded of their crosses and statues. Signs are posted outside forbidding anyone under the age of eighteen from entering. Pictures of the Madonna and Child are being replaced with pictures of "People's Leader" Xi Jinping. The Ten Commandments are painted over with quotes from Xi.

Party apparatchiks have been trying to hound the underground Catholic Church out of existence for the past several years, closing down churches and hunting down priests and bishops. But the state-controlled patriotic church is facing a surprising new wave of persecution as well, despite its close connection to the authorities.

On February 1, 2020, new and even more rigorous controls were imposed on all religious activity in China. The "Control Measures for Religious Groups," as they are called, deal with every imaginable aspect of the life of the patriotic church—from Mass and the sacraments to meetings of the parish council and collections. All of these must be reported in advance to the government's "Religious Affairs" office for its approval.

---

[28] The "Control Measures for Religious Groups" were announced by the Communist Chinese government on December 30, 2019 and came into force on February 1, 2020. Nardi, "The 2019 Regulation for Religious Groups in China."

[29] Tosatti, "Cardinal Joseph Zen To His Brother Cardinals: The Church is Being Killed In China."

For Chinese believers, who understand how the Communist Party works in practice, the most chilling line is this open-ended threat: "Religious groups must report to the appropriate government authorities all other matters that should be reported."

In other words, even if the new control measures do not specifically require you to report a certain activity, you can still be found guilty of violating them. This trap now allows Communist officials to charge any religious group at any time with carrying out an unauthorized religious activity on the grounds that "you should have reported that to us and you didn't."

The party's goal in promulgating the control measures, which consist of forty-one different rules, is twofold. First, it wants to stamp out all religious groups, such as the underground Catholic Church, that it does not directly control.

As the third rule warns right at the outset: "Without the approval of the Religious Affairs office of the people's government, or registration with the Civil Affairs office of the people's government, a religious group cannot carry out any activities."[30] In other words, without the permission of the authorities, you can't even organize a Bible study.

Groups such as the Early Rain Covenant Church and the Falun Gong, which the state has already declared to be illegal "heretical cults," will obviously never be allowed to register. But neither will the bishops and priests of the underground church, meaning that all the activities of their dozens of dioceses and thousands of parishes will be illegal too—unless and until they agree to join the schismatic patriotic church.

But the control measures also made it clear that there is simply no "safe haven" for the faithful in China, in or out of the patriotic church. In fact, the new rules are intended to turn religious groups into junior partners of the CCP, while at the same time gradually strangling them out of existence altogether.

---

[30] Nardi, "The 2019 Regulation for Religious Groups in China."

While the immediate goal of the new rules is to widen the schism between the Holy See and the Chinese faithful, the long-term goal is much more ambitious: it is to extinguish faith in God altogether, replacing it with faith in the CCP.

This is clear from reading rule 17, which says:

- religious groups must propagandize the principles and policies of the Chinese Communist Party, along with national laws and regulations, to all of their religious staff and followers;
- [they must] educate and guide all religious staff and followers to embrace the Chinese Communist Party's leadership, to embrace the socialist system, to uphold the path of 'Socialism with Chinese Characteristics,' and to obey all national laws and regulations;
- [they must] correctly resolve the relationship between national laws and religious commandments.[31]

If this sounds like the party wants to use religious groups to strengthen its own hold on power, that's because it does. Any diocese or parish that refuses to be used in this way will be declared heretical and face punishment: its churches will be closed and its priests arrested. As for the priests themselves, they can either serve as junior political commissars or they can go home. Does that sound like a safe haven to you?

Rule 5 adds that, in addition to "upholding the leadership of the Chinese Communist Party and obeying the Constitution and national laws," religious groups must "uphold the principle of independence [from all foreign groups] and the overall policy of the sinicization of religion."[32]

Sinicization of religion, it should be noted, means replacing the worship of God with the worship of the CCP and its "core leader," Xi Jinping. This is precisely what the Nazis attempted to do in the 1930s with its so-called Nazification program—namely, turn the Catholic

31   Nardi, "The 2019 Regulation for Religious Groups in China."
32   Nardi, "The 2019 Regulation for Religious Groups in China."

and Protestant churches of Germany into ardent supporters of the Third Reich and promoters of its ideology of National Socialism.

And this is exactly what the CCP seeks to do today, not just to the Catholic Church but to every church, mosque, Taoist shrine, and Buddhist temple in China.[33]

Pope Francis has been increasingly silent where China is concerned. In the years following the original signing of the Sino-Vatican agreement, he did not utter a word about the agreement or the intensifying wave of persecution that Catholics in China were enduring as a result.

Cardinal Joseph Zen, the retired cardinal archbishop of Hong Kong and a critic of the Sino-Vatican agreement, responded to the silence of the hierarchy by issuing a heartfelt letter to the entire college of cardinals reminding them of their "grave responsibility to help the Holy Father in guiding the Church," including the Church in China. He pointed out that the agreement has been kept so secret by its authors, such as Cardinal Parolin, the Vatican's secretary of state, that they did not allow him, one of only two Chinese cardinals, to review it. The letter to the cardinals closes by saying: "Your Eminence, can we passively witness the murder of the Church in China by those who should protect and defend her from her enemies? Begging on my knees, your brother."[34]

Neither Pope Francis nor Cardinal Parolin, who negotiated the agreement with China, responded to Cardinal Zen's letter. Nor did either defend the good cardinal when politically motivated charges were filed against him by the new rulers of Hong Kong—the CCP.[35]

Catholics in China understand, even if Vatican officials don't, that the same instruments of manipulation and control that officials used so effectively in imposing the "one-child policy" on them for almost four decades are engaged in carrying out the Sinicization of religious bodies.

---

[33] Mosher, "How China's Xi Jinping destroyed religion and made himself God."
[34] Tosatti, "Cardinal Joseph Zen To His Brother Cardinals: The Church is Being Killed In China."
[35] Mosher, "Pope Francis is more interested in not offending Communist China than in defending Cdl. Zen."

Xi Jinping Is Utterly Hostile to Religion

"Sinicization means that all religious communities should be led by the Party, controlled by the Party, and support the Party."

—Xi Jinping[36]

"[Religious groups that refuse to follow the Party's direction] are foreign hostile forces and extremist forces that are using religion to infiltrate and sabotage our country, leading our religions in a direction that deviates from the path of socialism, and plotting politically to defeat and subvert China . . . [and will be] resolutely suppressed and eradicated."

—*Study Times,* March 21, 2022[37]

Because it conflicts with these larger ideological goals of the Chinese state, the Sino-Vatican agreement has faced enormous political headwinds from its inception. It has clearly not created more "space" for Catholic believers in China, as Cardinal Pietro Parolin, the Vatican secretary of state, had hoped, but rather, it has enabled the CCP to cloak its persecution of the underground church by intimating that it has been at least tacitly approved by the Vatican.

Xi Jinping already has more power than the late Chairman Mao Zedong and aspires for more. He is not only the head of the Communist Party, as Mao was, but also the head of the government and the military, which Mao wasn't. The Chinese people mockingly call him the chairman of everything. His cult of personality is growing. Like Mao, he wants the Chinese people to worship him, not the God of the Bible.

In December 2021, CCP general secretary Xi Jinping gave a speech at the National Conference on Work Related to Religious Affairs.[38]

---

[36] Hu Zimo, "Xi Jinping asks for more Marxism, more surveillance of the Web, more Sinicization."

[37] Xia Qiao, "New Directives on Sinicization of Religion: 'Love the Party, Love Socialism.'"

[38] A news report in Chinese about the speech can be found at https://tv.cctv.com/20 21/12/04/VIDE6GtJIKDI9YQ4PEl2wTSj211204.shtml?spm=C31267.PFsKSaKh6 QQC.S71105.3.

Xi emphasized that "religion and religious organizations must be actively guided to adapt to socialist society" and that those working on "religious affairs" within the party must take the Sinicization of religion as their major task. And lest there be any misunderstanding that Sinicization simply means making modest adaptations to Chinese culture, he stated, "Sinicization means that all religious communities should be led by the Party, controlled by the Party, and support the Party."[39]

Three months later, on March 21, 2022, an article was published in the *Study Times*, an official publication of the Central Committee of the CCP, laying out how Sinicization was to be accomplished through total control of religious organizations, their staff, and their doctrines by the party.[40]

The party, it says, intends to "strengthen the ideological and political guidance of religious circles, improve the political consciousness of the religious circles, guide the religious community to support the leadership of the CCP and the socialist system, unite closely around the Party Central Committee with Comrade Xi Jinping at the core, and firmly follow the path of socialism with Chinese characteristics."

Even if Catholics consent to these manifold infringements on their religious liberty, their ideological reeducation will still be far from complete. They will still have to "diligently study Xi Jinping Thought on Socialism with Chinese Characteristics for a New Era, to study the history of the Party, the history of New China, the history of reform and opening up, and the history of socialist development in a targeted manner, and to educate themselves deeply on the theme of 'Love the Party, Love the Country, Love Socialism.'"

Of course, some will fail this course of study because, as the article explains, some religions are simply incapable of being Sinicized. Specific reference was made to religious groups that "copy the foreign

---

[39]   Hu Zimo, "China: First CCP National Conference on Religion Held Since 2016."

[40]   Xia Qiao, "New Directives on Sinicization of Religion: 'Love the Party, Love Socialism.'"

teaching model, take foreign values as their standard, and even accept the orders and domination of foreign forces."

Those who refuse to submit to party control will be considered "foreign hostile forces and extremist forces that are using religion to infiltrate and sabotage our country, leading our religions in a direction that deviates from the path of socialism, and plotting politically to defeat and subvert China." Any religion that refuses to follow the party's direction in all things will be "resolutely suppressed and eradicated."[41] It is hard to see how such a formulation leaves any room for fruitful collaboration between the Vatican and the CCP, especially on the appointment of bishops.

What these guidelines bring into sharp focus is that the CCP only allows religious organizations to exist because they serve, in effect, as an extension of the party. The directive says that any religious group that does not teach socialism and the party line and does not teach its members to love the party and socialism is a "backward" religion engaged in "illegal religious activities" and is to be stamped out.[42]

And, of course, neither Christians nor anyone else in China can be allowed to forget their other "savior," Mao Zedong. In recent years, Christians in China have been told not to celebrate the birth of Christ and are being locked out of their churches on Christmas Day to make sure they don't. Instead, they are being told to celebrate the birth of "the other great man" who was born the following day. That would be Chairman Mao, who was born on December 26, 1893, and who grew up to murder many Christians—and sought to murder their church too.[43]

If there is a tiny light at the end of the dark night that the Catholic Church is now experiencing in China, it is this: when the fifth underground bishop, Bishop Paul Ma Cunguo of Shuozhou, joined

---

[41]   Xia Qiao, "New Directives on Sinicization of Religion: 'Love the Party, Love Socialism.'"

[42]   Mosher, "China Orders Churches to Promote the Chinese Communist Party—or Else."

[43]   Li Mingxuan, "Forget Christmas, Celebrate Mao Zedong."

the Patriotic Association in a quiet ceremony in late 2020, his oath of allegiance was much different from those made by the previous four bishops.

Those who preceded him were required to publicly swear "to work for an independent, self-governing church," a condition clearly in conflict with the Magisterium. As circulated on social media, Bishop Ma's oath did not include this phrase. Instead, he reportedly promised to "be faithful to the one, holy, Catholic and apostolic church, commit to building up the Church, the Body of Christ, and contribute to evangelization" and also to "abide by God's command, fulfill his pastoral duties as a bishop and proclaim the Gospel faithfully."[44]

The only potentially questionable part of the oath—depending on how it is interpreted—was a commitment to ensure that his diocesan priests would abide by the country's constitution and laws, uphold the unity of the nation and social harmony, love the country and the church, and contribute to the "realization of the Chinese dream."[45]

Xi Jinping's "China Dream" is to create a high-tech, digital dictatorship so powerful that it will dominate the world.

I think it is safe to say that Bishop Ma's dream for the Chinese people is rather different: to lead as many as possible to the Gospel and from there, home to heaven.

---

[44]   UCA News, "China's state church installs fifth underground bishop."
[45]   Mosher, "Catholicism a Casualty of China's New Cultural Revolution."

CHAPTER 15
MAO'S ENDURING SPECTOR

"Totalitarian states . . . systematically falsify the truth, exercise political control of opinion through the media, manipulate defendants and witnesses at public trials, and imagine that they secure their tyranny by strangling and repressing everything they consider 'thought crimes.'"

—*Catechism of the Catholic Church*[1]

"The Chinese Communist Party must remain vigilant to the false ideological trends of the present time as listed below: . . .
(6.) Promoting historical nihilism, trying to undermine the history of the CCP and of New China. (7.) Questioning . . . the socialist nature of 'socialism with Chinese characteristics.'"

—*Communique on the Current State of the Ideological Sphere*[2]

Seven Political Perils

Xi Jinping took office in late 2012 determined to get back to totalitarian basics. Chief among these were—to paraphrase the Catholic *Catechism*—systematically falsifying the truth, controlling public opinion through the media, punishing dissidents in show trials, and, in general, strangling and repressing everything the Chinese Communist Party (CCP) considered to be "thought crimes."

---

[1]   *CCC* 2499.
[2]   "Communiqué on the Current State of the Ideological Sphere," General Office, Central Committee of the Chinese Communist Party, (Document 9, April 2013). Translation by the author. The document is available in translation at https://www.chinafile.com/document-9-chinafile-translation.

In order to accomplish this, Xi quietly launched a political campaign right out of Chairman Mao's playbook. He circulated a secret directive in April 2013 warning party members that the stakes were high: "Western anti-China forces" were trying to carry out a "Color Revolution" in China and overthrow the CCP. In the directive, which came to be known as Document 9, Xi urged party members to strengthen their resistance to "infiltration by outside ideas," renew their commitment to work "in the ideological sphere," and "handle with renewed vigilance" all ideas, institutions, and people deemed threatening to continued one-party rule.[3]

Xi listed seven "political perils" in Document 9—which has the force of law in China—that party members were to guard against at all costs. Of these seven political perils, the first five will come as no surprise. They have been on every Communist dictator's watch list from Lenin onward; they harken back to the heyday of Mao Zedong. Echoing Mao, they call on party members to be on the lookout for Western-inspired threats from those who:

1. undermine the current CCP leadership and system of governance by promoting Western constitutional democracy;
2. threaten the core values of socialism by insisting that freedom, democracy, and human rights are universal values;
3. attempt to weaken the party's hold on the masses by advocating the growth of Western-style civil society;
4. try to change China's basic economic system by promoting the free market; and
5. undercut the party's control of the press by spreading the West's idea of journalism, the so-called freedom of the press.

But if these first five perils come from abroad, the last two are, in a sense, of the CCP's own making. The party, it turns out, considers an accurate accounting *of its own history and ideology* to be a threat to its

---

[3]   "Communiqué on the Current State of the Ideological Sphere."

continued political dominance. Document 9 bluntly describes these homegrown perils as anyone or anything that:

6. undermines the CCP and the New China by being skeptical or negative about the official Party history;
7. questions whether or not "Socialism with Chinese characteristics" or the "Reform and Opening" is really socialism.

Why do the CCP and its current leader, Xi Jinping, see the truth about themselves and their rule as their nemesis? Because Mao Zedong and other CCP leaders—after the fashion of totalitarian rulers everywhere—have been, as the *Catechism* says, "systematically falsifying the truth" from the very beginning. He spun a wondrous tale of a wholly new kind of society, selfless and communitarian, while in fact systematically constructing its opposite, a highly stratified system of rigid classes with himself perched firmly on the very top rung.

In fact, both the party's history and its ideology are complete and utter fabrications: the fake history is intended to deprive the Chinese people of their past, while the phony ideology is intended to deceive them about their future. While Mao called religion "poison" and Marx considered Christians to be "cowards" because they refused to face life without the crutch of religion, the true cowards are Xi Jinping and his ilk because they refuse to face the people without the crutch of Maoist myths and Communist fables. It is Communism, not religion, that is the true "opium of the people" used to drug the masses into unthinking compliance with their Maoist masters.

Given everything we now know about the fabricated history of the CCP and its longtime chairman, it is no wonder that the party has gone to great lengths to cover up Mao Zedong's sordid past, which constitutes so much of its own. By now, it should be obvious to the reader that the founder of the Red Regime was a moral monster, one of the great butchers of human history. It is precisely to hide this hideous past that Document 9 condemns anyone who "rejects the Party's judgement on historical events and figures, who disparages our

Revolutionary forebears, or who vilifies the Party's leaders." Here you have—in the space of one sentence—three successive warnings not to take Mao's name in vain.

What is at stake for the CCP is not just Mao's reputation, of course, but the continuing legitimacy of the regime that he founded. Indeed, one way to read the mythology that the party has concocted around Mao is as one long historical justification for the party's continued rule. This "history" is not, under any circumstances, to be questioned. Those who do, Document 9 warns bluntly, "are fundamentally undermining the CCP's historical purpose, which is the same thing as denying that the CCP has a legitimate right to rule China for the foreseeable future." They are traitors and counterrevolutionaries, in other words.

You can judge for yourself whether an accurate account of the founder of the "New China" would destroy whatever legitimacy the CCP still enjoys and constitute a mortal peril to its continued rule since you're reading one right now. Certainly, the CCP is convinced that its control over narratives of the past is the key to its hold on the future.

"History is a maiden, and you can dress her up anyway you want," goes an ancient Chinese saying. Disguising several hundred million decomposing corpses is a lot more work, but the CCP under Xi Jinping is sparing no effort as it adds to the total.

Xi Jinping: Mao's True Son

"When the Soviet Party was about to collapse, there was not one person who was man enough to turn back the tide."

—Xi Jinping[4]

"When the prophets are silent and society no longer possesses any channel of communication with the divine world, the way to the

---

[4]   *Ming Pao,* February 16, 2013. *Ming Pao*'s translation of Xi's remarks, from which the quote comes, is a diplomatic rendering of a much cruder remark: "The Soviet Party fell apart because no one had the balls to keep it together." Mao, crude peasant that he was, would have been proud. See also Lam, "Xi Jinping wants to be Mao but will not learn from the latter's mistakes."

lower depths is still open and man's frustrated spiritual powers will
find their outlet in the unlimited will to power and destruction."

—Christopher Dawson[5]

Upon being elected general secretary of the Chinese Communist Party on November 15, 2012, Xi Jinping gave a secret talk to the other senior leaders on the reasons behind the demise of the Communist Party of the Soviet Union. Xi laid the blame on "traitors" such as Mikhail Gorbachev and Boris Yeltsin, saying, "When the Soviet Party was about to collapse, there was not one person who was man enough to turn back the tide."

Xi Jinping took power on his promise to be "man enough" to destroy any and all enemies, foreign and domestic, to the continued rule of the CCP. But his "will to power" did not end there. He was not content merely to monopolize the three highest offices in China—general secretary of the CCP, chairman of the Central Military Commission, and chairman of the People's Republic of China—as his two immediate predecessors had.[6] Instead, at the same time that he was warning of the "seven deadly perils" facing the CCP at large, he was ruthlessly purging his way to unchallenged control of the party itself.

But instead of openly denouncing those within the party he wanted out of his way as "right opportunists" or "revisionists" as Mao had, Xi engaged in a subterfuge worthy of the Great Snake himself. He launched an anti-corruption campaign.

The Chinese Communist political system is notoriously corrupt, rife with graft, kickbacks, and secret deals. Virtually every CCP official in a position of power in China seeks to monetize their power in one way or another, which means that virtually everyone is guilty of corruption. This is such a widely recognized and frequently denounced evil in China that the other senior leaders found it impossible to object. The new general secretary straightaway set up an anti-corruption commission to carry out

---

5   Dawson, *Religion and Culture*, 83.
6   Though Xi Jinping is referred to as "president," a title that has a democratic sound about it, his actual title in Chinese is chairman of the People's Republic of China.

a nationwide campaign. In Xi's first few years in office alone, the commission arrested *a quarter of a million officials*, confiscating their wealth and sentencing them to long prison terms. Local and provincial officials were so terrified by the anti-corruption campaign that soon the mere arrival of party investigators was prompting some to commit suicide.

What was publicly billed as an anti-corruption campaign, however, was actually a thinly disguised campaign of terror against Xi's political enemies. Among the first to be charged were two senior members of the Central Military Commission and the head of the State Security Commission, the widely feared Zhou Yonggang. In a pattern that would become familiar, Xi took over Zhou's domestic security portfolio himself, ensuring that the police, the secret police, and the courts all reported to him. The Central Military Commission slots he filled with generals from Fujian province, where he had formerly served as party secretary. These had gotten on Xi's helicopter early, as the Chinese say, and now were able to "ride that helicopter" to the very top of the power pyramid.

Now in firm control of the military and the security forces, Xi began to restructure the party itself to consolidate his power. He reduced the number of seats on the Standing Committee of the Politburo, the party's top decision-making body, from nine to seven, thus enhancing his own authority. He reorganized the Central Military Commission and drew new boundaries for the military districts, both actions that enabled him to appoint new commanders who had sworn personal oaths of loyalty to him.[7]

He appointed himself to head important party committees on foreign policy, Taiwan, and the economy, and then, still not satisfied with his grip on power, he created new bodies overseeing everything from the internet and national security to government restructuring and military reform and, naturally, put himself in charge. He has even appointed himself to be commander-in-chief of the Joint Battle Command of the People's Liberation Army, whose meetings he attends decked out in a combat uniform. While an American president sports two titles—president and

---

[7]   Zhiyue, "Is China's PLA Now Xi's Army?"

commander-in-chief—Xi Jinping now has twelve and counting.[8] He is, as the Chinese snarkily refer to him, "the Chairman of Everything."

To prove that he is a worthy successor to the founder of the Red Dynasty, Xi models himself on Mao in all things. He wears baggy, unfashionable Mao suits to party gatherings and has reinstituted such Maoist practices as "self-criticism" sessions. He publishes collections of his speeches and sayings in a format identical to Mao's own "Selected Works" and has made them required reading for tens of millions of party members. Party propagandists, at his direction, have created a personality cult right out of the Cultural Revolution.

The masses are encouraged to refer to their new leader as Big Daddy Xi, an echo of the old Confucian trope of the emperor as a father to his people. "Big Daddy Xi" has replaced the name of "Mao Zedong" in China's most famous song, "The East is Red." The new rendition goes like this:

> China has produced a Big Daddy Xi,
> No tiger is too big for him to fight.
> He fears neither heaven nor earth,
> Dreamers all look to him!

> China also has a Mama Peng,
> Gift her flowers beautiful and fresh.
> Protect her, and bless her,
> Rise up family, rise up country, rise up Chinese empire![9]

Quotations from Xi's works blossom on village walls and appear on the screens of smartphones. In private homes, in the exact same space once occupied by large posters of Chairman Mao, equally large posters of Xi's beaming face gaze down upon his subjects.

---

[8] Chan, "How Xi Jinping has taken on multiple roles … an amassed unrivalled power in China."
[9] While the song was not, as far as we know, written by state propagandists, it has certainly been vigorously promoted by the state media. The song can be heard, in Chinese with English subtitles, at "New Hit 'Xi Dada Loves Peng Mama' Goes Viral Online," CRIENGLISH, November 24, 2014, http://english.cri.cn/12394/2014/11/24/2361s853616.htm.

Big Daddy Xi's repeated invocation of Maoist phrases and practices suggests he knows *exactly* what he is doing in channeling the late chairman. For instance, he has called for everyone to study the "mass line," a phrase that retired party official Bao Tong compared to "a magical obedience spell" which is cast by party leaders whenever they want to warn the Chinese people that they "won't be allowed to take part in elections or express their opinions [about political matters]."[10] Invented by Mao (not Marx) to purge cadres who did not bow to his wishes, the "mass line" was first used by the chairman as a political weapon in the Yan'an days, the central period of the Chinese Communist from 1936 to 1948 following the Long March.

But most older Chinese will instinctively associate it with the Cultural Revolution, when the demand for Maoist groupthink reached hysterical proportions, leaving millions of those who were suspected of harboring heretical thoughts dead.[11]

Xi's actions have matched his words. He has ramped up the detention of dissidents of all stripes and launched an internet crackdown.[12] One of the first to be arrested in Xi's crackdown was billionaire Chinese American businessman Charles Xue, who was detained in Beijing in August 2013 on the charge of soliciting a prostitute. Xue was held in jail without bail for eight months, branded a "moral degenerate," and before his release, was forced to make not one but two public confessions on state television for broadcast throughout China. Xue's televised confessions were reminiscent of Stalin's show trials—and, even more chillingly, of the "struggle sessions" of the Cultural Revolution. In a "struggle session," a regular feature of life in the harshest period

---

[10]   Bao Tong, "The Communist Party's 'Magic Spell of Obedience' in China."

[11]   And sometimes eaten. One of the more heinous practices of the Cultural Revolution was what could be called "political cannibalism." See, for example, Duff-Brown, "Scholars Continue to Reveal Mao's Monstrosities: Exiled Chinese Historians Emerge with Evidence of Cannibalism and up to 80 million Deaths under the Communist Leader's Regime."

[12]   See Shao Jiang, "A Nightmarish Year Under Xi Jinping's 'Chinese Dream: 2013 Annual Report on the Situation of Human Rights Defenders in China."

of Chairman Mao's rule, the chosen victim was publicly humiliated, beaten, and forced to confess to crimes he had not committed.[13]

There is little doubt that Xue's *real* crime—in the eyes of Xi Jinping and his censors—was criticizing the failures of the party-state on his social media account on Weibo. After all, he was one of the biggest of the "big V's"—as "verified" (publicly identified) Chinese bloggers are called—and under the pen name of Xue Manzi, he had some twelve million followers. Hegemons have long put fear into their critics by using a tactic known in China as "killing the chicken to warn the monkeys." In this case, Charles Xue was the sacrificial "chicken": a high-profile victim who was publicly pilloried in order to intimidate the other chattering internet "monkeys" into silence.[14]

Xi has rounded up dozens of activists, from human rights attorneys to those representing peasants whose hand has been misappropriated. Even those calling for officials to be more open about their wealth— an action that would seem to fit in well with the theme of Xi's own anti-corruption campaign—are being targeted.

The anti-corruption campaign continued as well, despite repeated calls by former senior leaders to end them. In early 2014, Jiang Zemin called for a halt to the anti-corruption drive when he apparently began to fear that his two sons would be targeted.[15] Even Hu Jintao's faction suffered a loss in December 2014 when the CCP's anti-corruption agency descended upon his closest ally, Ling Jihua, who was shortly thereafter fired from all his posts.[16] Xi Jinping was sending a message

---

[13] There are *zero* references to Charles Xue's high-profile case on Chinese state television's English-language service, which is careful to showcase only "positive" news about the Chinese party-state.

[14] See Patience, "Charles Xue 'Confession' Highlights China's Blogging Back-lash."

[15] Anderlini, "Ex-President Jiang Urges Beijing to Curb Anti-Corruption Drive." Jiang's eldest son, Jiang Mianheng, was subsequently dismissed from his government positions in early 2015 but was never prosecuted.

[16] The Central Commission for Discipline Inspection is responsible for enforc-ing internal rules and regulations and combating corruption and malfeasance in the party. Since the vast majority of officials at all levels of government are also Communist Party members, the commission is in practice the top anti-corruption

to all of China that the only patronage that mattered under his reign was his. In the years that followed, each time a senior party or government official was arrested for corruption, Xi would fill the vacancy with someone from his own ranks. By 2022, after ten years in office, he had packed the Central Committee of the CCP with his own supporters.

Deng Xiaoping, seeking to avert the rise of another Maoist monster, had attempted to impose term limits on future general secretaries, decreeing that no one was to hold the party's highest office for more than two five-year terms. This did not stop Xi from being unanimously elected to a third term by the members of the Central Committee at the Twentieth Party Congress, all of whom owed their positions to Xi's patronage.

The entire congress, which ran from October 16 to 22, was carefully scripted, with the exception of one shocking incident that happened on the final day. An "election" for seats on the Central Committee had just been held. Folders listing the names of the 205 selected were distributed to Xi Jinping and the other senior leaders sitting on stage.

Former party leader Hu Jintao was among these dignitaries. In fact, he was sitting immediately to Xi's left, a tribute not only to his seniority but also to his service as one of Xi's most faithful backers. Hu had supported his designated successor as general secretary for a decade as Xi ruthlessly eliminated political rivals one by one, even countenancing the purging of his closest comrade.

The drama began when Hu opened his folder, and we saw a look of astonishment and dismay appear on his face as he scanned the list of names within. He turned and began to speak urgently to Xi. He had been promised that his faction would be allowed to fill some of the seats on the Central Committee, observers report, and he just discovered that not a single one of his nominees made the list.

---

body in China. The overseas Chinese news agency Boxun reported on December 8, 2014, that around $13.4 billion worth of gold, calligraphy works, and antiques had been confiscated from Ling Lihua's estate, characterizing these as bribes to Ling by those who wanted to obtain official positions. This is a number so large that it is scarcely credible.

Xi appeared to ignore him and gestured to someone off-camera. Xi's bodyguard appeared and began to bodily lift an uncooperative Hu out of his seat. Hu struggled to free his arm while continuing to talk to Xi. He reached for his folder, but the bodyguard took the folder away from him. While the hundreds of Communist officials present sat stone-faced and stared straight ahead, another security official came and led Hu away. The Chinese government later explained that Hu, as he was in poor health, needed to "rest." Xi didn't summon medical personnel, however, but security.[17] Xi Jinping, like Mao before him, had betrayed his closest ally and the man who was perhaps most responsible for his rise.

To add insult to injury, this betrayal took place in full view of the entire Party Congress, who were now all on notice that Xi Jinping had made a clean sweep. By eliminating Hu Jintao and his faction, the last check on Xi's power was gone.

What had emerged from the boiling cauldron of the Communist Party's factional politics, in other words, was a creature all too familiar to students of Chinese Communist history. A new red emperor, as great and terrible as the old one, had arisen, one who relentlessly persecutes his enemies and who, when he has no further use for an ally, humiliates him in full public view.

Following the Party Congress, Xi quickly moved to consolidate his power even further. By March 2023, he had rewritten the rules governing the operation of the State Council—China's cabinet— greatly weakening the powers of China's government ministers while enhancing his own.[18] Ministers are now required to immediately "report any major decisions, major events and important situations" to the Central Committee. The result is that the authority to make executive decisions has been shifted to the various party committees that Xi himself heads. To further underline Daddy Xi's dominance,

---

[17] The best overview of what happened comes from Chinese dissident Jennifer Zeng. See Zeng, "Timeline and Reason of Hu Jintao's Removal, 8 Features of Xi Jinping's New Yes Team."

[18] Gu Ting, "China deletes Marxism, Leninism, Maoism, other ideologies from government rulebook."

the new rules reference only "Xi Jinping Thought." Not only have the thoughts of Hu, Jiang, and Deng gone down the memory hole, but references to Maoism, Leninism, and Marxism have also gone missing. The omission of the entire Communist pantheon was clearly calculated to shock Communist sensibilities: Xi's exalted "Thought" is now the only one that matters.

It was at this moment, too, that Xi Jinping decided it was time to abandon the pretext of an "anti-corruption campaign" and go directly to purging the ranks of party officials who were not personally loyal to him.[19] While other factions had been earlier eliminated from senior positions around the country, followers of the now-disgraced Hu Jintao still held many posts. Xi now wanted them gone. He had learned from Mao that it was better not to leave brooding, resentful people in positions of power where they might cause future problems. The party ranks must be cleansed of such "two-faced people" and "black sheep," echoed the man who will lead the purge, Li Xi, who said, "The sword that punishes evil and promotes good should never sleep."[20] The purge that followed, however, had nothing to do with good and everything to do with evil. Factional fighting within Communist parties is not all that different from gang warfare, with one gang—or party faction— seeking to overthrow another and take over the political turf they once controlled, whether it be a county town or a whole province.

It now seems likely that Big Daddy Xi, like Mao, will die in office. As the years pass, and as he is increasingly beset by maladies of mind, body, and soul, he may also, like Mao, become increasingly isolated, fearful, and irrational. The wages of sin, one might say. His movements are already a closely guarded secret, as is his personal life. He doesn't

---

[19]   Gu Ting, "China's ruling party gears up to purge 'black sheep,' 'two-faced people' from ranks."

[20]   Li Xi is Xi Jinping's hatchet man. As the secretary of the Central Commission for Discipline Inspection of the CCP, he is the Politburo member directly responsible for carrying out the purge. He was selected by Xi to join the seven-man Standing Committee of the Politburo of the Chinese Communist Party at the twentieth Party Congress in October 2022.

hold press conferences, and he doesn't explain himself—ever—to the lesser beings that he rules. And his personal physicians will never be allowed to leave the country, as Mao's longtime doctor was given leave to do, much less write a tell-all memoir.

But even without someone memorializing his decline, he will be hard-pressed to avoid Mao's fate: a lethal cocktail of megalomania and paranoia brought on by wild excesses of public adulation combined with constant fear of betrayal and assassination.

Had one of Mao Zedong's sons been able to succeed him, a Mao dynasty might well reign in today's China, as the Kim dynasty still does in North Korea. But Mao's eldest son, Mao Anying, died at twenty-eight years of age, killed in an American air strike on the Red Army's headquarters in North Korea at the beginning of the Korean War. His only other son, Mao Anqing, suffered from schizophrenia and was never active in politics.

But in Xi Jinping, the Man of Stone has found a fitting successor. He may not carry Mao's genes—except through the Yellow Emperor—but in all other ways, he is Mao's creature and heir.[21] A loathsome master of subterfuge and machination, like his forerunner, he knows when to feint and when to attack, when to lurk and when to withdraw. Driven by a cold-blooded lust for power and possessing a ferocious instinct for self-preservation, he is Mao's true son.

He was born not of Mao's loins, but out of his lies.

The Socialist Road to Economic Ruin—Again

"To carry forward the spirit of the Long March and succeed in our present long march, we must remain committed to the great ideal of communism and the common ideal of socialism with Chinese characteristics."

—Xi Jinping[22]

---

[21] Xi Jinping has encouraged Chinese citizens to "inherit the Red Gene" by re-committing themselves to the revolutionary spirit and history of the CCP using the "Thought of Xi Jinping" as their guiding principle. If anyone has "inherited the Red Gene," whose progenitor was Mao Zedong, it is Xi himself.

[22] Xi Jinping, "Speech at the Ceremony Commemorating the 80th Anniversary of the Victory of the Long March."

"Property . . . is the economic guarantee of human liberty, the external manifestation of inner responsibility. Deprive man of the right to fashion things according to his own will, and you deprive him, at one stroke, of the social basis of his freedom."

—Archbishop Fulton Sheen[23]

Xi Jinping's rise to power was accompanied by troubling signs that he was a hardcore Communist. His "doctorate" (in quotes because there is some question whether he was the actual author) is in "scientific socialism," an oxymoron if there ever was one. Soon after assuming office, he gave a secret speech to senior leaders in which—sounding like every other Communist from Karl Marx on—he predicted "the eventual demise of capitalism and the ultimate victory of socialism."[24] On other occasions, he has invoked "the great ideal of communism," suggesting that the expropriation of private property may once again be in the cards.

Many observers, both in China and abroad, dismissed this as mere rhetoric. However much Xi may model himself on Mao in other respects, from his relentless political campaigns to his personality cult, they insisted that he would never be so foolish as to follow Mao down the Socialist road to ruin. Who would abandon, or recklessly experiment with, a successful economic policy that has produced over three decades of mostly double-digit economic growth for China? Yet, as Xi progressively reduces the public space in which private enterprise is allowed to operate, that is exactly what he is doing.

Big Daddy Xi maintains that he doesn't object to people getting rich, as long as they use their wealth to serve the party's interests. But the reality is that, as with all true believers in Communism, the Chinese dictator has been killing off free enterprise in China—one billionaire at a time.

In the beginning, he faced quiet opposition from other senior leaders, many of whose families had gotten fabulously wealthy by running a kind of protection racket: They would protect wealthy entrepreneurs

---

23   Marlin, *The Quotable Fulton Sheen,* 250.
24   O'Conner, "China's Xi Says Socialism Will Defeat Capitalism Because Communist Party is 'Glorious.'"

from government scrutiny, along with the exactions of other corrupt officials, in return for a share of the take. The Xi family, too, reportedly has overseas bank accounts stuffed with cash. But by 2017, Big Daddy Xi decided it was not enough to target corrupt officials; it was time to rein in China's entrepreneurs as well.

First, just to make sure that the wealthy complied with his dictates, he put a watch on them. Every major non-state-owned company in China was ordered to add a CCP representative to its board, and every company with more than fifty employees was required to set up a Communist Party branch. The wealthy were now living on borrowed time.

Placing party members on the boards of private corporations meant that wealth creators all of a sudden had targets on their backs. After all, in the minds of rapacious Communist officials, the best way to eliminate capitalism is to eliminate the capitalists themselves. And if some of the confiscated wealth from the capitalists winds up in their own pockets, so much the better. One after another, wealthy businessmen and women began being charged with various crimes. China's wealthiest woman, Whitney Duan, was snatched from her Beijing apartment by the security forces in 2017.[25] The anti-corruption campaign had begun claiming a whole new class of victims.

In 2020, the war on the wealthy in China picked up steam. Taking their cues from Xi's increasing hostility toward private enterprise, government officials at all levels began arresting, imprisoning, executing, and even "suiciding" their wealthy.[26] Literally, hundreds of Chinese billionaires and CEOs have been disappeared over the past few years. Some, like Whitney Duan, are still missing, while others have emerged a few weeks or months later in recorded propaganda videos, robotically expressing their undying devotion to the party and Chairman Xi.[27]

---

[25] Mosher, "China's Wealthiest Woman, Whitney Duan, Disappears Without a Trace."
[26] Mosher, "Communist Road Kill: Xi Jinping is Carry Out a War on China's Wealthy."
[27] O'Neill, "Scores of Chinese Billionaires and CEOs have Disappeared in State-Sanctioned Abductions."

Others are serving long prison sentences. In September 2020, Ren Zhiqiang, a real estate mogul who criticized Xi's handling of the pandemic, was jailed for eighteen years on corruption charges.[28] In August, Sun Dawu, a Chinese agricultural mogul, received a similar sentence for "provoking trouble."[29] This is a one-size-fits-all charge that, like "corruption," is frequently levied against those the regime targets.

In addition to reeducation or long prison terms, some Chinese billionaires have simply been executed.[30]

No one, however wealthy, is exempt. Even Jack Ma, once China's wealthiest man, was disappeared in late 2020 after he publicly criticized China's banking system.[31] Ma's company, e-commerce giant Alibaba, which he created using stolen US technology, has been downsized by regulators and its stock price has plummeted.[32] Ma himself is reportedly undergoing "reeducation" at the hands of party officials in a secret location. The party did release one brief "proof-of-life" video of the tech tycoon to quell rumors that he had been executed, but it appears doubtful that he will ever be free again.

China is eating its billionaires, one by one. And as tempting as it is to blame a single evil man for this outcome, as billionaire George Soros has attempted to do, the devil is also in the Communist system itself.[33] It was Mao who forged the one-party dictatorship that, by concentrating power in the hands of a few top leaders, created the deadly weapon that Xi is now wielding as an absolute dictator.

A Communist party's politburo is the perfect breeding ground for power-hungry megalomaniacs who dream of becoming the "chairman of everything." In other words, if Xi hadn't come along when he did,

28 *The Guardian,* "Ren Zhiqiang—who called Chinese president a 'clown'—jailed for 18 years."
29 Davidson, "Chinese billionaire pig farmer jailed for 'provoking trouble.'"
30 MacDonald, "China Executes Former Head of Asset Management Firm in Bribery Case."
31 Kennedy, "Why Alibaba's Joe Tsai gets to party but Jack Ma is punished by China."
32 Kennedy, "Who is Jack Ma? Where the Alibaba Co-founder came from and disappeared to."
33 Soros, "Xi's Dictatorship Threatens the Chinese State."

some other Mao clone would have. Atheistic Communism—"lawless and godless," as Mao once remarked—churns out Lenin, Stalin, Mao, and Castro clones like a donut shop churns out donuts. It was only a matter of time before this diseased tree produced another poisoned fruit.

Couple General Secretary Xi with a Communist Party apparatus that's naturally suspicious of everyone outside of its immediate control, whether those are members of religious groups or private entrepreneurs, and you have the perfect recipe for an all-embracing tyranny. And officials hardly need to be encouraged to help Xi kill the geese that lay the golden eggs in the hope that they can steal a few in the process.

We know how this tale ends. Whenever one-party dictatorships decide that producing tyranny is more important than producing the goods—as they all do sooner or later—economic collapse and famine follow.

Does anyone remember the New Economic Policy of the early Soviet Union? Vladimir Lenin so leveled the economy in his forced march toward Communism in the early 1920s that he was forced to allow private enterprise to return, lest everyone in Russia starve to death. Entrepreneurs stepped forward, only to be crushed by Stalin a decade later when Lenin's successor decided that it was time to once again exert total control.

The same sad scenario is now slowly playing out in China.

The Devil and Chinese Communism
Is a Match Made in Hell

"Communism is not love. Communism is a hammer we use to crush the enemy."

—Mao Zedong[34]

"In contrast to this Christian philosophy of forgiveness, there exists for the first time in the history of the world a philosophy and a political and social system based not on love, but on hate, and that is Communism."

—Archbishop Fulton Sheen[35]

---

[34] Mao Zedong, *On Practice and Contradiction.*
[35] Sheen, *The Cross and the Beatitudes,* 11.

It is hard to imagine two men who had less in common than Chairman Mao Zedong and Archbishop Fulton Sheen. The distance between the thoughts, words, and deeds of these two towering twentieth-century figures, one the leading Chinese Communist and the other the saintly archbishop, spans the distance between heaven and hell. Yet they strongly agreed on one thing. Communism, they both insisted, was inspired not by love but by hate, and that it was precisely that hate that gave it its terrible power to destroy.

Mao, for his part, exulted in the destructive power that this hate unleashed. "Communism is not love," he once gloated. Driving the point home, he added, "Communism is a hammer we use to crush the enemy." Coming from someone who wielded the hammer of Communism so effectively that he became the greatest mass murderer in human history, Mao's description of Communism as hate weaponized should give us all pause.

While Mao was celebrating the deadly utility of Communism, Archbishop Fulton Sheen was at pains to distinguish this ideology of hate from its opposite, Christianity, which is centered upon love. In his first book, entitled *The Cross and the Beatitudes*, he wrote, "In contrast to [the] Christian philosophy of forgiveness, there exists for the first time in the history of the world a philosophy and *a political and social system based not on love, but on hate, and that is Communism*."[36]

Sheen continued, "Communism believes that the only way it can establish itself is by inciting revolution, class-struggle, and violence. Hence its regime is characterized by a hatred of those who believe the family is the basic unit of society. The very Communistic gesture of the clenched fist is a token of its pugnacious and destructive spirit, and a striking contrast indeed to the nailed hand of the Savior pleading forgiveness for the clenched-fist generation who sent Him to the Cross."[37]

Mao Zedong, in the name of this hateful ideology, sent tens of millions of people to their deaths. None of his deadly actions ever seem

---

[36]   Sheen, 11, italics added.
[37]   Sheen, 11.

to have occasioned an ounce of contrition or a moment of remorse on his part. In fact, in a way that can only be described as diabolical, Mao seems to have celebrated death as a necessary weeding of the human garden. "What does it matter if a third of the population dies," he said. "Their bodies will fertilize the soil." That was what he thought of those he ground into oblivion: they were only useful as human compost.

"Hatred of God comes from pride,"[38] and few in the economy of evil have been as prideful, self-centered, and narcissistic as the man born in the Year of the Snake. A godless creature like Mao is a prefiguring of the antichrist, if not himself a lesser example of what awaits us at the end of time. He may not have made a conscious pact with the devil, as Marx seems to have come close to doing, but he certainly embraced every evil known to God and man. He longed to be the prince of this world—a dangerous ambition, indeed, since those who are driven by it generally wind up serving, whether they are aware of it or not, the real prince of this world, Satan himself.

We are in no position to impose a final judgment on Mao, or on any other human being, however much evil they may have wrought in their lives. Such dispositions are the sole province of God, who is the final arbiter of the souls He created. The only person that we can be certain is in hell is Judas Iscariot, about whom Our Lord said, "It would have been better for that man if he had not been born" (Mt 26:24). No one else is beyond the reach of redemption, although in Mao's case, it certainly would have been a very long reach.

In the last years of his life, Mao often remarked to visitors that he would soon be going to be with Marx. It seems clear from his descent into the depths of human wickedness that, given a choice—and we always have a choice—he would choose to reign in hell rather than serve in heaven. But hell, of course, already has a hellish master. It is hard to avoid the suspicion that behind Mao the Snake lurked the great dragon himself, waiting to devour him.

---

[38] *CCC* 2094.

While we are not allowed to know the eternal destiny of most souls, we surely must judge the ideologies of men and the political and social systems they create. This is especially true of the ideological system that Marx created, Lenin institutionalized, and Mao took to unprecedented heights of malevolence. Communism is based on hate, and the political system that it creates is a force multiplier for evil. Archbishop Fulton Sheen's "clenched fist" is a modern-day hammer of Baal, one that not only bedeviled the last century of humanity but still threatens to engulf the world—and the United States—in the present day.

In this book, I have outlined the industrial-sized massacres that the Maoist variant of Communism engaged in to, first, seize power and, later, to impose its will on the Chinese people. This was not a regrettable necessity, much less an accidental byproduct, of a noble effort to build a new and just society, as it is portrayed by its sympathizers, both Chinese and Western. Rather, it was a deliberate slaughter of any and all people—from elderly scholars to unborn babies—who were considered in some way to be a threat to the regime, its designs, or its leaders.

The history of the CCP is a century-long illustration of what Archbishop Fulton Sheen was referring to when he said, "Communism believes that the only way it can establish itself is by inciting revolution, class-struggle, and violence." What he doesn't say is that since evil is ultimately self-defeating, Communism can never truly "establish itself." Likewise, since hate is its very fuel, the violence must continue forever. There will always be some new enemy—a class, a religion, an ethnicity, a foreign adversary—to struggle with. There must be, lest the muscular rigor of the system be lost and the engine of totalitarianism grind to a halt. Such reckless, undying hate can only have one origin: Satan himself.

The ultimate instigator of the evil ideology that is Communism, based as it is on hate and not love, is the prince of darkness. That's why it is the sworn enemy of all that is good, true, and beautiful. Communism is not just a false gospel; it is, in a very real sense, the anti-gospel, Satan's latest and most successful attempt to turn man away from his Creator.

Lucifer's *non serviam* continues to echo down the ages and find human echoes. When you are looking at the history of Communism in China, North Korea, Vietnam, or Cambodia, you are looking at one of the many faces of Satan's rebellion against God.

As Catholics, we must reject the hatred preached and the violence practiced by Communism and embrace a life of mercy and compassion for others. We must echo Mary's fiat in our own lives, enthrone Jesus in our hearts, and live out the Father's commandments while we are on earth. We must commit to a life of sexual purity within the sanctity of Matrimony or Holy Orders. We must be open to the bearing of children and love, protect, and champion those God sends us. In this way, we will create a civilization of life and love, beginning with the primary building block of that civilization: our own families.

But even this is not enough. Just as we resist evil in our own lives and those of our families, we must also reject the evil ideology that enabled them. We are blessed to enjoy freedom of speech and to live in a democracy. We contribute to the public debate on issues of import. We elect the men and women who make the laws under which we all live. If we are to reject Satan and all his works, then as a country, we must reject Communism as well.

Mao began his journey to Communism by rejecting God. America needs to begin its journey back to Christian civilization by rejecting Communism, under whatever seductive guises it is presented to us.

BIBLIOGRAPHY

Aird, John. *Slaughter of the Innocents*. Washington: AEI Press, 1990.

Amnesty International. "China 2020." 2020. https://www.amnesty.org/en/lo cation/asia-and-the-pacific/east-asia/china/report-china/.

Amnesty International. "Vietnam 2020." Amnesty.org, accessed March 21, 2022. https://www.amnesty.org/en/location/asia-and-the-pacific/south-east-asia -and-the-pacific/viet-nam/report-viet-nam/.

Amnesty International. "Vietnam: Surge in Number of Prisoners of Conscience, New Research Shows." Amnesty.org, May 13, 2019. https://www.amnesty .org/en/latest/news/2019/05/viet-nam-surge-number-prisoners-conscience -new-research-shows/.

Anderlini, Jamil and Simon Rabinovich. "Ex-President Jiang Urges Beijing to Curb Anti-Corruption Drive." *Financial Times,* March 31, 2014. http:// www.ft.com/intl/cms/s/0/1bc9c892-b8c7-11e3-a189-00144feabdc0.html #axzz3U6tWnSra.

Associated Press. "United States 'abondoned Cambodia and handed it over to the butcher' during pullout 40 years ago: ex-ambassador." *Daily News,* April 10, 2015. https://www.nydailynews.com/news/world/u-s-abandoned-cambodia -1975-pullout-ex-ambassador-article-1.2180529.

Augustine of Hippo. *The City of God*. Catholic Way Publishing, 2015.

AZ Quotes. "Mao Zedong Quotes." AZ Quotes, accessed August 14, 2023. https:// www.azquotes.com/author/16154-Mao_Zedong?p=2.

AZ Quotes. "Pol Pot Quotes." AZ Quotes, accessed July 5, 2023. https://www.az quotes.com/author/22621-Pol_Pot.

Bao Tong. "The Communist Party's 'Magic Spell of Obedience' in China." Radio Free Asia Commentaries, September 16, 2013. http://www.rfa.org/english /commentaries/baotong/spell-09162013105548.html.

Barboza, David. "Billions in Hidden Riches for Family of Chinese Leader." *New York Times*, October 25, 2012. http://www.nytimes.com/2012/10/26/business/glo bal/family-of-wen-jiabao-holds-a-hidden-fortune-in-china.html?pagewanted= all&_r=0.

BBC News. "Vietnam Profile – Timeline." BBC News, April 22, 2018. https:// www.bbc.com/news/world-asia-pacific-16568035.

Becker, Jasper. *Hungry Ghosts: Mao's Secret Famine*. New York: Henry Holt, 1996.

Bennett-Jones, Owen. "Vietnam's Two-Child Policy." BBC, November 8, 2000.

Bergere, Marie-Claire. *Sun Yat-sen*. Redwood City: Stanford University Press, 1998.

Bodde, Derk. *Cambridge History of China*. Vol. 1. Cambridge University Press, 1986.

Braun, Otto. *A Comintern Agent in China, 1934-39*. London: Hurst, 1982.

Brewer, Kirstie. "How Two Men Survived a Prison Where 12,000 Were Killed." *BBC News*, June, 11, 2015. https://www.bbc.com/news/magazine-3309 6971.

Brown, Clayton. "China's Great Leap Forward." *Education About Asia* 17, no. 3 (2012): 31.

Burkhardt, V. R. *Chinese Creeds and Customs*. Volume II. Hong Kong: South China Morning Post, 1955.

Byron, John and Robert Pack. *The Claws of the Dragon: Kang Sheng - The Evil Genius Behind Mao - And His Legacy of Terror in People's China*. New York: Simon & Schuster, 1992.

Cambodia Tribunal Monitor, "Chronology of the Khmer Rouge Movement." *Cambodia Tribunal Monitor,* accessed January 29, 2022. https://cambodiatribunal.org/history/cambodian-history/chronology-of-the-khmer-rouge-movement/.

Castelfranco, Sabina. "Pope Calls for Chinese Catholics to Work Toward Reconciliation." *VOA*, September 26, 2018. https://www.voanews.com/a/pope-calls-for-chinese-catholics-to-work-toward-reconciliation/4588253.html.

Cervellera, Bernardo. "China-Vatican agreement: some positive steps, but without forgetting the martyrs." AsiaNews, September 24, 2018. http://www.asianews.it/news-en/China-Vatican-agreement:-some-positive-steps,-but-without-forgetting-the-martyrs-45023.html.

Chan, Minnie. "How Xi Jinping has taken on multiple roles … an amassed unrivalled power in China." *South China Morning Post*, January 27, 2017. www.scmp.com/news/china/article/2065833/how-xi-jinping-has-taken-multiple-roles-and-amassed-unrivalled-power.

Chandler, David P. *Brother Number One: A Political Biography of Pol Pot*. Boulder, San Francisco, and Oxford: Westview Press, 1992.

Chandler, David. *Terror and History in Pol Pot's Secret Prison*. Berkeley: University of California Press, 1999.

Chang, Jung and Jon Halliday. *Mao: The Unknown Story*. New York: Knopf, 2005.

Changming Hu and Shengsheng Liu. A Few Historical Facts on Mao Zedong's First Marriage. [In Chinese.] Research on Mao Zedong Thought, 1996.

Cheek, Timothy. *Mao Zedong and China's Revolutions: A Brief History With Documents*. New York: Palgrave, 2002.

Chen Muhua. "In order to Realize the Four Modernizations, We Must Control Population Growth in a Planned Way." *Renmin Ribao* [People's Daily], August 11, 1979.

"China 2020." Amnesty International. 2020. https://www.amnesty.org/en/location/asia-and-the-pacific/east-asia/china/report-china/.

China Power. "How does corruption hinder China's development." China Power Project, CSIS, April 26, 2023. https://chinapower.csis.org/china-corruption-development/.

Chindawongse, Suriya. "Pol Pot's Strategy of Survival." *The Fletcher Forum of World Affairs* 15, no. 1 (1991): 132. http://www.jstor.org/stable/45290122.

Chinese Communist Party. "The CCP's May 16th Circular (1966)." Alpha History, May 16, 1966, https://alphahistory.com/chineserevolution/ccp-may-16th -circular-1966/.

Chong, Woei Lien. *China's Great Proletarian Cultural Revolution: Master Narratives and Post-Mao Counternarratives.* Lanham: Rowman and Littlefield Publishers, 2002.

Chuang Tzu. "The Chuang Tzu." Dankalia (website). Translated by Lin Yutang. http://www.dankalia.com/literature/chuantzu/chn030.htm.

Clayton, Thomas. "Building the New Cambodia: Educational Destruction and Construction under the Khmer Rouge, 1975-1979." *History of Education Quarterly* 38, no. 1 (1998): 2. https://doi.org/10.2307/369662.

Clubb, Kathy. "Steve Mosher on the Sino-Vatican Agreement." The Freedoms Project, December 2, 2019. https://www.thefreedomsproject.com/item/462 -steve-mosher-on-the-sino-vatican-agrement.

Confucius. *The Book of Rites.* Edited by Dai Sheng. Translated by James Legge. Boston: Intercultural Press, 2013.

Courtois, Stéphane, Nicolas Werth, Jean-Louis Panne, Andrzej Paczkowski, Karel Bartosek, and Jean-Louis Margolin. *The Black Book of Communism: Crimes, Terror, Repression.* Translated by Jonathan Murphy and Mark Kramer. Harvard University Press, 1999.

Davidson, Helen. "Chinese billionaire pig farmer jailed for 'provoking trouble.'" *The Guardian,* July 28, 2021. https://www.theguardian.com/world/2021/jul/28 /chinese-billionaire-pig-farmer-sun-dawu-jailed-for-provoking-trouble.

Davies, Nick. "Vietnam 40 Years On: How a Communist Victory Gave Way to Capitalist Corruption." *The Guardian,* April 22, 2015. https://www.theguar dian.com/news/2015/apr/22/vietnam-40-years-on-how-communist-victory -gave-way-to-capitalist-corruption.

Dawson, Christopher. *Religion and Culture.* Washington, DC: Catholic University of America Press, 2013.

The Democratic Republic of Vietnam. *Declaration of Independence of the Democratic Republic of Vietnam.* September 2, 1946. http://inside.sfuhs.org/dept/his tory/US_History_reader/Chapter11/vietnamindep.pdf.

Dickens, Charles. *A Christmas Carol.* London: Chapman & Hall, 1843.

Dikötter, Frank. *The Cultural Revolution: A People's History, 1962-1976.* New York: Bloomsbury Press, 2016.

Dikötter, Frank. *Mao's Great Famine: The History of China's Most Devastating Catastrophe, 1958-1962.* New York: Bloomsbury, 2010.

Dikötter, Frank. *The Tragedy of Liberation.* New York: Bloomsbury Press, 2013.

Domes, Jurgen. *Peng Te-huai: The Man and the Image.* London: C. Hurst & Company, 1985.

Duff-Brown, Beth. "Scholars Continue to Reveal Mao's Monstrosities: Exiled Chinese Historians Emerge with Evidence of Cannibalism and up to 80 million Deaths under the Communist Leader's Regime." *Los Angeles Times,* November 20, 1994.

Ellis-Petersen, Hannah. "Cambodia: Hun Sen re-elected in landslide victory after brutal crackdown." *The Guardian, July 29,* 2018. https://www.theguardian .com/world/2018/jul/29/cambodia-hun-sen-re-elected-in-landslide-victory -after-brutal-crackdown.

Engels, Frederick. *The Origin of the Family, Private Property, and the State.* Edited by Eleanor B. Leacock. New York: International Publishing Company, 1972.

Fan You. "Tian Jiyun Addresses Population Meeting." *Guangming Ribao,* April 14, 1989, FBIS, No. 89-084, May 3, 1989.

Fischer, Louis. *The Life of Lenin.* London: Weidenfeld and Nicolson, 1964.

Fischer, Ruth. "Ho Chi Minh: Disciplined Communist." *Foreign Affairs* 33, no. 1 (1954): 86–97. https://doi.org/10.2307/20031077.

Fu, Zhengyuan. *Autocratic Tradition and Chinese Politics.* Cambridge: Cambridge University Press, 1994.

Fu, Zhengyuan. *China's Legalists: The Earliest Totalitarians and Their Art of Ruling.* Armonk, New York: M. E. Sharpe, 1996.

Gao Wenqian. *Zhou Enlai: The Last Perfect Revolutionary.* New York, NY: Public Affairs, 2007.

Giglio, James N. *The Presidency of John F. Kennedy.* 2nd ed. University of Kansas Press, 2006.

Global Security. "The Domino Theory." Global Security, accessed January 24, 2022. https://www.globalsecurity.org/military/ops/vietnam2-domino-theory.htm.

Gough, Kathleen. "Roots of the Pol Pot Regime in Kampuchea." *Contemporary Marxism,* no. 12/13 (1986): 14. https://www.jstor.org/stable/29765842.

Greenhalgh, Susan. *Just One Child: Science and Policy in Deng's China.* Berkeley, Los Angeles: University of California Press, 2008.

Gu Ting. "China deletes Marxism, Leninism, Maoism, other ideologies from government rulebook." *Radio Free Asia,* March 29, 2023.www.rfa.org/english /news/china/new-rulebook-03292023124017.html.

Gu Ting. "China's ruling party gears up to purge 'black sheep,' 'two-faced people' from ranks." *Radio Free Asia,* March 24, 2023. www.rfa.org/english/news/ch ina/purge-black-sheep-03242023131601.html.

The Guardian, "Ren Zhiqiang—who called Chinese president a 'clown'—jailed for 18 years." *The Guardian,* September 22, 2020. https://www.theguardian .com/world/2020/sep/22/ren-zhiqiang-who-called-chinese-president -a-clown-jailed-for-18-years.

Guy, Josephine. "Women and Child Abuse in China." *PRI Review* 11(4), September-October 2001.

Han Suyin. *The Morning Deluge.* Boston, Massachusetts: Little Brown, 1972.

Harden, Blaine. *Escape From Camp 14: One Man's Remarkable Odyssey from North Korea to Freedom in the West.* New York: Penguin, 2013.

Holcomb, Charles. *A History of East Asia: From the origins of Civilization to the Twenty-first Century.* Cambridge: Cambridge University Press, 2017.

Holubnychy, V. "Mao Tse-tung's Materialistic Dialectics," *China Quarterly* 19 (July–September 1964).

Hu Zimo. "China: First CCP National Conference on Religion Held Since 2016." *Bitter Winter,* December 8, 2021. https://bitterwinter.org/china-ccp -national-conference-on-religion/.

Hu Zimo. "Xi Jinping asks for more Marxism, more surveillance of the Web, more Sinicization." Bitter Winter, December 8, 2021. https://bitterwinter.org/chi na-ccp-national-conference-on-religion/.

Hucker, Charles O. *China's Imperial Past.* Stanford: Stanford University Press, 1975.

Human Rights Watch. "Cambodia: Khmer Rouge Convictions, 'Too Little, Too Late.'" Human Rights Watch, August 8, 2014. https://www.hrw.org/news /2014/08/08/cambodia-khmer-rouge-convictions-too-little-too-late.

Human Rights Watch. "Vietnam: Dozens of Rights Activists Detained, Tried." Human Rights Watch, January 13, 2022. https://www.hrw.org/news/2022 /01/13/vietnam-dozens-rights-activists-detained-tried.

Human Rights Watch. *World Report 2020: Events of 2019.* New York: Human Rights Watch, 2020.

Johnson, Sam. "I Spent Seven Years as a Vietnam POW. The Hanoi Hilton is No Trump Hotel." *Politico Magazine,* July 21, 2015. https://www.politico.com /magazine/story/2015/07/i-was-vietnam-pow-donald-trump-120436/.

Kengor, Paul. *The Devil and Karl Marx.* Charlotte, NC: TAN Books, 2020.

Kengor, Paul. *The Politically Incorrect Guide to Communism: The Killingest Idea Ever.* Regnery, 2017.

Kennedy, Dana. "Who is Jack Ma? Where the Alibaba Co-founder came from and disappeared to." *New York Post,* January 10, 2021. https://nypost.com/artic le/who-is-jack-ma-where-alibaba-founder-cam-from-disappeared-to/.

Kennedy, Dana. "Why Alibaba's Joe Tsai gets to party but Jack Ma is punished by China." *New York Post,* August 14, 2021. https://nypost.com/2021/08/14 /alibabas-joe-tsai-gets-to-party-but-china-punishes-jack-ma/.

Kennedy, John F. "Inaugural Address." National Archives, January 20, 1961. https://www.archives.gov/milestone-documents/president-john-f-kennedys -inaugural-address.

Kim Il Sung. "Let us Provide Active Support for the Revolutionary Struggle of the Chinese People." (1945), accessed May 6, 2023. www.marxists.org/archive /kim-il-sung/1945/09/15.pdf.

Kim Il Sung. "On Further Accelerating Socialist Rural Construction." Speech Delivered at the National Conference of Agricultural Workers, February 7, 1969 (DPR Korea: Foreign Languages Publishing House, 2023). http:// www.marxists,org/archive/kim-il-sung/1969/02/07.pdf.

Kim Il Sung. *With the Century,* "Comment to Cheondoist independence activ- ist Kim In Jin in 1936." (Pyongyang: Workers' Party of Korea Publishing House, 1992.

Lam, Willy. "Xi Jinping wants to be Mao but will not learn from the latter's mis- takes." *AsiaNews.it,* January 1, 2014. http://www.asianews.it/news-en/Xi-Jin ping-wants-to-be-Mao-but-will-not-learn-from-the-latters-mistakes-31787 .html.

Laux, John. *Church History: A Complete History of the Catholic Church to the Present Day.* Rockford, IL: TAN Books and Publishers, Inc., 1989.

Li Mingxuan. "Forget Christmas, Celebrate Mao Zedong." *Bitter Winter*, January 14, 2020. https://bitterwinter.org/forget-christmas-celebrate-mao-zedong/.

Li Si. "Memorial on the Burning of Books." *Shi Ji* 87:6b–7a. In Theodore de Bary, Wingtsit Chan, and Burton Watson, eds. *Sources of Chinese Tradition.* New York: Columbia University Press, 1960.

Li Yizhe. "On Socialist Democracy." In *On Socialist Democracy and the Chinese Legal System.* Edited by A. Chan, Stanley Rosen, and J. Unger. Armonk, New York: Sharpe, 1985.

Li Zhisui. *The Private Life of Chairman Mao: The Memoirs of Mao's Personal Physician.* New York: Random House, 1994.

Liu Binyan. "An Unnatural Disaster." *The New York Review of Books*, April 8, 1993.

Liu Xiaobo. "The Roots of Chinese 'Patriotism.'" *No Enemies, No Hatred: Selected Essays and Poems.* Cambridge: Harvard University Press, 2012.

Liu Ying. *Zai lishi de jiliu zhong* [In the Tidal Waves of History]. Beijing: Zhonggong dangshi chubanshe, 1994.

Long, Vincent. "St. John Paul II, 'Work is for man, not man for work.'" *Catholic Outlook*, December 2016. https://catholicoutlook.org/st-john-paul-ii-work-is-for-man-not-man-for-work/. .

Ma Licheng and Ling Zhijun. *Confrontation: Three Ideological Emancipation Records in Contemporary China.* [In Chinese.] China: Hubei People's Publishing House, 2008. https://books.google.com/books/about/%E4%BA%A4%E9%94%8B.html?id=svkQAQAAMAAJ.

MacDonald, Joe. "China Executes Former Head of Asset Management Firm in Bribery Case." The Associated Press, January 29, 2021. https://www.bloomberg.com/news/articles/2021-01-29/china-finance-official-executed-in-bribery-case?leadSource-uverify%20wall.

Mao Zedong. *Mao's Road to Power: Revolutionary Writings 1912-1949.* Vol. 1, *The Pre-Marxist Period, 1912–1920.* Edited by Stuart Schram and Nancy Jane Hodes. Armonk, NY: M. E. Sharpe, 1992.

Mao Zedong. *Mao's Road to Power: Revolutionary Writings 1912-1949.* Vol. 3, *From the Jinggangshan to the establishment of the Jiangxi Soviets, July 1927-December 1930.* Edited by Stuart Schram and Nancy Jane Hodes. Armonk, NY: M. E. Sharpe, 1995.

Mao Zedong. *Mao Zedong wenji* [Works of Mao Zedong]. Vol. 7. Beijing: People's Press, 1999.

Mao Zedong. *Mao Zedong zhuzuo zhuanti zhaibian* [Excerpts from Works of Mao Zedong by Topic]. Beijing: Central Document Publishing House, 2003.

Mao Zedong. *Mao Zhuxi shici sanshiqi shi* [Thirty-seven poems of Chairman Mao]. Beijing: Renmin chubanshe, 1964.

Mao Zedong. *On People's Democratic Dictatorship: written in commemoration of the 28th anniversary of the founding of the Chinese Communist Party, July 1, 1949.* Foreign Languages Press, 1959.

Mao Zedong. *On Practice and Contradiction*. Verso Books, 2007.

Mao Zedong. *Selected Works of Chairman Mao*. Vol. 1. Peking: Foreign Languages Press, 1967.

Mao Zedong. *Selected Works of Mao Tse-Tung*. Vol. 2. Beijing: Foreign Languages Press, 1967.

Mao Zedong. *Selected Works of Mao Tse-Tung*. Vol. 8. Hyderabad, India: Kranti, 1994.

Mao Zedong. *Selected Works of Mao Zedong*. Vol. 2. Beijing: Foreign Languages Press, 1938.

Mao Zedong. *Selected Works of Mao Zedong*. Vol. 4. Beijing: Foreign Languages Press, 1969.

Mao Zedong. *Quotations from Chairman Mao Tse-tung (The Little Red Book) & Other Works*. China Books & Periodicals, 1990.

"Mao Zedong, a persecutor of religions, is now worshipped like a god." PIME Asia News, December 28, 2016. https://www.asianews.it/news-en/Mao-Zedong%2C-a-persecutor-of-religions%2C-is-now-worshiped-like-a-god-39515.html.

Marlin, George et al., eds. *The Quotable Fulton Sheen: A Topical Compilation of the Wit, Wisdom, and Satire of Archbishop Fulton J. Sheen*. New York: Doubleday, 1989.

Marsh, Alan. "POWs in American History: A Synopsis." National Park Service, accessed January 25, 2022. https://www.nps.gov/ande/learn/historyculture/pow_synopsis.htm.

Marx, Karl and Frederick Engels. *Manifesto of the Communist Party*. Moscow: Progress Publishers, 1848.

Meadows, Donella H., Dennis L. Meadows, Jorgen Randers, and William W. Behrens III. *The Limits to Growth: A Report for the Club of Rome's Project on the Predicament of Mankind*. New York: Universe Books, 1972.

Meadows et al. "The Only Feasible Solution." In Mihajlo Mesarovic and Eduard Pestel. *Mankind at the Turning Point: The Second Report to the Club of Rome*. New York, E.P. Dutton: 1974.

Mencius. *Mencius*. Translated by James Legge. Pantianos Classics, 2016.

Military.com. "POW Blinks 'Torture' in Morse Code." Military.com, January 10, 2012. https://www.military.com/video/operations-and-strategy/vietnam-war/pow-blinks-torture-in-morse-code/1381254901001.

Mosher, Steven W. "After Vatican agreement, China's Communist leader is still trying to stamp out religion." *LifeSiteNews*, April 23, 2019. https://www.lifesitenews.com/blogs/after-vatican-agreement-chinas-communist-leader-is-still-trying-to-stamp-out-religion/.

Mosher, Steven W. "Are Chinese communists lying about number of babies born? They've got every reason to." *Lifesitenews*, January 22, 2020. https://www.lifesitenews.com/blogs/are-chinese-communists-lying-about-number-of-babies-born-theyve-got-every-reason-to/.

Mosher, Steven W. *Broken Earth: The Rural Chinese*. New York: MacMillan, 1983.

Mosher, Steven W. *Bully of Asia: Why China's Dream is a Threat to the World Order*. Regnery, 2017.

Mosher, Steven W. "Catholicism a Casualty of China's New Cultural Revolution." *National Catholic Register,* August 6, 2020. https://www.ncregister.com/com mentaries/catholicism-a-casualty-of-china-s-new-cultural-revolution.

Mosher, Steven W. "China Orders Churches to Promote the Chinese Communist Party—or Else." *The Epoch Times,* January 8, 2020. https://www.theepocht imes.com/china-orders-churches-to-promote-the-chinese-communist-party -or-else_3197447.html?ea_src=ai&ea_med=search.

Mosher, Steven W. "China's Wealthiest Woman, Whitney Duan, Disap-pears Without a Trace." *news.com.au,* September 14, 2021. https:// www.news.com.au/finance/money/wealth/chinas-richest-woman-whitney-duan-disappears-without-a-trace/news-story/2365755edd2ec3a974f9a47dd 8e41df0.

Mosher, Steven W. *Chinese Misperceived: American Illusions and Chinese Reality.* Harper Collins, 1990.

Mosher, Steven W. "Communist Road Kill: Xi Jinping is Carry Out a War on China's Wealthy." *The Epoch Times,* September 21, 2021. https://www.thee pochtimes.com/communist-road-kill_4008028.html.

Mosher, Steven W. "Expert condemns Vatican for 'betrayal' in secret agreement with Communist China." *LifeSiteNews,* September 22, 2018. https://www .lifesitenews.com/opinion/vatican-signs-secret-agreement-with-communist -china/.

Mosher, Steven W. "Faithful Chinese bishop on the run from communists high-lights Vatican/China deal disaster." *LifeSiteNews,* November 29, 2019. https://www.lifesitenews.com/blogs/faithful-chinese-bishop-on-the-run-fr om-communists-highlights-vatican-china-deal-disaster/.

Mosher, Steven W. "Female Infanticide in China." *Human Life Review* 1988 Spring, 14(2).

Mosher, Steven W. "How China's Xi Jinping destroyed religion and made himself God." *New York Post,* February 1, 2020. https://nypost.com/2020/02/01 /how-chinas-xi-jinping-destroyed-religion-and-made-himself-god/.

Mosher, Steven W. A Mother's Ordeal: One Woman's Fight Against China's One-Child Policy. New York: Harper Collins, 1993

Mosher, Steven W. "Parolin and the China Negotiations: First, Do No Harm." Population Research Institute, February 27, 2018. https://www.pop.org/pa rolin-china-negotiations-first-no-harm/.

Mosher, Steven W. *The Politically Incorrect Guide to Pandemics.* Washington, DC, Regnery, 2022.

Mosher, Steven W. "Pope Francis empowered Communists with Magisterial au-thority in Vatican/China deal." *LifeSiteNews,* September 28, 2018. https:// www.lifesitenews.com/opinion/pope-francis-empowered-communists-with -magisterial-authority-in-vatican-chi/.

Mosher, Steven W. "Pope Francis is more interested in not offending Commu-nist China than in defending Cdl. Zen." *LifeSiteNews,* September 27, 2022.

https://www.lifesitenews.com/blogs/pope-francis-is-more-interested-in-not
-offending-communist-china-than-in-defending-cdl-zen/.

Mosher, Steven W. "The Sino-Vatican Agreement—One Year Later." Lumen Fidei
Institute, January 21, 2020. https://www.lumenfidei.ie/the-sino-vatican-ag
reement-one-year-later/.

Mosher, Steven W. "Vatican to Allow Beijing to Name Bishops." Population Research Institute, September 19, 2018. https://www.pop.org/vatican-to-allow
-beijing-to-name-bishops/.

Mosher, Steven W. "Xi Jinping Places Catholic Church in China Under Direct Party Control." Population Research Institute, May 1, 2018. https://www.pop
.org/xi-jinping-places-catholic-church-in-china-under-direct-party-control/.

Nardi, Dominic J. "The 2019 Regulation for Religious Groups in China." United States Commission on International Religious Freedom, February 2020.
https://www.uscirf.gov/sites/default/files/2020%20Factsheet%20-%20Ch
ina_0.pdf.

Natsios, Andrew. "The Politics of Famine in North Korea." *US Institute of Peace* (1999).
http://www.jstor.org/stable/resrep12254.

The National Archives. "Scenes from Hell: Commander Jeremiah A. Denton, Jr.
-Report from Inside a Hanoi Prison, 1966." The National Archives, accessed
January 25, 2022. https://www.archives.gov/exhibits/eyewitness/html.php
?section=8.

National Archives and Records Administration. "Vietnam War U.S. Military Fatal
Casualty Statistics." National Archives and Records Administration, December 9, 2021. https://www.archives.gov/research/military/vietnam-war/casua
lty-statistics.

O'Conner, Tom. "China's Xi Says Socialism Will Defeat Capitalism Because Communist Party is 'Glorious.'" *Newsweek*, April 1, 2019. www.newsweek.com
/china-xi-socialism-defeat-capitalism-1381942.

OHCHR. "Report of the Commission of Inquiry on Human Rights in the Democratic People's Republic of Korea." 22, OHCHR, accessed January 31, 2022.
https://www.ohchr.org/EN/HRBodies/HRC/CoIDPRK/Pages/Reportofthe
CommissionofInquiryDPRK.aspx.

Olson, Gregory. *Mansfield and Vietnam: A Study in Rhetorical Adaptation.* MSU
Press, 2012.

O'Neill, Marnie. "Scores of Chinese Billionaires and CEOs have Disappeared in
State-Sanctioned Abductions." *news.com.au,* February 6, 2017. https://www
.news.com.au/lifestyle/real-life/news-life/scores-of-chinese-billionaires-and
-ceos-have-disappeared-in-statesanctioned-abductions/news-story/7d2d1cfe
add6b47ab66087d7f44d877f.

Owen, Taylor and Ben Kiernan. "Bombs Over Cambodia." *Yale University,* October 2006. https://gsp.yale.edu/sites/default/files/walrus_cambodiabombing
_oct06.pdf.

Park, Yoenmi. *In Order to Live: A North Korean Girl's Journey to Freedom.* New
York: Random House, 2015.

Patience, Martin. "Charles Xue 'Confession' Highlights China's Blogging Backlash." *BBC*, October 1, 2013.

Phillips, Tom. "China ends one-child policy after 35 years." *The Guardian*, October 29, 2015. https://www.theguardian.com/world/2015/oct/29/china-abandons-one-child-policy.

Pribbenow, Merle. "Treatment of American POWs in North Vietnam." Wilson Center, accessed March 21, 2021. https://www.wilsoncenter.org/publication/treatment-american-pows-north-vietnam.

Reuters. "Vietnam Plans Law to Ban Tests on Sex of Fetus." *Reuters*, November 16, 2001.

RMRB. "Firmly Destroy Old Habits, Insisting on Late Marriage." *RMRB*, August 31, 1969. American Consulate General, Hong Kong, *Survey of Mainland China Press*, No. 4495, September 15, 1969.

Roger Scruton Quotes (@Scruton Quotes). "Every practical application of Marxist theory has led not merely to tyranny, but to social and economic collapse." Twitter, January 14, 2017, 6:16 p.m. https://twitter.com/Scruton_Quotes/status/820409191496085504.

Rummel, R. J. "Death by Government." https://www.hawaii.edu/powerkills/NOTE1.HTM.

Rummel, R. J. "Statistics of Vietnamese Democide." University of Hawaii. https://hawaii.edu/powerkills/SOD.CHAP6.HTM.

Salisbury, Harrison. *The Long March: The Untold Story.* New York: Harper Collins, 1985.

Schoppa, Keith. "From Empire to People's Republic." In *Politics in China: An Introduction.* Edited by William A. Joseph. New York: Oxford University Press, 2019.

Schram, Stuart, ed. *Chairman Mao Talks to the People.* New York: Random House, 1974.

Schram, Stuart. *Mao's Road to Power.* Vol. 4, *The Rise and Fall of the Chinese Soviet Republic, 1931-34.* New York: Sharpe.

Selznick, Philip. *The Organizational Weapon: A Study of Bolshevik Strategy and Tactics.* Glencoe, Illinois: The Free Press, 1960.

Shao Jiang. "A Nightmarish Year Under Xi Jinping's 'Chinese Dream: 2013 Annual Report on the Situation of Human Rights Defenders in China." Amnesty International, March 6, 2014. http://www.amnesty.org.uk/blogs/countdown-china/nightmarish-year-under-xi-jinping%E2%80%99s-%E2%80%9Cchinese-dream%E2%80%9D-2013-annual-report.

Sheen, Fulton. *The Cross and the Beatitudes.* New York: P. J. Kenedy and Sons, 1937.

Short, Phillip. *Mao: A Life.* New York: Henry Holt, 2000.

Short, Phillip. *Pol Pot: The History of a Nightmare.* London: John Murray, 2004.

Silberstein, Benjamin Katzeff. "Let Them Eat Potatoes: Communism, Famine and the Case of North Korea." *North Korean Review* 17, no. 2 (2021): 38. https://www.jstor.org/stable/27067135.

Simon, Julian. *The Ultimate Resource.* Princeton: Princeton University Press, 1981.

Smedley, Agnes. *The Battle Hymn of China*. Victor Gollancz, London, 1944.

Smith, Christopher. "Judging a Civilization." *PRI Review* 11(4). September-October 2001.

Snow, Edgar. "A Conversation with Mao Tse-Tung," *Life*, April 30, 1971, 46-48.

Snow, Edgar. *Random Notes on Red China (1936-46)*. Cambridge: Harvard University Press, Chinese Economic and Political Studies, 1957.

Snow, Edgar. *Red Star Over China*. Middlesex, England: Penguin, 1973.

Song Jian. Tian Xueyuan, Li Guangyuan, and Yu Jingyuan. "Concerning the Issue of Our Country's Objective in Population Development." *Renmin Ribao* [People's Daily], March 7, 1980.

Song Jian. Chi-Hsien Tuan, and Jing-Yuan Yu. *Population Control in China: Theory and Applications*. New York: Praeger, 1985.

Song Jian. "Population Development—Goals and Plans." In Liu Zhen, Song Jian et al, eds. *China's Population: Problems and Prospects*. Beijing: New World Press, 1981.

Song Jian. *Song Jian kexue lunwen xuanji* [Selected scientific papers of Song Jian]. Beijing: Kexue Chuban She, 1999.

Soros, George. "Xi's Dictatorship Threatens the Chinese State." *The Wall Street Journal,* August 13, 2021. https://www.wsj.com/articles/xi-jinping-deng-xiaoping-dictatorship-ant-didi-economy-communist-party-beijing-authoritarian-11628885076.

Souza, Raymond J. de. "Figueiredo Report the First of Many to Come?" *National Catholic Register*, May 29, 2019. https://www.ncregister.com/commentaries/figueiredo-report-the-first-of-many-to-come.

Stanley, George F. G. "Dien Bien Phu in Retrospect." *International Journal* 10, no. 1 (1954): 38–50. https://doi.org/10.2307/40198089.

Sun Huilan and Fang Jinyu. "Population Burden: Root of All China's 'Troubles'--Factual Account of the Population Experts' Warnings on 'Population 1.2 .Billion Day.'" *LW*, February 27, 1995, FBIS, No. 95-079, April 25, 1995.

Teng-hui, Lee. *The Road to Democracy: Taiwan's Pursuit of Identity.* Tokyo: PHP Institute, 1999.

Terrill, Ross. "What Mao Traded for Sex." *Los Angeles Times*, March 8, 1998. https://www.latimes.com/archives/la-xpm-1998-mar-08-op-26719-story.html.

Time. "Religion: Chiang's Testimony." *Time,* April 26, 1943. https://content.time.com/time/subscriber/article/0,33009,802733,00.html.

Tosatti, Marco. "Cardinal Joseph Zen To His Brother Cardinals: The Church is Being Killed In China." *OnePeterFive,* January 8, 2020. https://onepeterfive.com/cardinal-joseph-zen-to-his-brother-cardinals-the-church-is-being-killed-in-china/.

Truong Nhu Tanh. *A Viet Cong Memoir: An Inside Account of the Vietnam War and Its Aftermath*. Vintage Books, 1946.

Tuong Vu. "Vietnam's Misunderstood Revolution." Wilson Center, June 19, 2017. https://www.wilsoncenter.org/blog-post/vietnams-misunderstood-revolution.

Ulferts, Gregory and Terry L. Howard. "North Korean Human Rights Abuses and Their Consequences." *North Korean Review* 13, no. 2 (2017). http://www.js tor.org/stable/26396124.

UCA News. "China Church further squeezed by revised regulations." *UCA News*, February 8, 2018. https://www.ucanews.com/news/china-church-further-sq ueezed-by-revised-regulations/81469.

UCA News. "China's state church installs fifth underground bishop." *UCA News*, July 20, 2020. https://www.ucanews.com/news/chinas-state-church-installs -fifth-underground-bishop/88840.

United States Commission on International Religious Freedom. *2019 Annual Report*. USCIRF, Washington, DC, 2019. https://www.uscirf.gov/sites/default /files/Tier1_NORTHKOREA_2019.pdf.

United States Holocaust Memorial Museum. "S-21, Tuol Sleng." United States Holocaust Memorial Museum, accessed January 28, 2022. https://www.ushmm .org/genocide-prevention/countries/cambodia/case-study/violence/s-21.

Waldron, Arthur. *The Great Wall of China: From History to Myth.* Cambridge: Cambridge University Press, 1990.

Wang, Chenyi. "The Chinese Communist Party's Relationship with the Khmer Rouge in the 1970s: An Ideological Victory and a Strategic failure." Cold War International History Project Working Paper 88, The Wilson Center, December 2018, accessed May 6, 2023. www.wilsoncenter/publication/the -chinese-communist-partys-relationship-the-khmer-rouge.

Whyte, Martin King, Wang Feng, and Yong Cai. "Challenging Myths About China's One-Child Policy." *The China Journal*, 74(2015): 144-159, at 151. https://scholar.harvard.edu/files/martinwhyte/files/challenging_myths_pub lished_version.pdf.

Wiest, Andrew. *Rolling Thunder in a Gentle Land: The Vietnam War Revisited.* Oxford: Osprey Publishing, 2006.

Williams, Thomas D. "China Expert: Communist Party Determined to 'Extinguish the Catholic Faith." *Breitbart,* August, 8 2020. https://www.breitba rt.com/national-security/2020/08/08/china-expert-communist-party-deter mined-to-extinguish-the-catholic-faith/.

Wood, Frances and Christopher Arnander. *Betrayed Ally: China in the Great War.* South Yorkshire: Pen & Sword Military, 2016.

Worden, Robert, Andrea Miles Savada, and Ronald E. Dolan. *China: A Country Study.* Washington, DC: Federal Research Division, Library of Congress, 1988.

Xi Jinping. "Speech at the Ceremony Commemorating the 80th Anniversary of the Victory of the Long March." *China Daily*, October 21, 2016. www.chinadai ly.com.cn/a/201701/24/WS6098e7bea31024ad0babd01d_2.html.

Xia Qiao. "New Directives on Sinicization of Religion: 'Love the Party, Love Socialism.'" *Bitter Winter*, March 24, 2022. https://bitterwinter.org/new-direc tives-on-sinicization-of-religion-love-the-party-love-socialism/.

Yathay, Pin. *Stay Alive, My Son.* New York: The Free Press, 1987.

Yoanna, Michael de. "From Torture to Freedom, Colorado Vietnam POW Recounts Captivity." *KUNC*, October 8, 2018. https://www.kunc.org/news/2018-10-08/from-torture-to-freedom-colorado-vietnam-pow-recounts-captivity.

Zen, Joseph Cardinal. *For Love of My People I will not Remain Silent.* San Francisco: Ignatius Press, 2019.

Zeng, Jennifer. "Timeline and Reason of Hu Jintao's Removal, 8 Features of Xi Jinping's New Yes Team." Jennifer's World (blog), October 25, 2022. https://www.jenniferzengblog.com/home/2022/10/26/timeline-and-reason-of-hu-jintaos-removal-8-features-of-xi-jinpings-new-yes-team.

Zheng Yongnian. *The Chinese Communist Party as Organizational Emperor.* New York: Routledge, 2010.

Zhiyue, Bo. "Is China's PLA Now Xi's Army?" *The Diplomat*, January 12, 2016. http://thediplomat.com/2016/01/is-chinas-pla-now-xis-army/.

Zhou Xun. *Forgotten Voices of Mao's Great Famine, 1958-62; An Oral History.* New Haven, CT: Yale University Press, 2013.